SOCCER
TACTICS AND SKILLS

The Football Association Coaching Book of
SOCCER
TACTICS AND SKILLS

CHARLES HUGHES

British Broadcasting Corporation
and
Macdonald
Queen Anne Press

A QUEEN ANNE PRESS BOOK

© The Football Association 1980, 1987

First Published in Great Britain in 1980 by
British Broadcasting Corporation
and
Queen Anne Press, a division of
Macdonald & Co (Publishers) Ltd
Orbit House
1 New Fetter Lane
London
EC4A 1AR

Limp edition first published in Great Britain in 1987
by Queen Anne Press, a member of
Maxwell Macmillan Pergamon Publishing Corporation

Reprinted 1988, 1990

Jacket photographs – Front: Brian Robson and Don Howe *Sporting Pictures (UK) Ltd*
Gary Lineker *All Sport*
Back: Bobby Robson *Colorsport*

British Library Cataloguing in Publication Data
Hughes, Charles
    The Football Association coaching book of Soccer Tactics and Skills.
    I. Soccer Coaching
    II. Title
    796.334'07'7.   GV 943.8

    ISBN 0-356-15169-7

Printed and bound in Hong Kong by Leefung-Asco Printers Limited

CONTENTS

FOREWORDS

Education is concerned with developing knowledge and sharing that knowledge with others. Much of football education is concerned with developing good habits and creating correct attitudes.

This book is very much concerned with explaining how to practise correctly, whether the practice is related to a basic technique or to a tactical situation in a full game. That is so important. My experience, after a life time coaching soccer, is that it is very much easier to develop good habits than it is to change bad ones.

The importance of correct attitudes is reinforced throughout the book. Charles Hughes properly makes the point that if coaches can bring about an improvement in attitude, that represents the biggest and quickest source of improvement at either individual or team level. Conversely, no amount of coaching will ever compensate for a poor attitude on the part of a player.

Developing good habits and creating good attitudes are the corner-stones of soccer education. Indeed, they are the corner-stones of education itself. We need better behaviour both on and off the field and we need it more today than at any previous time in the history of our game.

This book deals with the elements and principles involved with the techniques and tactics of the game, how to organise to practise those techniques and tactics correctly; how to develop the practices from the most basic of the full game; and the key factors for coaches to observe. The book is therefore definitive. One need not say more. The book, with its lavish illustrations, will speak for itself. It is a major contribution to world soccer education.

Bobby Robson

Bobby Robson

I was very pleased to have the opportunity of taking part in the coaching films on which this book is based along with a number of my England team-mates. Coaching is important to improve both individual technique and teamwork. I hope that schoolboys and senior players will read this book, as well as teachers and coaches, and that they will try the practices described in it. I know their knowledge of the game and their performance will improve because mine has improved through taking part in the very practices described.

You cannot become a star international player without practising correctly and without practising regularly. That is one reason why the best players as schoolboys do not always make the best professionals. Even for the players who never become professionals, they will get more fun out of the game if they can improve their own performance and also the performance of the team. I am convinced this book will help you to do just that.

Kevin Keegan

ACKNOWLEDGEMENTS

This book has been written in conjunction with the making of fourteen coaching films which have been a joint production between The Football Association and the BBC. I wish, therefore, to thank the many BBC staff who have played a part in the making of the series, especially Alan Hart, head of BBC Sport, and Bob Abrahams, the producer of the films.

I am also grateful to Elton John who wrote the original title music for the films and gave us such splendid support.

Five England international players, Kevin Keegan, Trevor Brooking, Luther Blissett, Peter Shilton and Ray Wilkins, took part in the films and we wish to record our gratitude to each one of them. Their attitude and their performance reflected enormous credit on them, their clubs, and the game of Association Football. We are also grateful to Terry Venables and Crystal Palace FC for making available twenty-two of their young players for the film production. Their splendid enthusiasm for the task in hand was very much appreciated by all those who took part in the series.

Excluding myself, twenty coaches took part in the films: Ron Atkinson, John Cartwright, Terry Casey, Dario Gradi, Ron Greenwood, Don Howe, Geoff Hurst, Mike Kelly, Colin Murphy, Bobby Robson, Robin Russell, Dave Sexton, Mike Smith, Bill Taylor, Graham Taylor, Terry Venables, Kevin Verity, Allen Wade, Howard Wilkinson and Keith Wright. We were privileged to have the benefit of their skill.

I am particularly grateful to Don Howe, arguably the best coach of Association Football in the world. He was with me throughout the shooting of the films and he has also been kind enough to read and comment upon the technical chapters of the book. I count myself fortunate to have had his advice readily available. I also wish to record my special thanks to Mike Kelly for his advice and guidance on the films and chapters concerned with goalkeeping; and to Tom Tranter who read and commented upon the chapter entitled 'Principles of Learning and Coaching'.

Bob Robson gave me and the whole project marvellous support. I am privileged that he has written a foreword to this book in his capacity as Manager of the England team. Likewise, I am grateful to Kevin Keegan for writing a foreword in his capacity as Captain of the England team at the time of making these films.

The production of fourteen films, and the writing of a book as large as this, involves a mountain of detailed administration. I have been fortunate to have the dedication and skill of two excellent assistants, Mandy Primus and John Thomson. They have greatly eased my task and I am grateful to them. I am also grateful to Brian Lee, the Director of Bisham Abbey, and his staff for the support they gave us during the shooting of the films.

The book owes much to its illustrations. I must record my thanks, therefore, to Chris Ridley who was commissioned by the BBC to take all the still photographs while the films were being shot; and to Logos Designs who drew the diagrams and line drawings and provided the lay-out for the book.

For two years my wife saw more of the film scripts and book manuscript than she did of me! I deeply appreciate her understanding and I thank her also for the meticulous way in which she checked all that I wrote.

Last, but certainly not least, I wish to place on record my thanks to Ted Croker, for writing the Introduction to this book, and the Chairman and members of the Instructional Committee of The Football Association for their support throughout this project.

INTRODUCTION

In 1979 The Football Association decided to go ahead with the production of a series of coaching films that would cover the subject of tactics and skills in a far more comprehensive way than had ever been tackled before. We knew that we were breaking new ground and that, apart from the problems we could foresee, others would undoubtedly emerge. This proved to be so, but at the same time the BBC solved many of our problems by approaching us to be involved in the series. This has given a professional expertise on the production side that we could have scarcely hoped for. Exactly the same professional approach has been applied to the production of this book.

This book was intended, originally, to be a back-up to the films, a natural essential. As you will see, it has become far more than this and will probably become a standard work in its own right. I have no doubt that anyone seeing the films will want to read the book and anyone reading the book will want to see the films. Possibly what the production of both has made clear to me is that the essential difference between the films and the book, that the one is static and the other is flowing, proves how totally complementary they are. There are many situations in the films, even with the use at times of freeze frames where the action is stopped to enable the position to be more clearly seen, when a longer look is needed.

To have confirmed one's inner beliefs is always satisfying and it is another aspect of this film and book project. The contribution that has been made by those involved in football, from the coaching and administrative staff in the Coaching Department and the help and involvement of Bob Robson, the England Team Manager, and many of his staff recruited from the various League Clubs, plus the outstanding contribution from professional footballers, from international players to apprentice professionals, has proved again how those who love the game are prepared to contribute to it.

We believe that this is a book that will be enjoyed world-wide by the most seasoned professional, the enthusiastic schoolboy, the man on the terraces and even the armchair critic who enjoys his soccer via the television screen. It may even tempt many of the latter to get out into the fresh air and realise how much more compelling soccer is if viewed live in a stadium, where the complete pattern of the game can be seen and enjoyed.

Ted Croker
Secretary
The Football Association

1
SYSTEMS OF PLAY

Those who believe that the most important single aspect in soccer is systems of play – and many people do – would be well advised to take heed of the well-known adage, 'A little learning is a dangerous thing.' It is quite extraordinary how people have become obsessed with systems of play. Yet it should be obvious that there is no system which will overcome inaccurate passing or shooting; none which will improve ball control; none which allows for players who will not support each other; and none which allows for players who cannot or will not run.

So why are so many people obsessed by systems of play? The main reason is that few people understand the real issues behind the success or failure of a team and, as a result, are influenced too greatly by what they hear and read. When the manager of a club announces on radio, television or in the press that his team will be playing 4–2–4, his audience usually accepts what he says without criticism. When the same manager, after a string of defeats, announces that the system is to be changed to 4–3–3, everybody believes that the root of the problem has been found and that success will immediately result. The fact is that people who do not understand the underlying issues in soccer place more reliance on what they are told and less on what they see.

It is important, therefore, that managers, and those in a position of influence, should state the facts as they really are and not cloud the issue with jargon. How many managers, for example, does one hear talking about the importance of set plays – corners, free kicks, and throws? Yet the facts show that at every level of the game, almost 50 per cent of goals originate from set plays. At the very highest level, and especially in key matches, that percentage is even higher. How many talk about the importance of a highly competent goalkeeper? Yet two world-class saves from a goalkeeper can be the difference between winning 1–0 and losing 1–2. These factors have nothing to do with systems of play. The fact is, however, that any team which has only a moderate goalkeeper and is not well organised at set plays will end the season in the ranks of the also-rans.

A team can play as many forward players as it wishes, but if it does not have the capacity to gain and retain possession of the ball the system employed will count for nothing. Likewise, a team can get as many players as it wishes behind the ball to defend but, if they lack the ability as individuals or as a team to mark players and space, the system will again count for nothing. If the ability of the players as individuals or as a team is lacking, no amount of system changing will affect the performance of the players.

Those who still feel that systems of play are crucial to the game of soccer should consider whether they are really talking about systems or attitudes. If incentives in league soccer were changed to give four points for a win and one point for a draw, one would expect more emphasis to be placed on attacking. This would be brought about by a change of attitude on the part of managers and players alike in relation to risk taking and would not necessarily involve a sudden change in the system of play adopted. Managers and coaches often effect remarkable improvements in the second-half performance of their players and these are nearly always due to a change in attitude to the game rather than a change in the system of play.

The importance of a team's mental attitude to the game and its surroundings is well illustrated by the fact that a team can play with the same players and operate the same system in home and away matches and yet achieve vastly different results. In international matches this is more understandable since the conditions in terms of travel, food, climate, playing surface and crowd may be very different. But the same applies in local matches where the grounds of the two clubs may only be a couple of miles apart. The fact is that the attitude of most players, and therefore most teams, is different when they play away to when they play at home. There is a greater expectation of success at home than away, which is not surprising. Most of us feel more relaxed, comfortable and confident in our own homes than we do in someone else's home.

There is a further point which is worth making. Teams can be arranged in exactly the same way in terms of the number of players in back positions, midfield positions and forward positions, but any two teams will play differently. The reason for this, apart from the obvious fact that the players will be different, will be the respective instructions given by the managers or coaches. The purpose of giving an instruction is to get a reaction, a performance. Much of the time it is not so much what one says but how one says it which produces the desired reaction. Any two managers will be different in this respect.

If some of our top managers and coaches have been responsible for placing an undue and inappropriate emphasis on systems of play, the media have certainly given systems of play an inordinate amount of publicity, thereby accentuating the problem.

The television presentation of matches is usually preceded by a consideration of whether the teams will play 4–3–3 or 4–2–4 or whether they will play with or without a sweeper. The press has certainly created the impression that Sir Alfred Ramsay put the English game into decline by declining to win the World Cup with wingers in his team. They seem to have lost sight of the fact that in 1966 England happened to have three or four world-class players in their team and were playing at home. Wingers were used in the preparatory matches, and indeed in the final tournament, but were found to be ineffective.

The task of the coach or the manager is twofold: to get the best out of the players as individuals and as a team; and to ensure that the sum of the whole exceeds the sum of all the separate parts. If one of the parts is ineffective it will affect the sum of the whole. One does not need to be very astute, therefore, to select a different part.

Events and results in British soccer since 1970 have indicated that we had more outstanding individual players in the period 1966–1970 than we have had since that time. That, one feels, is a more complete explanation for the decline of the England team in the early seventies than the fact that Ramsay selected teams without wingers.

That simple illustration, one trusts, puts into perspective the matter of systems of play. It also brings into focus the power of the media.

Sadly, the backlash of all this is in the schools with the result that too great an emphasis has been placed not only on systems of play, but also on the playing of eleven-a-side football. The development of young players would be better served by playing small-sided games. It would be even better served if schoolmasters would dedicate themselves to the task of teaching techniques and developing those techniques by simple progressive practices, leading to small-sided games and eventually, when the players are technically and physically equipped, ending in the eleven-a-side game.

This book, and the coaching films which have been made in conjunction with it, are directed to the proposition of what to coach and how to coach it – how to coach techniques, how to develop skill and how to coach and combine the understanding and skills of the players in the eleven-a-side game.

The time has surely come when more of us should be talking and writing about the real technical issues in soccer. We should be destroying myths and exposing what amounts to confidence trickery. We should be seeking the support of the media as a vehicle through which to launch a positive and extensive worldwide educational programme. We should be persuading schoolmasters, and others who coach young players, of the importance of their task. Should they fail in their task, should the foundations be less than sure, then a soccer superstructure will fail to arise.

Association Football is not only the World Game, it is the major source of enjoyment for countless millions. Teaching and coaching can and should be a catalyst for that enjoyment. The better and more skilfully one coaches, the more one enjoys coaching, and the better the players become whom one coaches. The better the players become, the more skilful they are, the more enjoyment and success they will derive from playing. The more understanding spectators have of the skills of the game, the more they will enjoy watching the game, and the more they will appreciate and enjoy watching skilful players and skilful teams.

The purpose of this book and of the films is to contribute towards world soccer education. Education, of course, is a never-ending process. But all of us who teach and coach would do well to remember that we are the trustees for the rising generation. May we be worthy of our stewardship.

PRINCIPLES OF LEARNING AND COACHING

THE PRINCIPLES OF LEARNING

Much teaching and coaching is based on the misguided notion that practice makes perfect. That is not necessarily so. Practice makes permanent and that fact applies with equal certainty to both good and bad practice. Incorrect practice, therefore, will eventually produce permanent bad habits. This fundamental truth requires to be understood. Those who believe in coaching understand the benefits which will accrue from correct practice and the formation of good habits and sound knowledge. Those who do not understand this basic truth have no basis for belief.

There are two further misguided notions concerning the coaching of soccer which should be dispelled at the outset. The first of these is that soccer players are born with natural flair and do not require coaching. This notion is not supported by the facts. The essential fact is that the progress of civilisation through the ages is largely a commentary on the progress of education, whereby each generation has handed on to its succeeding generation more knowledge and better techniques of teaching and learning. So it is that man can run faster and jump higher, has ascended the highest pinnacle on earth and has set foot on the moon. These achievements are the result of the practical application of advanced knowledge harnessed to assiduous and purposeful practice and training. Suffice it to say that it is unlikely that soccer players have been granted immunity from this process of evolution.

This thesis is consistent with the fact that youngsters are not born equal – indeed, they are unequal physically, mentally and psychologically. Nor is this thesis inconsistent with the fact that those who are born and brought up in a soccer environment will have better opportunities to develop their talents than those who are not.

It is, therefore, self-evident that we are not born with equal talents and that we do not have, environmentally speaking, equal opportunities. The great challenge of teaching, however, is to recognise potential talent and develop that potential to its full realisation.

The other misguided notion to which reference should be made is that techniques practised in isolation cannot be transferred into the game. If a player is a poor technical performer in a situation where he has no opposing player, then there is nothing of technical merit to transfer into the game. It should, however, be understood, that the player who is technically proficient without opposing players will not necessarily be as proficient when opposing and co-operating players are brought into the practice.

The misconception of the affects of transference of training is often characterised by a desire to teach by trial and error. It is dangerously assumed that one can learn equally well by performing unsuccessfully as by performing successfully. Whilst it is desirable that performers should be challenged and stretched, the teaching progressions should be such that any new learning situation should be balanced towards the probability of success. This is not the least of the skills of coaching, and the accruing habit of success is not least in order of importance to the performer.

Effective coaching and learning of Association Football is very much bound up with establishing correct attitudes, correct habits and correct movements. First, in order of importance, is the attitude towards learning by both the coach and the player. This attitude should be characterised by two qualities:

- An open mind.
- An enquiring mind.

An open mind is essential to receive new ideas; it is essential for mental vitality and it is essential for progress. A closed mind indicates that a man believes he knows it all. It also indicates that he is not only feeling old but has become old.

An enquiring mind is essential to evaluate new ideas. Not all ideas are good and it is a mistake to accept a new idea on the sole criterion of it being new – this is as foolish as to discount it without evaluation. One should question new ideas, analyse them and establish if they are correct in principle. Only after the most careful consideration should any idea be accepted or rejected.

What then is technique? And what is skill?

Technique is the execution of a single performance – a pass, a control, a jump, or a turn. Decisions are involved which means that the performance involves both physical and mental elements.

Skill, in soccer terms, is the ability to be in the right place at the right time and to select the correct technique on demand. Skill, therefore, is concerned with making judgments and selections. There are some games which are predominantly games of technique. Soccer is predominantly a game of judgment. How do we reach that conclusion? By a simple analysis of the facts:

- In a 90-minute game of soccer the ball is only in play for approximately 60 of those minutes. For the remainder of the time the ball is out of play.
- Out of the 60 minutes in which the ball is in play, each team, in an even game, will have possession of the ball for 30 minutes.
- During the time in which the ball is in play the ball will frequently be in flight and outside the playing distance of any one of the 22 players.
- An individual player in a team, on average, cannot have possession of the ball for more than two minutes.

  Question: What is the player doing for the other 58 minutes that the ball is in play?

  Answer: Making judgments, decisions and selections.

Added to all this is the probability that soccer is the most fluid of all games. All the players and the ball can move through 360 degrees and there are a minimum number of laws and relatively few stoppages. Situations, therefore, change rapidly, requiring from the players a high degree of mental alertness and concentration.

All of which brings us back to the fundamental question which is not, how does one coach, but rather, how does a young player learn.

How a young player learns

Young players have a desire to achieve and a desire to prove themselves to others. In order to motivate them successfully, the coach needs to take into consideration the following factors:

He must be interested. The player who is not interested has a closed mind and that, if it cannot be changed, is a recipe for disaster.

He should have enthusiasm – a desire to be involved and to participate. One should be suspicious of any young player who lacks enthusiasm. It is worth remembering that people who are enthusiastic want to do more not less.

He should see good examples and be set good standards. Seeing good players play live, or on film, is important. By observing what good players do, standards are set; standards, one must add, not only of performance but also of behaviour. By observing what others do, particularly those whom we respect and admire, attitudes and habits are formed. One cannot therefore overestimate the responsibility which falls on outstanding players and coaches alike in setting and establishing standards for young players. Through harnessing this means of learning, coaches can bring about a permanent change for the better in both attitudes and habits.

He will learn through correct practice and through the frequency of that practice. The quality of the practice is more important than the frequency. Given, however, the quality, the greater the time devoted to practice, the better will be the results.

He will learn by knowledge of results. The more progress a player can be seen to be making, the more the player is likely to be encouraged to practice. Like taking medicine, we may not always like it; but if there is clear evidence that it is doing us good we will continue to take it. Correct practice involves setting players performance targets so that progress can be measured. This task belongs entirely to the coach.

He will learn by being challenged. Progress involves a continuous process of reaching beyond one's grasp. Progress is not achieved by constantly working within one's limits – one does not climb higher by looking down. Players will improve by being set more difficult tasks and by playing with and against better players, the proviso being that the task is not too difficult nor the opposing players too good. Coaches must set these challenges carefully for young players calculating on the probability of success.

He learns by faith. At the end of the day a man will not achieve more than he believes to be possible. The question is, what is possible? Many of us under-estimate what we could achieve. At the same time, most of us are inspired by hope; but many hopes are not realistically based. Coaches should inspire and encourage players to strive harder to establish and improve hopes and ambitions which are attainable.

The elements in a skilful performance

Having established how a player learns, what does he need to learn in soccer? What are the factors involved in skilful performance? There are three major areas: technique; understanding; and fitness.

Technique. Techniques in soccer are the tools of the trade. The better the techniques, and the wider the range of techniques at the disposal of the player, the better he is likely to be. A player, therefore, who is one-footed, no matter how efficient technically that one foot may be, would be even better if he were as efficient technically with the other foot. There is no substitute for good technique.

Understanding. Understanding means understanding what one can do and what is necessary. To attempt something which one knows one cannot do is, to put it mildly, unskilful. Understanding what is necessary requires knowledge, vision and perception; thus the excellent technical performer may not be skilful, since he may not understand or perceive when and where to use his various techniques.

It has already been established that, for the most part, players will not be performing techniques with the ball during a game of soccer. A skilful player, therefore, must understand how to position to the best advantage of his team and team-mates. In order to do this successfully, the principles of the game should guide his thinking. Without a thorough grasp of these principles, real understanding is not possible.

A player must also understand the relative importance of the various areas of the field, the state of the game, and the physical conditions, when calculating between safety and risk. Coaches sometimes refer to good soccer as if it were a finite state. Efficiency is what we must strive to achieve: efficiency as an individual and as a team. Part of that efficiency is embodied in a player's appreciation of when, where and how to take risks and when, where and how to perform with safety.

Understanding and skill in football is therefore a composite of many factors.

Fitness. Fitness requires a combination of physical and mental fitness. It is, in our present state of knowledge, impossible to determine where physical fitness ends and mental fitness starts. It is also impossible to state with any certainty the influence which a player's physical state has upon his mental state, or vice versa. The two are not only inter-related: they are woven like a golden thread through the whole of soccer.

Fatigue causes techniques to deteriorate, concentration to lapse and judgment to falter. Thus, skill is not a realisable asset unless it is accompanied by fitness. Without attempting to draw final conclusions, an analysis of the times at which goals are scored in matches gives some interesting statistics. 30 matches were analysed during which 76 goals were scored.

23 goals (30 per cent) were scored in the last 15 minutes of the game.

17 goals (22 per cent) were scored in the last 5 minutes of the game.

These statistics are an indication that fitness is an important factor, and perhaps the major factor, during the closing stages of a game.

Arising from the three major areas of technique, understanding and fitness, there emerge five elements in skilful performance:

Mental concentration. This has to be ingrained as a habit and an attitude of mind. Without concentration, and thinking about what one is doing, the game is reduced to a lottery and the game as a battle of wits does not take place.

Correct techniques. The wider the range of techniques the greater the possibility of being equal to the technical demands.

Seeing and perceiving. There is a vast difference between seeing and perceiving. There are some players who are essentially 'one-eyed', only seeing the play on one side of the field. Usually it is the side they happen to be on at the time. Often an incorrect body position of the player or a poor supporting angle precludes the player from having a wide range of vision. Players need to learn to play with their heads up, surveying constantly the changing positions of the ball and players. They also need perception to interpret what all that information means. Without perception, seeing means very little.

Decisions and judgments. Knowledge and perception are fundamental to decision-making. It is necessary to be able to sift the essential from the non-essential and the first priority from the second and lower priorities. It requires an alert, decisive and positive frame of mind to make such a judgment. Players should be encouraged to understand that soccer is a game of decisions. It is better to make a wrong decision than no decision at all.

Action. This is the application and the implementation of the decision with single-minded purpose. Soccer is very much a game of mistakes and the biggest mistakes are not to make a decision or to change one's mind in the midst of applying a decision.

THE PRINCIPLES OF COACHING

Having outlined how young players learn, and the various factors involved in a skilful performance, it is logical to turn next to the task of coaching. What are the principles involved in effective coaching?

Know the subject

It is self-evident that to coach well, one does need to know the game of soccer from the technical and tactical standpoint. Paradoxically, one of the advantages of soccer is also a disadvantage.

Soccer has a marvellous spectator appeal. It is a fast moving game, the laws are minimal and uncomplicated, and the purpose of the game is easy to grasp. Everybody has an opinion on whether we should play with or without wingers, whether we should play this system or that. Discussions are riddled with clichés and half-truths and team selection is never wrong – the team which the spectator selects never plays and therefore never loses. It never wins either, of course, but in the emotional trauma which team selection excites, and the dedicated search for a magic formula which does not exist, it is perfectly understandable that such a detail should be completely overlooked.

It is against that background, and the influence which such opinions may have on players and coaches alike, that coaches must keep a steady gaze and never lose sight of the basic truths. Those truths are embodied in the principles and key factors of technical performance and the principles and key factors of tactical play – the grammar of the game. Without that basic knowledge a coach cannot begin to do his job.

Know how people learn

Earlier in this chapter key factors in learning were discussed. Without knowledge of those factors, effective coaching is not likely to take place. It is the task of the coach to create an effective learning situation. If that situation has been created correctly, from an organisational point of view, then it is likely that some learning will take place even without direct coaching.

Know the key factors in coaching

1. Purpose. Without a purpose, direction is not possible. Purpose is concerned with factors which are usually long term. For example, the purpose may be to improve the attacking play of the team. Many factors come into attacking play, perhaps involving techniques and skills which the players at present do not possess. From the overall purpose, therefore, emerge short-term objectives which serve that purpose.

2. Objectives. In the example quoted above, there may be several objectives. These can be divided roughly into two sectors:

- Play with the ball, e.g. passing, control, dribbling, crossing the ball.
- Play without the ball, e.g. combining movement, supporting overlap runs, cross-over plays, diagonal runs.

A coach cannot teach all these factors at once, so it is necessary to determine a priority order and logical sequence of coaching within the overall objective.

3. Priority order and logical sequence. To further the example already quoted, if the attacking play is poor, and the passing is inaccurate, it is best to start with short passing rather than long passing. It is better to concentrate on those techniques and movements which will achieve greater possession of the ball, and make more frequent progress towards the opponent's goal, before dealing with crosses to the near and far posts.

It is not difficult to determine priorities or a logical sequence, but it does require an understanding of two factors:

- One cannot coach effectively several different facets of the game at one time.
- Out of any two factors, one will always take logical precedence over the other.

If a coach gets two factors out of logical sequence, learning becomes more difficult because it makes less sense. Also, it usually assumes knowledge of techniques not yet acquired. If one persists in coaching the right things, but at the wrong time, effective learning will not take place. Careful thought, therefore, must be given to planning priorities and logical sequence.

4. Planning and organisation. Planning is concerned with a consideration of the best use of the facilities, equipment and players. It is also concerned with the provision of equipment such as balls, cones, portable goals, training shirts and field markings. Planning takes place in advance of the event and makes sound organisation possible. Organisation of an actual coaching session involves the following considerations:

The area of the field for practice. This may involve the use of grids or it may involve the use of an appropriate part of the pitch, e.g. a flank area in the attacking third of the field for near-post crosses. The area in use should be clearly marked, preferably with cones.

The number of players involved in the practice. The number of players must be appropriate to the area, and the area must be appropriate to the number of players. It is just as big a mistake to provide too much space as it is to provide too little. Sound organisation, therefore, in terms of area and numbers of players is a prerequisite to effective practice. Defenders and attackers should, of course, wear distinctive clothing in the form of training shirts or bibs.

Realistic practice. In all practices where there are opponents and co-operating players, it is important that the players should position realistically. If players are not realistically placed, they embark on an unrealistic practice which is unrelated to the game. It is not only important that players should position realistically; they should also perform realistically on commencement of the practice and on the recommencement of each successive practice.

One of the most important aspects of achieving realistic practice is the use of full-sized portable goals. Small five-a-side goals produce unrealistic shooting and are of little help to goalkeepers. In this book, where it is indicated that goals will be used, it means full-sized portable goals unless otherwise stated.

The two most vital aspects in soccer have to be scoring goals and stopping shots. The fact that the majority of practices give realistic practice at neither borders on lunacy.

The start of the practice and the type and quality of service. Many practices flounder because insufficient thought is given to how the practice should start. Most practices, for example, should start with a moving ball so that the players are already alert and reacting to the ball before the ball is played in. Most practice situations are a reconstruction of a fluid situation.

The type of service is also important. If players are practising defensive heading, it is important that the service is the type with which the defending players will have to deal in a game. The quality of the service is also important. It must be accurate to the 80 per-cent level. If the correct type or quality of service is missing from the practice, beneficial practice cannot take place.

The catchwords for organisation are simplicity and clarity. All players should understand the organisation and the purpose of the practice. Each player should also understand his function within that organisation. Each time a practice develops, the five facets of organisation should be reviewed and, where necessary, readjusted.

5. Observation. Analysis is the basis of diagnosis. There are aspects of soccer which, in our present state of knowledge, defy analysis – for example, the attitude of players to being a goal up or a goal down. There are, however, many technical and tactical aspects which can be analysed.

Coaches should accept, as a matter of principle, that where it is possible to obtain the facts, the facts should be obtained. It can be appreciated that some coaches and teachers do not believe in analysis; but they should understand that their opinions will carry more force and conviction if they are supported by facts.

Observation, therefore, takes place on two levels – objective and subjective. It is a logical extension to continuing the priority order, and a logical sequence of coaching. If, therefore, determining priorities and a logical sequence is concerned with what to coach, observation is concerned with what to look for and in what logical order. The process of observing a coaching session may be summarised in the following logical sequence:

Observe that the organisation is correct. Observe also that the practice is being carried out according to the organisational requirements.

Observe that the attitude of the players is correct. Players should show that they are interested, stimulated and working purposefully. If this is not the case in the opening minutes of a practice then it is almost certainly the fault of the coach. Quite frequently the fault will relate to shortcomings in the organisation or imprecise instructions.

Observe the general performance of the group. The performance may be concerned with practising a technique or a tactic. There will be key principles to observe and a logical sequence in which to observe them. For example, if the group is practising ball control, as an isolated technique, the first principle to observe is that the players are successful in moving into the path of the ball. If the group performance in respect of this principle is poor, then the practice should be stopped and the necessary coaching points and corrections made. The group then resumes practice and the observation by the coach starts again.

Observe the specific performance of the individual. It may be that in the group the performance of one or more individuals is unsatisfactory. It is then necessary to observe each individual performance closely to establish the root cause of the problem. These are the questions which the coach should be seeking to answer:

1. Is the task physically within the player's capabilities? If not, there is no point in pursuing the practice.

2. Is there an inhibiting factor – possibly apprehension or fear? Fear could be the root of the problem in, for example, heading or tackling. When this problem occurs it will sometimes be necessary to make the practice a little easier. What is usually required though is more encouragement.

3. Is the problem purely technical? If so, which technique and which principle? The answer to the problem is to ensure that the player understands what he is doing wrong and how he should practise to put it right. Concentrated practice should then take place.

4. Is the problem tactical? If so, is the problem basically:

i) Lack of knowledge or understanding? If this is the fault, then the principle and the key factor involved should be isolated, and concentrated practice given.

ii) Lack of perception? The problem may be that the player does not see what is happening. Is the area too crowded? Is everything happening too quickly for the player? Is the player playing with his head down? If the area is too crowded, or the play too quick, then the remedy is to reduce the number of players or increase the space, or both. If the player is playing with his head down, then the need is for concentrated one-touch practice.

iii) Lack of application? The problem may be that the player understands what is wanted, but fails in the final execution. If that is the case, then the problem is reduced to one of technique. It could be that, in the final execution, the player was either attempting the difficult or the impossible in an area where it would be more sensible to calculate on the side of safety. If that is the case, the solution to the problem is to give the player a clearer understanding of the areas of safety and risk, and change the attitude of the player to his performance in those areas.

The skill of observation is closely related to the ability to think logically and analytically – essentially the products of a trained mind.

6. Communication. The ability to organise and observe counts for little in coaching if one lacks the ability to communicate. A coach can communicate in two ways:

By showing. Visual communication could be by picture or film, but usually it will be by physical demonstration. The demonstration could be of a technique or a tactical movement. In both cases the following qualities should be evident:

- The performance as demonstrated should be correct, and preferably an excellent example.
- The demonstration should be simple. Complication leads to confusion and failure.
- The demonstration should have clarity and should isolate and highlight the key factor.
- The demonstration should set the standard and challenge the players in terms of achievement.

By speaking. Demonstrations will often be accompanied by verbal explanation, the object of which is to assist clarification. Communication through speaking is a skill in itself. Its importance is grossly underestimated, but the difficulty in terms of performance in front of a group is grossly overestimated.

The difference between speaking in front of one person and speaking in front of thousands is almost entirely one of confidence. Coupled with confidence should be the ability to speak effectively. There are certain ground rules to effective communication which coaches should understand:

- Be convinced that there is something of value to say. If there is any doubt about it, the best advice is to keep quiet.
- Think before speaking. Even a short time spent in considering what to say and how best to say it will pay dividends.
- Be certain of the meaning of words. Misuse of words inevitably leads to misunderstanding.
- Avoid jargon – particularly professional jargon. The majority of people will not understand jargon and its use can only lead to confusion.
- Speak clearly in terms of volume and speed. In varying the speed, try also to vary the pitch. This makes the presentation more compelling.
- Speak concisely. Short words are better than long words and one word is better than two. This greatly assists clarity. It also assists in reducing the complicated to simple proportions.
- Make all instructions positive. Instructions should be affirmative, i.e. 'Do this' rather than 'Don't do that'.
- Watch the group while speaking. This is compelling and helps the group to concentrate on what is being said.

When the action starts, observe the performance. If the instructions are not carried into action the communication has not been effective. Effective communication is not the complicated business some would have us believe. Effective communication, like effective playing, just requires that the simple things be done well.

COACHING IN THE GAME

The skill of a coach will be put to the most severe test when coaching in an eleven-a-side situation. Coaching in the game is the culmination of all that has gone before and is designed to produce a good team performance. It is the final progression and, of all the progressions, produces the biggest dividend in terms of cashing in on all that has gone before.

Generally speaking, coaching in the game is the worst aspect of coaching since it is so little understood and practised. What coaching in the game frequently amounts to is an indifferent practice game with the coach uttering a stream of unrelated, often confusing and distracting, hints and tips from a position on the touch-line. These people mean well, and are probably very enthusiastic in their approach, but that is not how learning takes place.

Some people take the view that coaching in the game is not necessary. They are mistaken. Coaching techniques and small practices is like making the pieces of a jigsaw. Coaching in the game is fitting those pieces together. To expect the pieces to fall into place by themselves is the height of optimism. It does not and will not happen.

Coaching in the game, like any other form of coaching, has to be structured to be effective; it has to be logical and it has to be systematic. There are three important considerations to coaching in the game.

What to coach

Coaching in the game should be directed towards those factors which the players must perform well as a team. The factors divide into two groups:

Defence

- Restricting time and space.
- Challenging and covering.
- Defending at set plays.

Attack

- Creating and exploiting space.
- Passing and movement.
- Attacking at set plays.

In relation to the above, the coach should encourage the players to understand how to make two calculations:

- The calculation between safety and risk.
- The calculation of playing the percentages, i.e. determining what will be successful most times in a given situation.

Coaching in the game is, however, no different from coaching anything else. Priority order and logical sequence are of the utmost importance.

Where to coach

Because of the calculations, particularly between safety and risk, players need to gain the experience, through practice, of performing as a team in each of the thirds of the field.

Team play in attack should be developed through the defending third of the field, the middle third of the field, and the attacking third of the field. Likewise, team play in defence should be developed through the attacking third of the field, the middle third of the field, and the defending third of the field.

It should not go unnoticed that attacking starts in the defending third and defending starts in the attacking third.

How to coach

There are five basic methods of coaching in the game:

Game control. If a team requires practice in a particular aspect of play in a specific area, then it is helpful to control and limit the play to that area. For example, if a team requires practice at creating space in the middle third of the field, then the practice can be controlled in, and limited to, that area. An objective should be set – for example, getting an attacking player on the edge of the final third of the field, in possession of the ball, and facing the opponent's goal. Once the objective is achieved the practice should be restarted. In this way, time is concentrated on the aspect of play which needs to be improved. Care should be taken that players are always realistically positioned before each practice commences.

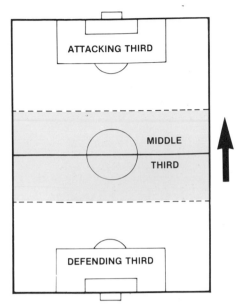

The various aspects of team play already referred to should be coached first in the relevant thirds of the field. The play should then be expanded to two thirds of the field and eventually allowed to go free over the whole pitch. The coach should further control the practice by being the person to start the practice. This is achieved by playing the ball to the particular player or into the specific area required.

Game condition. A form of concentrated practice is achieved by controlling the play in a specific area of the field. Practice, however, becomes much more concentrated if a specific condition is imposed. For example, if concentrated practice at quick passing is required, then the condition of one-touch play can be imposed. If concentrated practice is required at overlap running, then the condition that a player must run outside the player to whom he passes the ball can be imposed.

A condition can be imposed for any aspect of play. It must, however, be understood that a condition is necessarily artificial. Sometimes some conditions produce an element of unrealistic play. It is therefore wise to impose conditions for only relatively short periods – ten or fifteen minutes would normally be acceptable.

Freezing the game. This is a method of stopping the game in order to demonstrate to the players the advantages or disadvantages of their positions. Two points are of particular importance when using this method:

■ There should be a prearranged signal, e.g. a double blast on the whistle, to indicate to the players that play is being frozen.
■ The players, having stopped in their tracks, must remain still. If players wander even two or three yards, the whole picture becomes distorted.

The coach himself must be particularly observant and quick to see a situation which needs freezing. Any hesitation in stopping play will result in the situation changing. It is also important that the coach should freeze play on a theme – for example, coaching supporting angles and distances in attack. If that is the theme in a particular session, then play can be stopped frequently to make the necessary points. It is, however, a bad mistake to stop the play several times to deal with several different themes.

Reconstruction and rehearsal. While freezing the game, it is sometimes helpful to reconstruct and rehearse what went wrong. By this method, if play has been stopped to draw attention to players in poor positions, then play can be reconstructed to show how these players could have been in better positions. It can also be shown how play could then be developed from those positions.

Having reconstructed the play, the players should be rehearsed in moving into those positions: first, by walking; second, by running; and third, by repeating the whole practice at match speed. It is never, of course, sufficient for players to be

25

rehearsed in moving into different positions. They must understand why those different positions are more advantageous.

Thinking ahead. This is a method whereby the coach thinks aloud for the player, anticipating for him. Very often this method is used to advantage following reconstruction and rehearsal. When play is focused on a particular theme, the coach helps the player to adjust and quicken his thinking. There is an obvious danger in this method – the player may rely entirely on the thinking of the coach and cease to think for himself.

All these methods of coaching in the game are, to a greater or lesser extent, necessarily artificial. All sessions, therefore, should end with a period of unrestricted play. That is the only valid test of the effectiveness of the coach and the methods he has used.

The qualities of a good coach

1. Enthusiasm. This is a self-motivating factor. Many of the other qualities a coach requires emanate from this basic quality. Enthusiasm is not a substitute for skill, but no amount of skill will ever compensate for lack of enthusiasm.

2. Integrity. Needless to say there is no substitute for integrity. If a coach lacks integrity, it were better that he did not occupy a position of influence on his fellow human beings.

3. Persistence. Nothing in life worth achieving is achieved easily. Persistence is continuity in a line of action. It is also an act of faith in sticking to the task, and belief in the correctness of the action.

4. Patience. Patience, we are told, will always be rewarded. Progress sometimes comes very slowly and the higher one reaches, the slower the progress becomes. Patience, therefore, is very much a characteristic of top performers – coaches and players alike.

5. Good standards. A good coach will set and demand good standards, especially in relation to attitude.

6. An open and enquiring mind. It is self-evident that progress is based on change and change is based on the development of new ideas. From the process of questioning and enquiring, new ideas are born; by the same process, fallacious ideas are exposed.

7. A logical and analytical mind – the ability to diagnose. Effective coaching and learning is based on a logical approach to analysis and synthesis.

8. Knowledge of how players learn. The various ways in which players learn have been discussed in this chapter. Without that knowledge it is not possible to coach effectively.

9. Knowledge of the principles of effective coaching. Knowledge of the game itself is important, but on its own is not sufficient. It is the adherence to the principles of effective coaching that maximises the dissemination of that knowledge.

10. The ability to inspire. Some coaches have the ability to instil in players an immense sense of purpose. It is when a man has a high sense of purpose that normal expectations in performance and achievement are exceeded.

3
CREATING SPACE (1)
AS AN INDIVIDUAL

Soccer matches are won by exploiting space. Before a team can exploit space, it must first create it. Space is created either by an individual player or by co-ordinated team-play. It can also be given away by the mistakes of the opposition, although players should always plan on the basis that their opponents will give away nothing. Giving away space is considered in the chapters concerned with defending, and creating space by co-ordinated team-play is the subject of the next chapter. This chapter looks at the requirements of the individual.

The player whose ball control is poor needs more space in which to control the ball than the player whose control is good. It is logical, therefore, to start with ball control when considering the matter of creating space at the individual level of performance. To achieve good ball control, a player must understand the principles of ball control and he must practise.

1 Moving into the line of flight
Vince Hilaire moving into the line of flight of a ball which has been played wide of him on the ground.

THE PRINCIPLES AND PRACTICE OF BALL CONTROL

1 Move the controlling surface into the line of flight

If this principle is violated, the player misses the ball. It is clear, therefore, that the first principle of ball control to practise is that of moving the controlling surface into the ball's path.

ORGANISATION FOR PRACTICE

The practice takes place in a grid measuring 30 yards by 20 yards. With young players the area could, with advantage, be reduced. If several grids are needed, each area should be marked with a cone at each corner to save confusion. Two players, O and X (Diagram 1), use each area and are positioned at either end of the grid. O passes the ball on the ground wide of X for X to move to and control. X then passes the ball wide of O for O to control. The practice is then repeated.

The players are instructed to pass the ball on the ground wide of their partner so that he has to move into the path of the ball. Lofted passes should not be used at this stage. The players are encouraged to develop the habit of controlling the ball and creating a passing angle for themselves in one movement – on most occasions in soccer it is a mistake to kill the ball dead.

DEVELOPMENT OF THE PRACTICE

1. Practise controlling the ball with the inside of the foot and passing the ball with the same foot.
2. Practise controlling the ball with one foot and passing the ball with the other foot.
3. Practise controlling the ball with the outside of the foot and passing the ball with either foot.

POINTS FOR THE COACH TO OBSERVE

1. Make sure the practice is being performed correctly, according to instructions. The ball must be played on the ground and it must be played wide of the player making the control.
2. The player making the control should move into the path of the ball early, for early decisions make time. The more proficient a player is in this respect, the wider the server can pass the ball.
3. In controlling the ball, the player should control and make a new angle for the pass in one movement. The process should be as follows:

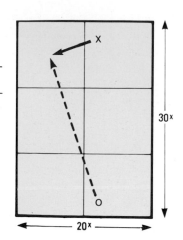

Diagram 1

30ˣ

20ˣ

2a

2b

2c

3a

3b

2 Controlling and creating a passing angle in one movement

2a Hilaire controls the ball with the inside of his left foot and plays the ball wide to his left in one movement.

2b He moves on to the ball.

2c He passes the ball with the inside of his left foot on the second touch.
Note how well his head is down for both the control and the pass.

The three photographs also show well how Hilaire has controlled with the inside of the foot and passed with the same foot.

3 Control with one foot passing with the other foot

3a Hilaire controlling the ball with the inside of his right foot and altering the angle of the ball.

3b Hilaire passing the ball with the inside of his left foot.

- Move the controlling surface into the path of the ball.
- Control and make a new passing angle in one movement.
- Head up and observe the position of the other players as one moves to the ball.
- Head down and pass.

4. Players applying the technique of control in a game should learn to glance away from the ball to check passing possibilities while the ball is in flight. It is a mistake to keep the eyes on the ball throughout its flight.

2 Select the controlling surface early

The second principle in controlling the ball is to decide early which surface of the body is going to be used for the control. Once again early decisions give time: time to become composed and time to concentrate on the technical performance. There are two types of ball control – the wedge and the cushion.

The wedge control. In this type of control the ball is normally wedged between the controlling surface and the ground, as happens when the sole of the foot is used. The lower chest, however, can also be used as a wedge to force the ball down towards the ground. The wedge is characterised by a rigid controlling surface.

The cushion control. In this type of control the controlling surface is withdrawn on impact, rather like a boxer riding a punch. Withdrawing the surface has the effect of 'cushioning' or absorbing the pace of the ball.

4 Control the ball with the outside of the foot and pass with the same foot

4a Hilaire moves into the line of flight and prepares to control the ball.

4b Hilaire controlling the ball with the outside of his right foot sweeping across the ball.

4c Hilaire passing the ball, also with his right foot.

4a

4b

4c

ORGANISATION FOR PRACTICE

The dimensions of the practice area are now increased to 40 yards by 20 yards to facilitate a lofted service and a greater range of controlling techniques. For young players the area could, with advantage, be reduced, but sufficient space is required to enable the player passing the ball to make a lofted pass.

In Diagram 2, O passes the ball wide of X at varying heights so that X first has to move into the line of flight, and then has to select the appropriate body surface with which to control the ball. Once again, X is encouraged to effect the control and create a new passing angle in one movement. The practice is then reversed by X passing the ball back to O. The angle, flight, and pace of the service should all be varied.

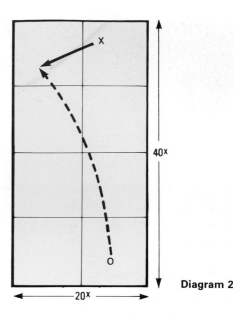

Diagram 2

DEVELOPMENT OF THE PRACTICE

1. Using any technique for controlling a flighted ball, players should practise:

- Moving sideways to make the control.
- Moving forward to control the ball as early in flight as possible.
- Making the control as late as possible and turning with the control to screen the ball from a potential opponent.

2. The three previous elements should be combined so that the service is as varied as possible in terms of angle and flight, and the controlling player is made to move sideways, forwards or backwards to make the control.

3. The ball should be controlled and a volley pass made before the ball touches the ground. Instructions need to be given for a high service to make the performance of this technique possible.

POINTS FOR THE COACH TO OBSERVE

1. Make sure the practice is being performed correctly according to instructions. The ball must be played in the air and the angle and flight should be varied.

2. The player should decide early which surface he is going to use to control the ball. It is helpful to ask the player to nominate the controlling surface while he is moving to the ball by shouting, for instance, 'head', 'chest', 'thigh' or 'foot'.

3. The player controlling the ball should make the control and create a new angle for the pass in one movement. The process is the same as in the previous practice.

5 Wedge control

Hilaire about to wedge control the ball with the outside of his right foot. The ball is wedged between the outside of the boot and the ground as his right foot sweeps across the ball from left to right.

6 Cushion control

Hilaire in position to cushion the ball by using the upper part of his chest. The surface of his chest is withdrawn on the impact of the ball thus absorbing its pace.

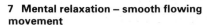

4. The movement from control to pass should be rapid but smooth.

5. Observe in the practice on control and volley pass that the player is balanced as the pass is made and the pass is a volley from the control, not a volley from a bounce off the ground.

3 Be mentally relaxed

If a player becomes tense, his movements become jerky rather than smooth and flowing. Even in the wedge type of control, when the surface presented to the ball is rigid, it is important for the player to be mentally relaxed. Relaxation is a product of confidence – knowing what one can do; tension is a product of uncertainty and fear.

4 Keep the head steady

The principle of keeping the head steady runs like a golden thread through the whole of ball control. It is no overstatement to say that in ball control a steady head controls one's destiny.

A popular but mistaken coaching point is to tell players to keep their eyes on the ball. A simple test will show that this is not usually possible. If you throw a ball in the air and catch it, it is a near certainty that the catch will be made in front of the chest and that at the moment the ball enters the hands the eyes will not be focused on the ball.

Practising against opposition

Some players can both relax mentally and keep their head steady during an isolated practice. Once opponents are brought into the practice, however, a certain anxiety creeps into their play. These players become more concerned with the opponent than the ball.

7 Mental relaxation – smooth flowing movement

7a Hilaire in the air as he performs a high chest control with poise and relaxation.

7b Well balanced as he, followed by the ball, comes to ground.

7c A lovely composed, balanced and flowing movement as he makes the pass.

8 Head and eye position in relation to the control

8a Hilaire inadvertently proves a point by catching an inaccurate service. Note the position of the head and eyes in relation to the ball.

8b No hands this time! Again note the position of his head with the ball at eye level.

31

9 Control the ball away from the opponent

9a Kevin Keegan prepares to control the ball.

9b He controls and screens the ball away from his opponent.

9c He controls the ball away from his opponent and turns to attack the goal.

9d He prepares to shoot for goal with the defender in no position to challenge.

At some stage in the teaching of techniques opposition has to be brought in. Players must be given practice in performing their techniques in circumstances where there are opponents and co-operating players. Time, space, movement and angles now become important factors in the judgment of how to control the ball. Practice to encourage the development of such judgment should not be complicated.

ORGANISATION FOR PRACTICE

In Diagram 3, O passes the ball to X_1 who in turn passes the ball for X_2 to control and pass back to X_1. O waits for X_1 to make the pass to X_2 and then moves to challenge X_2. The distance of O from X_2, and the angle between them, can be varied in order to give X_2 more time to begin with and then less time as he becomes more skilful. O repeats the practice from the same starting position each time.

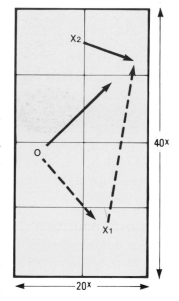

Diagram 3

POINTS FOR THE COACH TO OBSERVE

1. The player controlling the ball should control the ball away from his opponent, thus creating more space and time.
2. Observe that the control creates a passing angle.
3. Observe the quality of the final pass delivered and the number of touches on the ball before delivery. Skilful players should be able to pass the ball on the second touch.

Pressure training to improve ball control

It should be understood that pressure training has no value to a player who has not reached the stage of technical competence sufficient to deal with a rapid number of services in a short space of time. Obviously the more competent, technically, a player is, the quicker and more accurately he will deal with any one service or sequence of services. The art of playing soccer is largely the art of doing simple things quickly and well. Pressure training is a means of training players who can perform techniques well to perform them more quickly.

ORGANISATION FOR PRACTICE

In Diagram 4, X is under pressure. An S player serves the ball to X who controls and passes to any S player. O attempts to intercept the pass. Both O players must

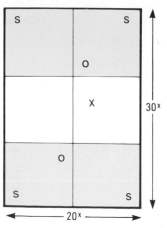

Diagram 4

10a

10b

10c

10d

11a

11b

10 Control to create a passing angle

10a Luther Blissett prepares to control the ball on the turn in front of goal.

10b He controls the ball with the inside of his left foot into the space away from the challenging defender and turns to face the goal.

10c He moves on to the ball, placing his body between the ball and the challenging player.

10d He shoots for goal having evaded the challenge by skilful ball control.

11 Control and pass on the second touch

11a Hilaire makes a chest control on the first touch and alters the angle of the ball.

11b He makes a trap-pass on the second touch.

stay in their respective areas, the S players must remain in their corners, and X should stay in the middle.

The coach controls the practice by nominating the server but not the final receiver. X must control the ball in the middle two squares. The practice can be conditioned so that X always has to control and turn before passing the ball.

POINTS FOR THE COACH TO OBSERVE

1. Ensure that the servers have a sufficient supply of soccer balls and that all players understand the organisational requirements for the practice.
2. The player under pressure should control the ball and adjust the passing angle in one movement.
3. The ball should be passed on the second touch.
4. The pass should be of a high quality and well disguised. The quality of both the control and the pass must be good, otherwise the purpose of the pressure training becomes self-defeating.

BALL CONTROL AS A MEANS TO AN END

Controlling the ball must always be seen as a means to an end. The better the control, the better will be the end performance. The end performance is always one of three possibilities: a pass; a dribble; or a shot. There are two situations in which the control will be made: facing one's opponent's goal; or with one's back to the opponent's goal.

Controlling the ball when facing an opponent and the opponent's goal

ORGANISATION FOR PRACTICE

In Diagram 5, the situation is two-v-one. O_1 passes the ball to X_1 and follows in to try to defend against X_1 and X_2. X_1 controls the ball and must decide the best way to reach the line at the end of the grid. He can either combine with X_2 to beat O_1, or dribble past O_1 himself. The practice should first take place without the off-side law operative, the law being introduced when the players have a good command of the practice.

DEVELOPMENT OF THE PRACTICE

An extra opponent is positioned five yards outside the grid behind X_1 (Diagram 6). The practice follows exactly the same procedure as above but O_2 is allowed to recover and combine in defence with O_1 once X_1 has made contact with the ball. The presence of O_2 injects a greater sense of urgency into X_1 and X_2.

POINTS FOR THE COACH TO OBSERVE

1. There should be a variety of services from O_1 to X_1.
2. Once X_1 has made a good control he should observe the movements of X_2 and decide quickly whether to attack at speed by dribbling or passing. The speed of the attack is important.
3. There should be a positive attempt to attack the back of O_1 and no more than one pass should be made in front of O_1.
4. If O_1 is not being attacked at speed by the player with the ball, he should be attacked at speed by the player without the ball who should run past O_1 into the space behind him.
5. The quality of the pass or the dribble should be such that X_1 or X_2 crosses the 30-yard line with the ball under full control.

Increasing the practice to three-v-two

ORGANISATION FOR PRACTICE

In Diagram 7, the situation is three-v-two. O_1 passes the ball to X_1 and selects to either challenge X_1 or mark X_3. X_2 is marked by O_2. X_1 must again decide the best way to reach the 30-yard line. He can either combine with X_2 and X_3 or dribble the ball himself.

DEVELOPMENT OF THE PRACTICE

An extra opponent is positioned five yards outside the grid behind X_1 (Diagram 8). O_3 is allowed to recover and combine in defending with O_1 and O_2 once X_1 has made contact with the ball. Once again, the effect of this progression is to inject a greater sense of urgency into X_1, X_2 and X_3.

POINTS FOR THE COACH TO OBSERVE

1. In addition to the points already made under the two-v-one practice, the coach should observe closely the ability of the attackers to prevent the defenders from covering each other and marking the important spaces.
2. Observe the ability of the attackers to draw the defenders to one side while exploiting space on the opposite side.

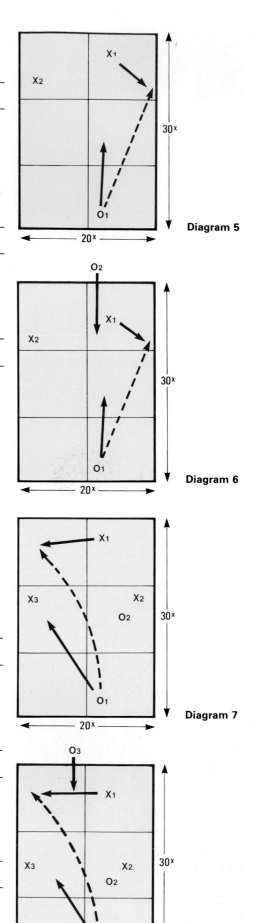

Diagram 5

Diagram 6

Diagram 7

Diagram 8

12

3. Observe the ability of the attackers to isolate one of the defenders in a three-v-two situation.
4. Observe the ability of the attackers to combine movements towards the ball with movements away from the ball, in order to make the defenders' task more difficult.
5. Observe the ability of X_1 to take the ball early and attack at speed.

Controlling the ball with one's back to the opponent and the opponent's goal.

ORGANISATION FOR PRACTICE

In Diagram 9, the situation is one-v-one in the centre of the grid, X being marked by O. There is a server, who is also a target man, at each end of the grid. S_1 passes the ball to X who either turns and passes the ball to S_2 or passes the ball back to S_1. The receiver and marker are alternated so that both players benefit from the practice – unless concentrated practice is required for one player.

12 Control in a situation with one's back to the opponent's goal
Keegan controlling the ball with his back to the opponent and the opponent's goal.

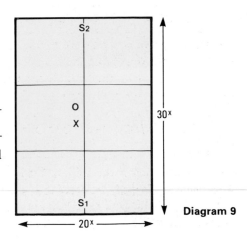

Diagram 9

13a

13b

13c

13d

13e

13f

13g

13 Moving away from the opponent at an angle

13a Keegan moves away from a central position with the defender behind him.

13b Moving away to his right.

13c Continuing at an angle of about 45 degrees.

13d and 13e Watching carefully the line of the pass.

13f and 13g Preparing to receive the ball on his right foot with his body between the defender and the ball.

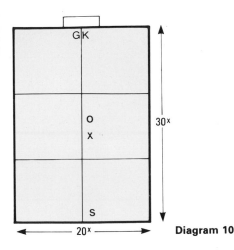

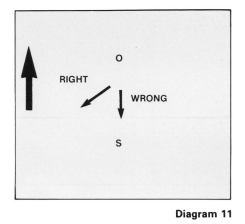

Diagram 10

Diagram 11

DEVELOPMENT OF THE PRACTICE

The practice can be developed and reality increased by introducing a goal and a goalkeeper (Diagram 10). The emphasis is now on X turning, or at least making an angle for himself, so that he can take a shot at goal.

POINTS FOR THE COACH TO OBSERVE

1. The player receiving the ball should feint to move in one direction before checking and quickly moving away from his opponent in the opposite direction in order to receive the server's pass.

2. The player receiving the ball should dictate the angle and speed of the pass. By moving away at an angle, as in Diagram 11, X can observe the movement of O. X will create space in a central position if O follows, or will have the space in which to turn if O does not follow.

3. X should receive the ball on his outside foot so that his body is screening the ball from his opponent. Also, if O does allow X to turn, X has a wider passing angle.

Creating space by moving towards the passer before checking and moving away from the passer.

ORGANISATION FOR PRACTICE

In Diagram 12, the situation is again one-v-one in the centre of the grid, X being marked by O. There is a server at each end of the grid. X and S should combine to create space by adopting one of two ways to put the ball past O:

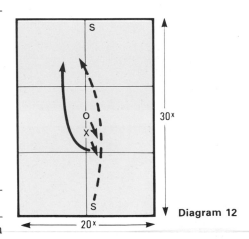

Diagram 12

■ S passes the ball to X who screens the ball at the same time as drawing O closer to S, thereby creating space behind O. X, having created the space, plays the ball back to S, turns and sprints past O to receive the ball in the space created.

■ X draws O towards S, creating space behind O. X then turns and sprints past O into the space and receives the ball from S.

DEVELOPMENT OF THE PRACTICE

The practice can be developed by introducing a goal and a goalkeeper. The length of the grid should be increased to 40 yards to give more space for the delivery of the ball into the space behind O.

14a

14b

14c

14 Controlling the ball on the outside foot – screening the ball from the opponent

14a Keegan preparing to control the ball on his right foot, away from the defender.

14b The control is made with the outside of his right foot.

14c He screens the ball and turns on the defender.

15 Creating space by moving towards the passer before checking and moving away from the passer

15a Keegan moving away from the defender and towards the passer.

15b He receives the ball and plays it back to Ray Wilkins.

15c and 15d He turns to attack the space created behind the defender.

15e Keegan has turned through 180 degrees and is into his running stride. The defender has only turned through 90 degrees and is not yet into his running stride.

POINTS FOR THE COACH TO OBSERVE

1. X should not feint or check his movement since he is trying to draw O out of the space. The tighter, therefore, that O marks X, the more likely it is that space will be created.

2. The movement of X towards S should be of moderate speed, with a sudden change of pace when X decides to turn to attack the space behind O.

3. X's movement towards S can be either straight (Diagram 13), in which case O will have to turn through 180 degrees, but S will have to play the ball over the head of O; or at an angle (Diagram 14), drawing O out of a central position so that X can turn to attack the space to the inside and back of O. The advantage of the second approach is that the ball can be played on the ground.

It should be understood that players who can turn with the ball in a confined space are a considerable asset to any team. They cause defenders to be extremely nervous. Short players with a low centre of gravity are best equipped physically for the technique of turning. Tall players with a higher centre of gravity will turn more slowly. It should also be noted that it is in the final third of the field that the technique of turning an opponent will pay the highest dividend.

THE DEVELOPMENT OF ISOLATED GRID PRACTICES INTO SMALL-SIDED GAMES

The skill in progressing from isolated grid practices depends on the following factors:

Selecting the appropriate number of players. It is a mistake to progress from an isolated grid practice of perhaps two-v-one or three-v-two into a full eleven-a-side game. Because increased numbers bring about increased variables which result in there being more decisions to make in less time, the number of players in the practice should be increased gradually. By progressing first to a five- or six-a-side game, the probability of achieving a successful practice will be maximised.

Diagram 13

Diagram 14

Deciding the dimensions of the area. When calculating the area appropriate to the number of players, use as a rough guide the fact that an eleven-a-side game is usually played with twenty-one players in half, or rather less than half the pitch. The dimensions of the pitch are approximately 115 yards by 75 yards for senior players. For a six-a-side game, therefore, an appropriate area would be 60 yards by 40 yards for senior players.

Achieving concentrated practice on a theme. To achieve concentrated practice in ball control it is desirable to limit the players to two touches, one for controlling the ball and another for passing. Having concentrated on coaching ball control, it is a mistake to allow free play as players will run with the ball and thus defeat the purpose of the coaching. Conditioned play, therefore, should take place for a period of ten to fifteen minutes, followed by a period of free play. It must not be assumed, however, that optimum results can be achieved in a period of fifteen minutes. Learning and developing skills and techniques is a continuous process and one that needs regular coaching. It is important, therefore, to have frequent, but fairly short periods of concentrated practice on the central theme of controlling and passing the ball.

Analysis shows that as far as attacking play is concerned, the techniques which are most frequently required are those of ball control and passing. Without the first, the second becomes very much more difficult. The first touch is therefore vital and should not be taken for granted in the practice game.

Achieving game control. The ultimate goal in coaching is to achieve the performance in the eleven-a-side game that one has coached in smaller situations. It is the most difficult aspect of coaching, but it is the final progression from isolated grid practices and small-sided games and produces the biggest dividend. The purpose of coaching the various individual techniques for creating space in the game is twofold:

■ Players practise performing those techniques in a realistic situation and are made to combine them with other players.

■ Players as a team are made to combine their understanding of when to take risks.

To achieve the first of these requirements, concentration on a theme is necessary. The same two-touch condition which was imposed in the small-sided game is equally appropriate to coaching in the full game. To achieve the second requirement, however, requires concentrated practice in a particular area of the

16 Moving away at an angle before checking and attacking the space inside the defender

16a Keegan moving away from the defender at an angle, almost before Geoff Hurst, the coach, is in a position to observe.

16b He continues his movement at an angle.

16c He receives the ball on his outside foot.

16d and 16e The defender attempts to tackle. (Do not be confused by the goal in the background – it is on the side of the pitch and not part of the practice.)

16f The ball is played back to the supporting player.

16g Keegan immediately turns to attack the space inside the defender. Note that at this moment the two players are moving in opposite directions.

16h Keegan is into his running stride and is attacking the space inside the defender. The defender is caught square and flat footed.

16e

16f

16g

16h

field. Different types of control are appropriate to different areas on the field; for example, receiving the ball and turning on opponents usually involves a risk which is more appropriate to the attacking third of the field.

It is advantageous for the coach to control the practice by selecting a position from which he can play the ball into the area where the practice is to be concentrated. He should instruct the players to position realistically in relation to the position of the ball. In this way, the coach can concentrate the practice in the defending third, the middle third or the attacking third of the field so that concentrated practice is achieved on a selected theme in a selected area.

The coach may allow the play to develop through one third of the field, two thirds of the field or, on rare occasions, all of the field before stopping the practice and restarting from the original positions. This method of coaching in the game is certainly the best means of achieving game control and concentrated team practice. It should, of course, be developed into free play.

POINTS FOR THE COACH TO OBSERVE

1. When a practice is stopped, the players should walk back to their starting positions rather than run back. This will give the coach time to make his coaching points and will reduce the physical tempo of the session.
2. The players should always start in realistic positions.
3. All players should be concentrating before the practice is started.

CREATING SPACE (2)

AS A TEAM

What players do as individuals is always important in soccer. But without co-ordinated team-play, excellent individual performances count for very little. With co-ordinated team-play, the performance of the individual is maximised. There are a number of ways in which space can be created by two or more team-mates combining their understanding and their movements.

CREATING SPACE BY CROSS-OVER PLAYS

The creation of space is usually associated with increasing the distance between defending players. The function of a cross-over play is to do the opposite, to draw two defenders close together and thereby create space either side of them.

Cross-over plays can be executed across the field (side-to-side) or down the field (end-to-end). The player with the ball and a team-mate move towards each other and cross. As they cross, the player without the ball either takes the ball or acts as a decoy for his team-mate who continues to dribble. Three points are of particular importance in the execution of a successful cross-over:

- The movement when the players cross should be accompanied by a rapid acceleration by each player.
- The player dribbling the ball should do so on the foot farthest from the opponent, so screening the ball from him.
- The two players should communicate clearly to establish which one is taking the ball and which one is acting as a decoy.

If the screening of the ball is correctly executed, defenders will find it difficult to get a clear view of the ball. If, in addition, the change of pace is rapid, defenders will find it impossible to react with sufficient speed to mark the attackers. Space is thus created and with it the opportunity to play the ball forward.

1b

1a

1c

1d

1 Cross-overs – taking the ball from the dribbling player

1a Wilkins about to take the ball from Keegan.

1b Wilkins comes away with the ball.

1c Keegan occupies two players while Wilkins moves (out of shot) into space.

1d Wilkins, in space, shoots for goal.

ORGANISATION FOR PRACTICE

In Diagram 1, the situation is two-v-two in a 30-by-20-yard grid with a server, who is also a target man, at each end. S_1 passes the ball to either of the X players, each of whom is closely marked by an O player. The X players must perform a cross-over and create sufficient space in which to pass the ball to the feet of S_2.

The practice is repeated with a ball being served by S_2. If concentrated practice is required, the X players will position to receive and the O players to defend. If concentrated practice is not required, the ball is served to the O players and the X players defend – this time S_1 is the target.

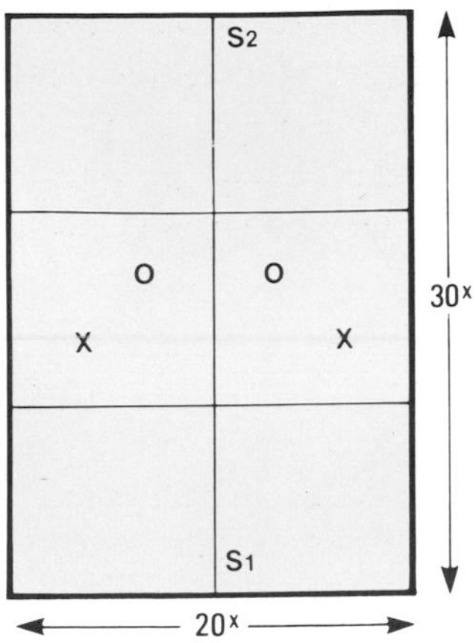

DEVELOPMENT OF THE PRACTICE

The practice can be developed by introducing a goal and a goalkeeper. The same area can be used, although it is probably better to increase the length to 40 yards. Once a goal is introduced, a different technique may be developed whereby the player without the ball takes the ball off the dribbling player by shooting first time.

POINTS FOR THE COACH TO OBSERVE

1. The ball should be screened by the dribbling player.
2. There should be clear communication between the two players to determine which one is taking the ball.
3. Players should make a rapid change of pace at the moment of cross-over.
4. Feint plays should be encouraged. The player with the ball could, for instance, feint to back-heel the ball before dribbling away with it.
5. If the player dribbling the ball is not taking it on he should simply leave it, rather than stop or pass it.
6. When cross-over plays fail, it is usually for one of two reasons: either the two attacking players approach each other too quickly; or they are confused as to which one is to take the ball.

CREATING SPACE BY OVERLAP RUNS

The objectives in making an overlap run are to create space and to exploit space. Overlap runs are always made from positions behind the ball, so that the player without the ball runs outside the player with the ball into a forward position. Overlap runs are usually made on the flanks but can equally well be made in infield positions.

It is important to know when to play behind the ball and support the player in possession, and when to make an overlap run and move into a position in advance of the ball. When the player in possession no longer needs support, that is the time for the supporting player to move forward. When the player in possession is allowed to turn, and has the space in which to play the ball forward, that is the moment when an overlap run can make an extra forward player.

Overlap runs to create space

It will frequently happen that the player in possession of the ball will be challenged by an opponent who also has a covering player.

In Diagram 2, X_1 is in possession of the ball and is challenged by O_1 who is covered by O_2. X_2 is supporting X_1. If X_2 makes an overlap run past X_1 and also runs past O_2, X_2 will either achieve space himself or, much more likely, will draw O_2. This destroys the covering position of O_2 for O_1 and leaves X_1 challenged only by O_1 and with space to attack.

Diagram 1

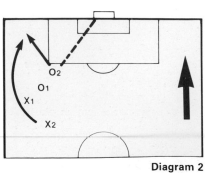

Diagram 2

2a

2 Cross-overs – ball on farthest foot from the opponent

2a Wilkins with the ball on the foot farthest from the opponent.

2b Brooking takes the ball in his stride with Wilkins still screening the ball.

2b

3a

3b

3 Cross-overs – player without the ball acting as a decoy

3a Keegan dribbling the ball and Wilkins acting as a decoy.

3b Keegan continues to dribble the ball and both players accelerate away. Note the defender is flat-footed and the other defender, No 3, is still watching Keegan as Wilkins is about to move past him.

4a

4b

4c

4d

4 Overlap runs – drawing the defender

4a Keegan has turned on his opponent and Brooking moves to get in advance of the ball.

4b Brooking has affected the position of the defender, No 4, and Keegan is taking advantage of the defender's position to move inside.

4c The defender, No 4, is now square and a second defender, whose left foot is just in shot, is also in a poor position.

4d The covering player, No 7, is now in shot and his position has also been affected by Brooking's overlap run. Nothing can now stop Keegan from passing the ball forward.

The advantages of this type of overlap run are that the covering defender's position is destroyed, in terms of the angle and the distance from the challenging player, and he is drawn out of his normal line of retreat. The more defenders can be drawn towards the touch-line, the more space is created in central positions.

It is important that players making overlap runs should remember that, once they have decided to go forward, they must keep on running past not only the player with the ball but also the covering defending player. Clear communication between the overlap runner and the player with the ball is also important. A call of 'hold it' is usually sufficient to alert the player in possession to the fact that he must allow more time for the run to be made.

Overlap runs to exploit space

The challenging player will not always be covered. If this is the case, then an overlap run produces a two-v-one situation in the attacker's favour.

In Diagram 3, X_1 moves slowly towards O_1, thus widening the angle for the ball to be played to X_2 who has made an overlap run. It is important that X_1 passes the ball in front of X_2 so that he can run on to it. It is also important that the pass should place X_2 well clear of O_1.

5 Overlap runs into space to receive the ball

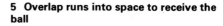

5a Brooking makes an overlap run past Wilkins who is in possession of the ball.

5b Brooking in space to receive the pass, Wilkins in space to deliver the pass.

5c Brooking receiving the ball at the back of the defence and in position to score a well-worked goal.

5a

5b

5c

It is worth pointing out that some players elect to make a run behind O_1 rather than outside X_1 (Diagram 4). If this occurs on a flank there are two particular disadvantages:

- Because of the angle of his run, the range of vision for X_2 is not as good as in the overlap run of Diagram 3. In the overlap run X_2 is running with the ball played in front of him. He can therefore see both the ball and the target area.
- The receiving position for X_2 is not so good because he is running across the path of the ball and away from the target area.

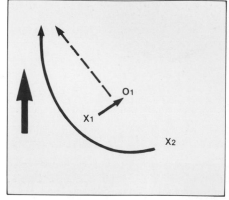

Diagram 3

ORGANISATION FOR PRACTICE

Practice takes place in a 30-by-20-yard grid, using a portable goal. The situation is three-v-two, plus a goalkeeper. In Diagram 5, X_2 starts the practice by playing the ball a couple of yards and X_1 and X_3 make checking movements to create space. X_2 then elects to pass to either X_1 or X_3, and then decides to support or move forward on an overlap run. After each attack the play is stopped and the players walk back to their starting positions to reform.

DEVELOPMENT OF THE PRACTICE

1. In Diagram 6, X_2 starts the practice by passing the ball to X_1. X_1 and X_3 combine to create space so that X_2 can make the overlap run to receive the final pass. The end result can be achieved in three basic ways:

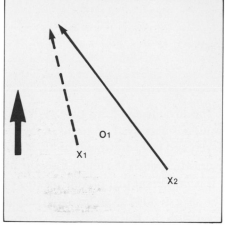

Diagram 4

- X_1 and X_3 move towards each other, X_1 passes to X_3 and X_3 plays the ball first time into the space for X_2.
- X_1 and X_3 effect a cross-over play so that X_3 can pass on to X_2.
- X_1 and X_3 move towards each other to create space and X_1 makes a reverse pass into the space for X_2.

2. The practice can be further developed by extending the length of the grid to 40 yards and introducing a recovering player, O_3 (Diagram 7). O_3 starts 10 yards behind X_2 and is allowed to recover when X_2 passes the ball to X_1 or X_3.
3. The final development of this particular practice is to allow O_3 to position on the goal-side of O_2. O_3 becomes active when X_2 plays the ball.

Although the practice is three-v-three, it should not be considered a small-sided game as it is important to the practice that the marking should remain tight at all times. The players are now encouraged to combine the skill of checking with cross-overs and overlap runs. They should be encouraged to attempt difficult individual techniques and to calculate on the side of risk.

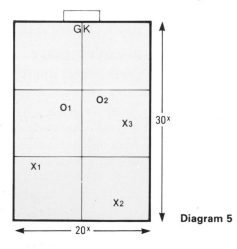

Diagram 5

POINTS FOR THE COACH TO OBSERVE

1. The movement forward from behind the ball should be made at the correct time. If the player in possession of the ball needs support, then a supporting position should be adopted. If, however, the player in possession of the ball has turned and is in a position to pass the ball forward, then that is the moment for the player behind the ball to make his run.
2. The players must communicate with each other. The player making the overlap run should warn the player in possession, telling him to hold the ball. This is a very important element in synchronising the run of the player off the ball with the pass or dribble of the player in possession.
3. The movement of the player making the overlap run should be outside the player in possession of the ball. This will create a better range of vision and a better angle for receiving the pass.
4. The player making the overlap should run past the player in possession and keep running towards the back of the defence. It is a common fault for players to

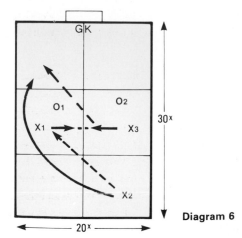

Diagram 6

slow down or even stop running once they achieve a position level with the player with the ball.

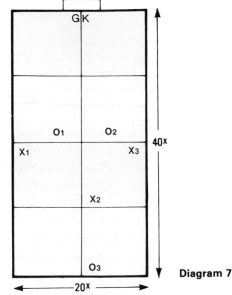

Diagram 7

CREATING SPACE BY ONE-TOUCH PLAY

To survive at the highest level, teams must have the capacity to play accurate one-touch soccer. The nearer one gets to one's opponent's goal, the more important it is to have the ability, as a team, to play accurately and quickly.

One would be mistaken to think that one-touch play is too difficult for those of modest talents. Popular thinking dictates that one should start with something much easier, like two touches or even three touches. To embark on such thinking is to miss the whole point and purpose of one-touch soccer. The purpose of such practice is to increase the ability of the players in the following areas:

1. Range of vision. The majority of young players play with their heads down, rarely observing what is happening around them in terms of the movement of players. This is sometimes due to players being overconcerned with the ball and not sufficiently concerned with surveying the scene. Two touches of the ball allow the player to look, control, and look again before passing. The probability is, however, that between looking, controlling, and looking again, the state of play will have changed. This often leads to indecision and slow play.

The great advantage of one-touch play is that it encourages the players to look and survey the scene, and compels them to make a passing decision before the ball arrives. In the unconditioned game, circumstances will dictate whether or not there is an advantage to be gained in playing the ball first time. The circumstances will differ greatly but, in order to be in position to make the correct decision, one needs to have the range of vision to see the movements of players and the perception to evaluate those movements.

2. Speed of decision. The point has already been made that soccer is very much a game of decisions. It is, of course, important that the decisions should be correct. In order to out-think opponents, however, it is also important to have the capacity to make decisions quickly. One-touch play educates players to think quickly and make early decisions.

3. Ball speed. It is obvious that one-touch soccer is the quickest method of passing the ball. Sometimes it is an advantage to let the ball run to increase space and angles, and to allow more time to survey the state of play before playing the ball. On other occasions it is best to play the ball early. Defenders will react to the movement of the ball. If, therefore, the point of attack is changed frequently in a bout of one-touch interpassing, the movement of the ball will be quicker than the reaction of the defenders. The result will be a space created for the attackers.

4. Movement of attackers. Defenders will not only react to the movement of the ball, they will also react to the movement of the players. When there is a combination of the ball, and the attacking players, moving quickly, the degree of difficulty, in terms of making decision, is at its highest for defenders.

One-touch soccer encourages attacking players to move quickly into positions to help the player playing the ball. Furthermore, it encourages the player playing the ball to move quickly to a new position once the ball is played.

Hopefully it can now be appreciated why one-touch soccer should be regarded as an integral part of soccer education. The formula for success is to practise a little and often – perhaps 15 to 20 minutes every training session.

ORGANISATION FOR PRACTICE

Practice involves six-v-six, including two goalkeepers, in a 40-by-30-yard grid (Diagram 8). The area is small in relation to the number of players because it is essential that the marking is tight and that the players have to work hard to create space. There is a one-touch condition on both teams.

DEVELOPMENT OF THE PRACTICE

Progression in the practice can be achieved by either making the area smaller (for example, 35 yards by 25 yards), or introducing more players (for example, seven v seven). The main progression, however, is to bring the one-touch creation of space into the eleven-a-side game. This aspect is considered on page 57.

POINTS FOR THE COACH TO OBSERVE

1. Adherence to the one-touch condition is all-important and players who play the ball more than once should be penalised.
2. Young players, possibly through fear of mistakes, will often think and play in a negative way. One can expect many passes to be played backwards. Should this occur, it will be necessary to impose a further condition that only one back-pass can be made before the ball is played forward. This will apply equally to the goalkeeper who may be used as an easy safety valve unless the previously imposed condition prevents this from happening.
3. Players should be made to appreciate when they can let the ball run to advantage. Still playing the ball on the first touch, but playing it late (for example, when the ball is played back), it may be possible to achieve the following advantages from allowing the ball to run:

■ Opponents may be drawn towards the ball.
■ More space and wider passing angles may be created.
■ Attackers may be given more time to make penetrative runs and observe those runs.

4. Observe that the players appreciate when to move towards the ball to play the ball early – especially in the attacking third of the field and when opponents are marking tight from behind.
5. Observe the movements of the attacking players, especially the player who has just made a pass. Does he move or stand still? It is not always wrong to stand still, but he must be in a position of advantage.
6. Observe that the point of attack is being changed and that space is being created. Once this space has been created, it should be exploited by a penetrative pass.

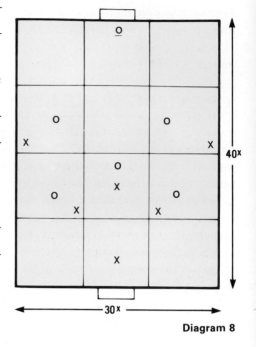

Diagram 8

CREATING SPACE BY SPREADING OUT END-TO-END AND SIDE-TO-SIDE

Soccer is a game of opposites. The objectives of the game are diametrically opposed and depend on whether a team is attacking or defending.

When a team is defending, the object is to restrict the amount of time and vital space available to the attacking players. As a team retreats and funnels back towards its own goal, so that vital space becomes centred in and around the penalty area (Diagram 9). Once the retreat is completed, defending players find themselves in close proximity to each other.

When a team is attacking, the creation of space and time are of paramount importance. This is achieved by attacking players spreading out from either side-to-side or end-to-end, or both. It is also achieved by quick thinking and quick movement on the part of each player.

In the creation of space, quick thinking is every bit as important as quick movement. Quick thinking is only possible if players are concentrating. There is a tendency to relax mentally when the ball changes hands. If this happens, the initiative quickly passes to the opposition. However, if players think and react quickly, they can ensure that having taken possession of the ball they can also seize the initiative.

In Diagram 10, X_2 has made a pass back to his goalkeeper, X_1. Once X_2 is certain that the ball will reach him, he moves off to a wide-angled position and makes himself available to receive the ball. If O does not follow X_2, which is most likely, space is created for X_2 in a flank position. If O does follow X_2, space is created in a central position.

If players, as a team, spread out quickly once possession is achieved, problems are posed for the opposition in terms of marking and covering. Six points are of particular importance in coaching a team to spread out from side-to-side and end-to-end:

- Not only should the runs be made at different angles and into different spaces, but players should also run in such a way that they can keep the ball in view.
- The positions adopted should make it difficult for the opposition to mark players and cover each other.
- The position in which an attacking player receives the ball should give him as wide a field of vision as possible.
- Selection of the pass is important. The ball should be played to the player who is in the best position to penetrate – which is not necessarily the player in the biggest space.
- The quality of the pass delivered is vital. Having created space, that same space can be lost by poor ball control or a poor quality pass.
- If space has been created, then the next stage is to exploit that space. If players persist in playing the ball back or square across the field, the opportunities to exploit space will soon be lost. Having created space, therefore, players must think in terms of exploiting it and making rapid progress towards shooting at the opponent's goal.

ORGANISATION FOR PRACTICE

Practice takes place in the defending third of the field using four defenders, a goalkeeper and three attackers. The coach acts as the server and plays the ball directly to the goalkeeper (Diagram 11). As the ball is travelling to the goalkeeper, and once the defenders are certain that it will reach him, the four defenders spread out.

Diagram 12 shows the new positions adopted by the X players. Once the ball is in the hands of the goalkeeper he rolls it, in this case, to X_4. X_3 responds by making a forward run behind O_2 to make a forward pass from X_4 possible. Back players should be encouraged to make this type of run when space is available and when the player in possession of the ball does not require their support.

In Diagram 13, the ball has been played to X_5 who is being challenged by O_3. X_4 makes a run into the space behind and beyond O_3 to receive a pass from X_5. Note that the goalkeeper, X_1, has moved into a supporting position in place of X_4 and that X_3 has moved across into a central position.

In both examples of this practice, once an X player receives the ball in space

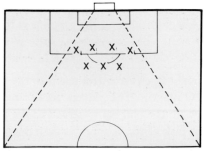

Diagram 9

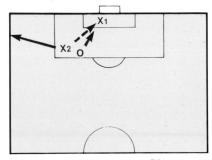

Diagram 10

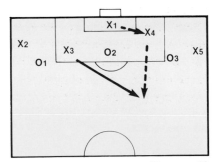

Diagram 11

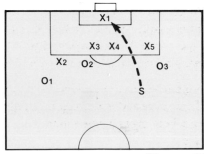

Diagram 12

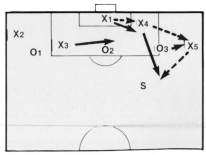

Diagram 13

behind the O players the ball is returned to the server. The players then reform, as in Diagram 11, and the practice is restarted.

DEVELOPMENT OF THE PRACTICE

The next stage is to introduce into the practice three further X players marked by three O players. The players are arranged in the midfield and practice commences again with the ball being served to the goalkeeper (Diagram 14).

The task of X_6, X_7 and X_8 is to move forward and achieve one of two possible objectives: to get behind their markers so that the ball can be played to them in space behind their opponent; or to create space for the back players to utilise as in Diagrams 12 and 13.

In Diagram 15, the players have spread out side-to-side and end-to-end. X_7 has achieved a position behind his marker, O_5, and the goalkeeper has played the ball direct to X_7 in space. In Diagram 16, space has been created between the back players and the midfield players. X_3 has moved into that space to receive a pass from X_4. In both examples of this practice, the object is to get an X player over the half-way line in full control of the ball. The ball is then returned to the server and the players reform and restart the practice.

Further development of this practice can take place by varying the service and playing the ball to any one of the X players, or by playing the ball to one of the O players so that the X players must first win possession before spreading out. The second development gives the players practice at concentrating when the ball changes hands.

POINTS FOR THE COACH TO OBSERVE

1. The players should be alert and in their correct starting positions before the ball is served.
2. Observe the angles of the runs made.
3. Observe that the spaces between the attacking players are such that they make marking and covering difficult for the defending players.
4. Observe the way in which the attacking players are positioned to receive the ball in relation to the path along which the ball has to travel, and the field of vision for playing the ball once it is received.
5. Observe the selection of the pass in relation to its safety and penetration.
6. Observe the quality of the pass in terms of:
   (i) Timing the release – giving time for the players to spread out.
   (ii) Accuracy – the line of best advantage – to feet or to space?
   (iii) Pace – fast enough, so that the space created is not surrendered, but giving ease of control.
7. Progression – by timing the release of the pass with forward runs into spaces behind opponents.

CREATING SPACE BY DIAGONAL RUNS

In the previous section, the development of the practice stopped at a point where it might have appeared logical to include the forward players. It is, however, necessary to consider the skill of making diagonal runs with particular reference to players in forward positions. This is not to suggest that players in other parts of the field will not make diagonal runs to advantage.

A diagonal run is, as the name implies, a run made diagonally across the pitch. These runs can be made in either of two directions:

■ From the centre of the field diagonally towards a flank (Diagram 17). These runs are often referred to as inside-to-outside runs.

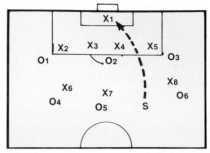

Diagram 14

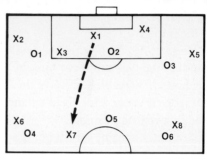

Diagram 15

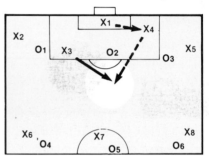

Diagram 16

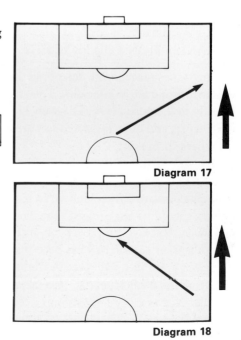

Diagram 17

Diagram 18

6 Diagonal runs – inside to outside

6a Keegan and Blissett making diagonal runs from central positions towards the right flank.

6b They have taken their markers into positions on the flank.

6c Just in shot is an attacker who has made a diagonal run from the left flank to a central position.

6d The ball is delivered into the space, in the right full-back position, to Brooking. Note the defenders making a desperate effort to recover.

7a

7b

7 Diagonal runs – outside to inside

7a The space appears to be in a central position for Brooking (top right of picture) to attack.

7b The central space is attacked by the outside-left making a run from the flank to the inside. Brooking is running into the space created.

7c Brooking moves into the space created by the diagonal run of the outside-left on the blind side of the full-back.

7d Brooking receives the ball in space.

7c

7d

8a

8b

8c

8 Diagonal split runs to create central space

8a Keegan taking his marker towards the ball. Blissett taking his marker away from the ball.

8b The split runs of Keegan and Blissett have created the central space for Brooking to move into.

8c The ball and Brooking arrive in the space created and Brooking shoots for goal.

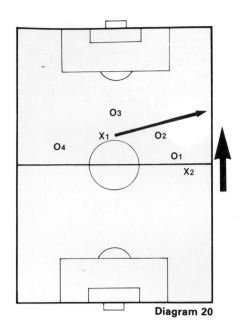

Diagram 20

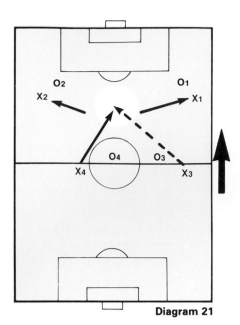

Diagram 21

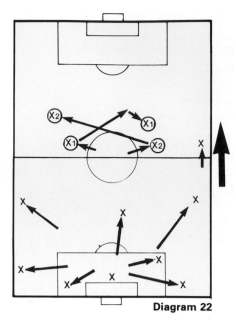

Diagram 22

■ From a flank position diagonally towards the centre of the field (Diagram 18). These runs are often referred to as outside-to-inside runs.

The purpose of the diagonal run is to create space or to exploit space already created. Sometimes the run required will be quite short and deep – 10 to 15 yards (Diagram 19). At other times the runs will be much longer and shallower – 40 to 50 yards (Diagram 20).

In Diagram 19, X_1 passes the ball square to X_2 and runs diagonally from inside to outside. His run opens up the possibility of exploiting space behind O_1, or creating space inside O_1. Because X_1 was running from inside his own half, and because of the position of O_2, the run has to be a steep diagonal.

In Diagram 20, X_1 has made a much longer run into the space behind O_1 and O_2. Because X_1 is in the opponent's half of the field, and because of the position of the O players in relation to the off-side law, the run has to be a shallow diagonal. Forward players frequently have to make both short and long shallow diagonal runs because of the off-side law.

Diagonal runs made by players in forward positions cause defenders considerable problems. Defenders would like attackers to play up and down the field in straight lines. This greatly assists defenders in marking, covering, and retreating towards their own goal. Diagonal running, therefore, is another of those opposites which are designed to give the opposition what they do not want. Diagonal runs present defenders with the problems of being taken out of their normal line of retreat and having to decide how far to go, when to mark players, when to mark space, and how to cover each other.

Good diagonal running by players in forward positions will frequently create space which can be exploited by players moving forward from deep positions. In Diagram 21, X_1 and X_2 have made diagonal runs in opposite directions, called 'split runs' because they split the two central defenders, O_2 and O_1. X_3 has possession of the ball and X_4 makes a diagonal run from a deep position into the space created by X_1 and X_2. The assumption in the diagram is that O_4 has not observed the movement forward of X_4. The movement of X_4 behind O_4 is called a 'blind-side' run because it is on the opposite side of O_4 to the ball. Defending players on the opposite side of the field to the ball are particularly vulnerable to diagonal blind-side runs. This is largely due to the fact that defenders in those positions tend to watch the ball to the exclusion of their opponent and position themselves in such a way that they have their back to their opponent and are unable to observe his movements.

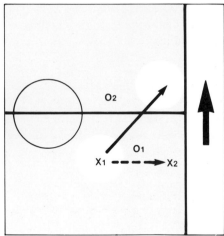

Diagram 19

ORGANISATION FOR PRACTICE

By using a method of coaching called 'shadow play', it is possible for a team to practise diagonal runs and combine these runs with stretching side-to-side and end-to-end. Shadow play takes place with eleven players on the field and no opponents. It is designed to give players a feeling for the movements and an opportunity to develop imaginative play without being inhibited by opponents.

In Diagram 22, the two circled forward players have made diagonal split runs followed by a second diagonal run in the opposite direction. In addition to these runs, X_1 makes a diagonal run away from the opposing goal to meet the pass with his back to goal. X_2 would continue his diagonal run forward to a position from which he can attack either the far post or the near post. As the ball is played forward by the X team, the opposition is stretched both side-to-side and end-to-end.

Shadow play contributes towards developing a team's understanding of the wide variety of attacking movements. Its value is considerable if used at the right time, in the right way, and for the right purpose.

DEVELOPMENT OF THE PRACTICE

The development of shadow play and the bringing together of all the methods practised for creating space, both as individuals and as a team, should take place by coaching in the eleven-a-side game.

Game control. The coaching should take place in thirds of the field, placing emphasis on the players' adoption of the appropriate attitude towards safety or risk. The type of service from the coach should also ensure that the team being coached in attacking play must sometimes have the task of winning possession of the ball from its opponents. This will develop concentration when the ball changes hands.

Achieving concentrated practice. Concentrated practice can be achieved by focusing on a selected theme in a particular third or thirds of the field. For example, the coach may ask the players to concentrate on making cross-over plays in the middle third of the field. To assist in this play the opposition would be asked to mark their opponents man-to-man. By focusing on cross-over plays the coach must understand that the players may make cross-over plays when there is a better alternative. It is for this reason that in every session the play must be

9 Diagonal blind-side runs

9a Blissett in possession of the ball and Keegan starting his diagonal run to get behind the defender on the blind side.

9b Blissett plays the ball past the defender into space. Keegan is moving into that space and has still not been seen by the defender.

9c Keegan, at the back of the defence, in possession of the ball and about to beat the goalkeeper.

allowed to go free for a period. In this way, the coach finds out if the players have the skill to perform the correct technique at the correct time.

On certain aspects of play, even more concentrated practice can be achieved by imposing a game condition:

- Emphasis on ball control – impose the condition of two touches.
- Emphasis on quick play – impose the condition of one touch.
- Emphasis on overlap runs – impose the condition of pass and follow where the passer runs outside the player to whom the ball was passed.

POINTS FOR THE COACH TO OBSERVE

1. General points to observe:
   (i) When play is stopped the players should know if that is the end of the practice or the coach wishes to freeze the play in order to make a coaching point.
   (ii) Players should always start the practice in realistic positions.
   (iii) Ensure concentration on the part of all players before each practice starts.

2. Observe in all parts of the field:
   (i) Concentration as the ball changes hands.
   (ii) Spreading out side-to-side and end-to-end.
   (iii) Receiving positions.
   (iv) Quality of passing.
   (v) Quality of control and selection of pass in relation to safety and risk.
   (vi) Speed and penetration of play.

3. Observe primarily in the middle and attacking thirds of the field:
   (i) Cross-over plays.
   (ii) Overlap runs.
   (iii) Diagonal runs.
   (iv) Control with one's back to the opponent.

5
PASSING AND SUPPORT

The two most important techniques in soccer, and the two techniques which are used most frequently during games, are those of controlling the ball (see pages 28 to 42) and passing the ball. On rather more than 80 per cent of occasions when a player receives the ball, he will pass the ball to a team-mate – on other occasions he will either shoot or dribble. Nothing, therefore, will destroy a team, or an individual, quite so quickly as inaccurate passing. Optimum efficiency in passing cannot be achieved without three things: correct techniques; a range of techniques; and an understanding of how to apply those techniques to bring about skilful passing.

A comparison between high level and low level performance reveals that at a high level more passes are played short (30 yards or less) than long, and more passes are played on the ground than in the air.

In coaching and learning the art of passing, some simple truths need to be grasped:

- If a player cannot pass the ball accurately without opposition, there is absolutely no reason to believe that the introduction of one or more opponents will lead to a technical improvement.
- If a player cannot pass the ball accurately over a short distance, there is absolutely no reason to believe that he will be more accurate over a longer distance.
- If a player cannot pass the ball accurately on the ground, there is absolutely no reason to believe that he will be more accurate at passing the ball in the air.
- If a player is not comfortable and composed in receiving balls on the ground, there is absolutely no reason to believe that he will be more comfortable and composed when receiving balls in the air.

It is necessary to grasp the above fundamental truths in order to establish priorities and logical progressions in coaching and learning the art of passing.

The art of effective play in soccer is the art of doing the simple things quickly and well, and persisting in following that formula. It is the amateur, in all sports, who gambles, without calculation, on the difficult and the spectacular. The professional concentrates much of his effort on taking the unforced errors out of his game. The amateur, through poor understanding and sheer foolhardiness, persists in introducing unforced errors into his game. The fact that his opponents usually do the same only serves to mask a multitude of sins.

The fundamental difference between the professional and the amateur is as much one of attitude as it is of technique. It is the responsibility of teachers and coaches to ensure that young players start with the correct attitude. This is best achieved by coaching the right technique at the right time and in the right order. Thus good habits are developed from the start. This leads to the logical conclusion that one should start by coaching passing without opposition, over a short distance (in a 10-yard grid), and on the ground.

1 The Push Pass

1a The part of the foot used to make contact with the ball.

1b Placement of the non-kicking foot – note also head down.

1c Kicking foot at right angles to the line of pass – head still down.

1a

PASSING TECHNIQUES – GROUND PASSES

Passing the ball with the inside of the foot

The 'push pass' is the most reliable technique for passing the ball on the ground over short distances with accuracy.

The kicking foot. The foot is turned outward so that the side of the boot makes contact with the ball at right angles to the line of the pass. The ankle must be firm. In order to keep the ball low, the contact of the boot on the ball must be through the horizontal mid-line of the ball.

1b

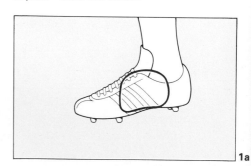
1c

The non-kicking foot. The foot should be placed far enough to the side of the ball to allow a free-swinging movement of the kicking leg.

Position of the head. The eyes should be looking down at the ball and the head should be steady.

Advantage
- It is the best guarantee of accuracy because of the large surface of the boot presented to the ball.

Disadvantages
- The pass is easy for defenders to predict.
- It is not suitable for long passing or power shooting as it is difficult to generate power in such a technique.
- It is not an easy pass to make when running at speed as it is not possible to position correctly without interrupting the stride pattern.

ORGANISATION FOR PRACTICE

Practice takes place in a 10-yard grid. A pass is made with a dead ball. In Diagram 1, X passes the ball to the feet of O. O must stop the ball by slightly altering the angle and giving himself space to move towards the ball and pass the ball back to the feet of X. It is important that the player receiving the pass should always stop the ball and alter the angle in one movement.

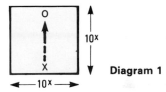

Diagram 1

DEVELOPMENT OF THE PRACTICE

1. Once the players are accurate over 10 yards, they should be encouraged to play the ball in two touches: the first touch to stop the ball and alter the angle; the second touch to pass the ball while it is still rolling.
2. Further progress can be made by players passing the ball with a first-time pass. Having made the pass, the player should move across his grid. In Diagram 2, X passes the ball to O and then moves to a new position. O passes the ball to X in his new position and then moves to a new position himself. This encourages the players to look up and observe the target before passing.
3. Still further progress can be made by extending the grid to 20 yards by 10 yards. Passing over the longer distance should start with the two-touch routine and then progress to using only one touch.

Diagram 2

The player should always move across his 10-yard line after passing the ball.

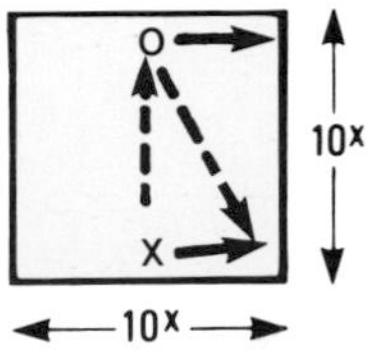

POINTS FOR THE COACH TO OBSERVE

1. Observe that the players are practising according to instructions.
2. Observe the action of the kicking foot and its point of contact with the ball.
3. Observe the position of the non-kicking foot.
4. Observe the position and steadiness of the head.

Passing the ball with the instep

Passing the ball with the instep (the laces) is not as easy as with the side of the foot. More practice is therefore required to perfect the technique.

The kicking foot. The toe must be kept pointing down towards the ground so that the instep makes contact with the ball through the horizontal mid-line. If the toe is not kept pointing down, the kicking foot is likely to make contact with the ball through the bottom half and the ball will rise off the ground. The foot should also make contact with the ball through the vertical line. This will ensure that the ball goes straight. The approach to the ball is from an angle of about 30 degrees and the boot of the kicking foot goes through the vertical line at an angle. Very rarely is the boot of the kicking foot in a vertical position (Diagram 3).

Diagram 3

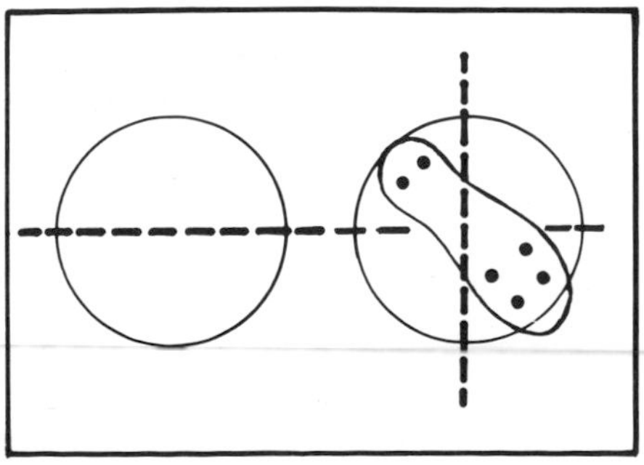

2 Contact on the ball

2a Contact the ball through the horizontal mid-line and the ball stays down.

2b Contact the ball below the horizontal mid-line and the ball goes up.

The non-kicking foot. The foot should be alongside the ball and a few inches away from it otherwise the kicking foot is likely to contact the ball through the bottom half and the ball will rise off the ground.

Position of the head. The eyes should be looking down at the ball and the head should be steady.

Advantages

- It is easy for the passer of the ball to disguise his intentions and therefore difficult for defenders to predict the pass.
- It is a good technique for power and pace and is therefore of value for long passing and shooting.
- It is a technique which can be used when running at speed without interrupting the stride pattern.

Disadvantage

- It is a difficult technique to perform because a relatively small part of the boot strikes the ball, and a relatively small area of the ball has to be hit to achieve accuracy.

Left: Low drive with the instep
Keegan – toe down and striking through the horizontal mid-line. Note that the head is steady and the eyes are firmly on the ball.

Below: Position of the non-kicking foot
Blissett's non-kicking foot in perfect position alongside the ball.

ORGANISATION FOR PRACTICE

The practice, and development of the practice, is exactly the same as that for passing the ball with the inside of the foot.

POINTS FOR THE COACH TO OBSERVE

1. Observe that the players are practising according to instructions.
2. Observe the action of the kicking foot and its point of contact with the ball.
3. Observe the position of the non-kicking foot.
4. Observe the position and steadiness of the head.

Passing the ball with the outside of the foot

Passing the ball with the outside of the foot is an essential technique in the armoury of players who wish to play at a high level. The technique can be used over short distances, and in tight situations, to flick the ball through quite wide angles with heavy disguise. Over longer distances the technique can be used to swerve the ball past opponents.

The kicking foot in the flick pass. The foot is positioned to the inside of the ball and the ball is 'flicked' by an outward rotation of the foot. To keep the ball down, contact with the ball should be made through the horizontal mid-line. This technique can only be used over short distances.

The kicking foot in the swerve pass. The foot comes across the body and across the ball from outside to inside, contacting the ball just left of centre for a right-footed kick, thus imparting spin and swerve to the ball from left to right. The foot should make contact with the horizontal mid-line of the ball in order to keep the ball low. The ball should be positioned in the centre of the stance.

The non-kicking foot. For both the flick pass and the swerve pass the foot should be placed a little behind and to the side of the ball. This position facilitates the movement of the kicking foot.

Position of the head. The eyes should be looking down at the ball and the head should be steady.

Advantages
■ The flick pass can be made with the minimum of foot movement and the maximum disguise.
■ The swerve pass can be used to bend the ball round an opponent.
■ The swerve pass can be used over long distances and is therefore a valuable technique for shooting.
■ The swerve pass can be used when running at speed without interrupting the stride pattern.

Disadvantages
■ The flick pass can only be used over short distances.
■ The more swerve required the more difficult it is to control the kick.

ORGANISATION FOR PRACTICE

The practice of flick passing with the outside of the foot, and the development of the practice, is exactly the same as that for passing the ball with the inside of the foot and the instep. For practice in swerving the ball past opponents, however, the players should be in a 20-yard grid and preferably passing the ball down a line in order to see the amount of swerve imparted to the ball (Diagram 4).

3 The flick pass
The flick pass allows heavy disguise but can only be played over short distances.

4 The flick pass when marked from behind

4a Preparing to receive the ball – knee bent.

4b Extension and outward rotation of the kicking leg.

4c Play the ball in one direction, move off in the opposite direction.

POINTS FOR THE COACH TO OBSERVE

1. Observe that the players are practising according to instructions.
2. Observe the action of the kicking foot and its point of contact with the ball.
3. Observe the position of the non-kicking foot.
4. Observe the position and steadiness of the head.

Swerve pass using the outside of the foot

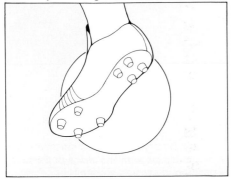

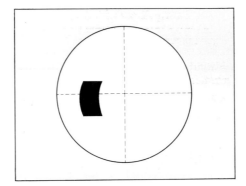

5a Foot comes across the ball, right to left with the right foot.

Swerve pass using the inside of the foot
6a Foot comes across the ball, left to right, with the right foot.

5b Contact on the ball is made just left of centre with the outside of the foot.

6b Contact on the ball is made just right of centre with the inside of the foot.

5c The follow through of the foot is across the body. This is facilitated by the non-kicking foot being behind the ball.

6c The follow through is away from the body.

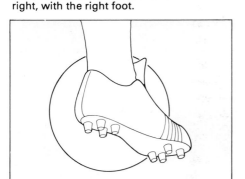

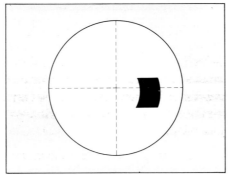

Passing the ball with the inside of the foot for swerve

This pass, which should not be confused with the push pass, can be used over short or long distances and a great deal of spin and swerve can be imparted to the ball.

The kicking foot. The foot comes across the ball from inside to outside. There is an outward rotation of the kicking leg. The ball is struck by the forward part of the inside of the kicking foot in the region of the joint of the big toe. Contact with the ball is made just right of centre, for a right-footed kick, thus imparting spin and swerve to the ball from right to left. The foot should make contact with the middle of the ball to keep it low.

The non-kicking foot. The foot is positioned 8 to 12 inches to the side of the ball and slightly behind it.

Position of the head. The eyes should be looking down at the ball and the head should be steady.

Advantages
■ The ball can be bent round an opponent.
■ The pass can be used over long or short distances and is a valuable technique for shooting.
■ If contact is made slightly below the horizontal mid-line, the ball can easily be lifted a few inches over a defender's outstretched legs.

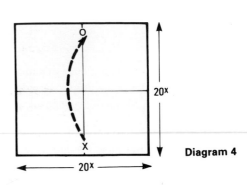

Diagram 4

- A great deal of swerve can be imparted to the ball and the swerve is easier to control than the swerve with the outside of the foot.
- The ball is drawn away from the goalkeeper when it is crossed from a flank.

Disadvantage
- The ball will never go straight and will always be spinning – possibly making control a little more difficult.

ORGANISATION FOR PRACTICE

The practice follows the established pattern. For practice in swerving the ball past opponents, however, as with swerve passing with the outside of the foot, the players should be in a 20-yard grid and preferably passing the ball down a line.

POINTS FOR THE COACH TO OBSERVE

1. Observe that the players are practising according to instructions.
2. Observe the action of the kicking foot and its point of contact with the ball.
3. Observe the position of the non-kicking foot.
4. Observe the position and steadiness of the head.

7 Swerve pass with the inside of the foot – position of the non-kicking foot
Non-kicking foot behind the ball to facilitate movement across the ball of the kicking foot.

PASSING TECHNIQUES – LOFTED PASSES

The range of techniques available to a player who wants to be a good passer of the ball must include the technique of lofting the ball. There are occasions when the only way in which to exploit space behind opponents is to loft the ball over their heads. There are three basic techniques which can be used to achieve this objective: the lofted drive; the chip; and the volley. Within these three basic techniques, there are four different techniques for achieving the lofted drive and two different techniques for achieving the volley.

The chief characteristic of all the passes is that the kicking foot must strike the ball through the bottom half, that is below the horizontal mid-line. There is no other contact on a ball which will cause a ball to rise. Which technique should be selected in any given situation will depend fundamentally on three considerations: the length of the pass; the space in front of the nearest defender over whom the ball will travel; and the space behind the defender where the ball will pitch.

The lofted drive with the instep from a slightly angled approach

The kicking foot. The ankle should be extended and firm and contact with the ball should be made through the vertical mid-line and through the bottom half of the ball.

The non-kicking foot. The foot should be slightly to the side of the ball and behind it.

Position of the head. The eyes should be looking down at the ball and the head should be steady.

Advantages
- The ball can be played over distances of more than 40 yards.
- The ball can be played with considerable pace, thus giving defenders little time in which to make up ground.

Disadvantages
- The ball will not have a steep trajectory. It is, therefore, difficult to clear defenders who are less than 10 to 12 yards away from the kicker.

8 Lofting the ball
To loft the ball contact must be made below the horizontal mid-line.

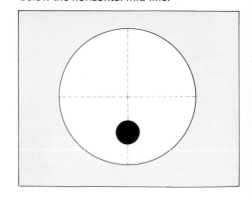

■ There will be little or no spin imparted to the ball. The ball, therefore, will continue to roll after pitching. An acute sense of pace will be required if the ball is played into space.

The lofted drive with the instep from a wide-angled approach

The kicking foot. The foot should be pointed outwards and the ankle should be firm and extended. The foot should sweep through the bottom half of the ball.

The non-kicking foot. The foot should be positioned some 12 to 18 inches to the side of the ball, and behind it.

Position of the head. The eyes should be looking down at the ball and the head should be steady.

Advantages
■ The ball can be played over distances of more than 40 yards.
■ The pass is not difficult to control.
■ A certain amount of back-spin can be imparted to the ball, thus slowing the run of the ball in space.
■ A steeper trajectory can be achieved than that with the instep pass from a slightly angled approach.

Disadvantage
■ The ball cannot be hit with as much pace as some other methods of kicking. Defenders, therefore, have a little more time to adjust their positions while the ball is in flight.

10 Lofted drive with the instep from a slightly angled approach

10a The placement of the non-kicking foot is slightly behind the ball.

10b Contact on the ball is through the bottom half.

10c The body leans slightly back.

11 Lofted drive with the instep from a wide-angled approach

11a The front view showing the leg extension of the kicking foot and the position, to the side of the ball, of the non-kicking foot.

11b The back view showing the contact sweeping through the bottom half of the ball.

The lofted drive with the outside of the foot

The kicking foot. The foot should come across the ball and across the body from outside to inside, imparting swerve and spin to the ball. The foot makes contact through the bottom half of the ball, slightly to the left of centre for the right-footed player.

The non-kicking foot. The foot should be positioned to the side of the ball and behind it.

Position of the head. The eyes should be looking down at the ball and the head should be steady.

Advantages
- The ball can be played over distances of more than 40 yards.
- The ball can be played with pace.
- The ball can be swerved away from defenders, thereby making interception more difficult.
- The ball can be swerved into the path of an attacking player.

Disadvantages
- The kick is difficult to control over long distances.
- The ball will not have a steep trajectory.
- The ball will continue to roll after pitching. It is difficult, therefore, to judge the pace of the pass into space.

The lofted drive with the inside of the foot

The kicking foot. The foot should come across the ball from inside to outside with an outward rotation of the kicking leg. The ball should be struck by the forward part of the inside of the kicking foot. The foot makes contact through the bottom half of the ball, slightly to the right of centre for the right-footed player.

The non-kicking foot. The foot should be positioned to the side of the ball and behind it.

Position of the head. The eyes should be looking down at the ball and the head should be steady.

Advantages
- The ball can be played over distances of up to 40 yards.
- The ball can be played with pace.
- The ball can be swerved away from defenders, thereby making interception more difficult.
- The ball can be swerved into the path of an attacking player.
- The kick is relatively easy to control.
- A reasonably steep trajectory can be achieved.

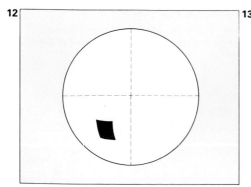

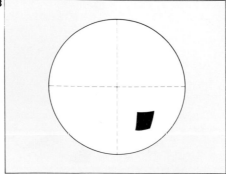

12 Lofted drive with the outside of the foot

Contact is made through the bottom half of the ball and left of centre for the right-footed player.

13 Lofted pass with the inside of the foot

Contact is made through the bottom half of the ball and right of centre for the right-footed player.

Disadvantage

■ The main disadvantage is that the ball will continue to roll after pitching so that it is difficult to judge the pace of the pass into space.

ORGANISATION FOR PRACTICE

The practice takes place in an area measuring 40 yards by 10 yards. In Diagram 5, O_1 passes the ball to X_1 who plays a lofted pass to X_2. X_2 controls the ball and passes to O_1 who returns the ball for X_2 to make a lofted pass to X_1. O_1 is confined to the middle two squares but must threaten the line of flight. The same method is used for practising each of the four techniques, each of which should be practised first with the stronger foot and then with the weaker foot. Eventually, unrestricted practice is allowed.

DEVELOPMENT OF THE PRACTICE

In Diagram 6, O_1 passes the ball to X_1 who controls the ball and plays a lofted pass to X_2. The X players should continue to pass to each other, controlling with the first touch and passing with the second. O_1 and O_2 are confined to the middle two squares. Their task is to threaten the line of flight and force the passer to pitch the ball deep into the receiver's square.

POINTS FOR THE COACH TO OBSERVE

1. Observe that the players are practising according to instructions.
2. Observe the action of the kicking foot and its point of contact with the ball.
3. Observe the position of the non-kicking foot.
4. Observe the position and steadiness of the head.

The chip pass

The kicking foot. The action of the kicking leg should be a stabbing movement, or downward thrust, which should bring the foot into contact with the ball at a point where it touches the ground. This action imparts vicious back-spin on the ball.

The non-kicking foot. The foot should be no more than 3 or 4 inches to the side of the ball.

Position of the head. The eyes should be looking down at the ball and the head should be steady.

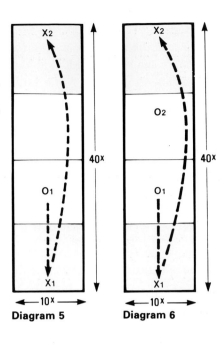

Diagram 5   Diagram 6

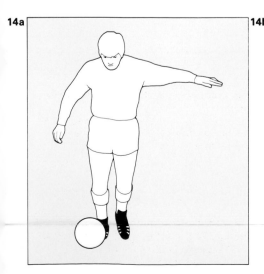 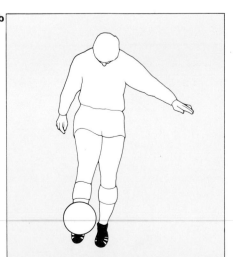

14 The chip pass

14a The approach is straight.

14b The action of the kicking foot is a stabbing action to the underneath of the ball. Vicious back-spin is thus imparted to the ball.

Advantages

■ Because of the vicious back-spin which is imparted to the ball, a very steep trajectory can be achieved. It is, therefore, possible to play over the heads of opponents who are only 5 or 6 yards away from the ball.

■ Because of the back-spin on the ball, it is possible to stop the ball in small spaces.

Disadvantages

■ The pass can only be played over distances of up to 20 to 25 yards.

■ Players running on to the ball may find it difficult to control because the control would be made against the spin.

ORGANISATION FOR PRACTICE

The practice takes place in a grid measuring 20 yards by 10 yards. In Diagram 7, O passes the ball to X_1 who must chip the ball over the head of O to pitch, and stay, in the square occupied by X_2. X_2 then passes the ball to O and the practice is repeated with O serving the ball to X_2.

In the early stages of this practice, it is important that the receiver should not try to control the ball. The ball should be allowed to pitch and thus establish if there is sufficient back-spin on the ball to keep it inside the grid.

Diagram 7

DEVELOPMENT OF THE PRACTICE

It is much easier to chip a ball which is rolling towards the passer than it is to chip a ball which is rolling away. On many occasions, the chip pass will have to be made in a game when the ball is rolling away from the passer. The practice in Diagram 7, therefore, should be repeated, with the X players controlling the ball, and then making a chip pass with the ball rolling away from them. O should always threaten the line of flight by moving along the 10-yard line. He should not enter the square of the passer.

POINTS FOR THE COACH TO OBSERVE

1. Observe that the players are practising according to instructions.
2. Observe the action of the kicking foot and its point of contact with the ball.
3. Observe the position of the non-kicking foot.
4. Observe the position and steadiness of the head.

15 Volley with the instep from a straight approach

15a In line and preparing to volley.

15b Ankle extended as the knee is raised.

15c Contact with the instep (laces) through the vertical mid-line.

15d Balanced and head still down after contact.

Volley pass with the instep from a straight approach

The kicking foot. The foot should contact the ball through the vertical mid-line and through the bottom half of the ball, *not* underneath the ball. The ankle should be extended.

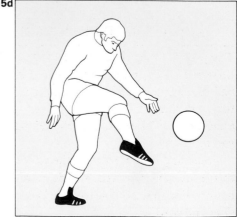

15a

15b

15c

15d

The non-kicking foot. The foot should always be behind the ball. If, however, the ball is played early in flight, the non-kicking foot will be farther behind the ball. If the ball is played late in flight, the non-kicking foot will be nearer to the ball.

Position of the head. The eyes should be looking down at the ball and the head should be steady.

Advantages
- The ball can be played over the heads of opponents who are only a few yards from the ball.
- The ball can be played early to enable quick exploitation of possession.
- The ball can be played over long distances.
- The ball can be played with considerable pace.
- The ball can be 'dipped' by imparting top spin to the ball.

Disadvantages
- The pass is difficult to control in terms of its accuracy.
- The pace of the pass is difficult to control.

The volley pass with the instep from a sideways approach

This type of kick is often referred to as a 'hook volley'. The essential feature is that the body is positioned sideways to the line of the ball. The leading shoulder should fall away to allow the kicking leg to swing through smoothly.

The kicking foot. The foot should point outwards and the kicking leg should swing forward and across the body. Contact with the ball is made just below the horizontal mid-line.

The non-kicking foot. The foot should be well to the side of the ball in order to allow the swing and follow-through of the kicking leg. The body rotates on the standing leg.

Position of the head. The eyes should be looking down at the ball and the head should be steady.

Advantages
- The ball can be played over the heads of opponents who are only a few yards from the ball.
- The ball can be played over long distances.
- Considerable pace on the ball can be achieved.
- The ball can be played early.

Disadvantages
- This type of volley is even more difficult to control than the previous one in terms of accuracy.
- The pace of the pass is difficult to control.

16 Playing the ball early in flight
The non-kicking foot is well back if the ball is played early in flight.

17 Playing the ball late in flight
The non-kicking foot is much nearer to the ball if the ball is played late in flight.

ORGANISATION FOR PRACTICE

The practice starts in a grid measuring 20 yards by 10 yards. In Diagram 8, X throws the ball up in front of him, allows the ball to bounce and then volleys the ball to O. O controls the ball and repeats the practice. The players must practise first with their stronger foot and then with their weaker foot. Once the players are accurate over 20 yards, they should extend the distance to 30 yards and then to 40 yards.

Practising the volley from the sideways position is much the same but in this case a server is used. In Diagram 9, S throws the ball for X to make a hook volley to O. O controls the ball and returns it to S who then throws it for O to volley to X.

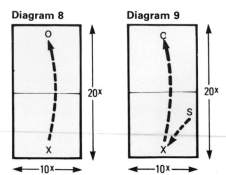

DEVELOPMENT OF THE PRACTICE

When the players are accurate over a distance of 30 to 40 yards, the practice can be developed by introducing an element of opposition. In Diagram 10, O_1 throws the ball for X_1 to volley to X_2. O_1 begins by throwing a ball which bounces in front of X_1, thus allowing a little more time for X_1 to make the volley. The degree of difficulty is increased by varying the flight of the service and by requiring X_1 to volley the ball before it touches the ground. O_1 and O_2 must threaten the flight of the ball within the confines of the middle two squares. When X_2 controls the ball, he returns it to O_2 who throws the ball for X_2 to volley to X_1, thus repeating the practice.

POINTS FOR THE COACH TO OBSERVE

1. Observe that the players are practising according to instructions.
2. Observe the action of the kicking foot and its point of contact with the ball.
3. Observe the position of the non-kicking foot.
4. Observe the position and steadiness of the head.

DEVELOPING THE SKILL OF PASSING

It should now be evident that a player cannot be a good passer of the ball without good techniques. It should also be understood that a player cannot apply even the best techniques unless he has a full understanding of what is happening around him and how to respond to circumstances. The application and transference of good technique into the skill of passing is based on two factors: selecting the pass; and making the pass.

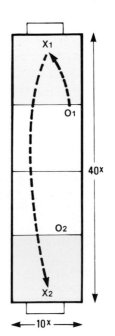

Diagram 10

Selecting the pass

Selecting the pass involves assessing the game's state of play and then deciding what technique best suits the circumstances. The decision is based on a consideration of the following factors:

What one sees. If players play with their heads down, they will see very little in terms of passing possibilities. Added to this, if players are not relaxed when they receive the ball, they will tend to squander the time which is available to them.

Players, therefore, should be educated to look and to see. This means that players must lift their heads and observe the play around them.

How this vital element is taught is of the utmost importance. Get this element wrong and very little else of value can be added. The majority of those who have responsibility for coaching young players are getting it comprehensively wrong. One observes very young players playing eleven-a-side games where nearly twenty of the players are packed into a very small area of the pitch. Imagine the thoughts of a young player having received the ball and looking up. He will probably see total confusion and, in the confusion, he may be excused for not being relaxed. He may also be excused for not seeing one of his team-mates unmarked.

It must be stressed that the education of young players should start with small numbers in a situation where the probability of success is weighted towards the player in possession of the ball. In simple terms, this means more attackers than defenders (for example, four-v-one in a 10-yard grid), so giving the young player time to look (Diagram 13). What he sees will be in his favour. From such a start three things will happen:

- The players will develop the habit of looking and seeing.
- The players will become more confident.
- The efficiency of the players in passing the ball will improve.

When this point is reached the time is right to increase the degree of difficulty for the attacking players.

The position of one's own team-mates. Having learned to look, the player in possession of the ball should learn to see which of his team-mates is in the best position to receive a pass. The pass which puts the most opponents out of the game is the most penetrative. The player in a position to receive such a pass, therefore, is in the position of most advantage, for it makes penetration possible.

The position of the opposing players. The defender who can have the most influence on the player with the ball is the immediate opponent. If the immediate opponent is in a good challenging position and is preventing the ball from being played forward, then the sooner the ball is passed to a team-mate who is in a position to pass the ball forward the better. If the immediate opponent is not in a position to prevent the ball from being played forward, then the ball should be played forward to the team-mate in the most penetrative position.

It could be that the opposing players are so well positioned that there is no attacking player in a position to penetrate. In these circumstances the attackers should remember that defenders will react to the movement of the ball. If the ball is passed quickly and accurately, and the point of attack is changed rapidly, the defenders will have to adjust their positions. Since the ball, however, will travel quicker than the defenders, space will almost certainly be created and progress forward should then be possible.

The area of the field and the calculation between safety and risk. In general terms, the nearer an attacker is to his own goal, the more he should calculate on the side of safety in passing the ball. The nearer an attacker is to the opponent's goal, the more he should calculate on the side of risk in his passing.

Tactical objectives. Tactical objectives will vary within a game. One of the major factors affecting tactics will be the scoreline. The emphasis may be on penetration and taking risks if a team is losing, or it may be on ball possession and safety if a team is winning. Whatever the objective, it is a very dubious tactic to emphasise possession without penetration.

Knowing one's technical capabilities. The biggest *risk* of all is to attempt a technique of which one is not capable. But the biggest *mistake* of all is only to attempt the technique at which one is a master. Somewhere between these two extremes, of attitude rather than technique, lies the balanced skilful performance.

18 Volley with the instep from a sideways approach

18a Adopt a sideways position early.

18b Ankle extended as the knee is brought through in advance of the foot.

18c The kicking leg almost parallel with the ground.

18d Contact on the ball with the instep (laces) just below the horizontal mid-line.

18e The body rotates round the non-kicking leg after contact.

Depending upon his technical competence, a risk for one player may be perfectly safe for another. A player should know, in relation to any one technique, what his capabilities are so that he can play the percentages in relation to his own technical performance. He does this by refusing to attempt what is for him impossible, but attempting the difficult at the right time and in the correct area of the field. We all want to see adventurous and attacking football, but it is not possible without a good range of techniques for passing the ball.

Making the pass

Other than the need to pass the ball accurately, there are three qualities which contribute towards a skilful pass:

Disguise. Defenders will always try to make the play predictable. Attackers must do the opposite and try to make the play unpredictable. Attacking players achieve this objective by pretending or disguising their intentions. They can do this by shaping up to pass in one direction as a disguise for passing in a different direction; by pretending to pass the ball and then holding it; and by pretending to stop the ball and then letting it run. All these ploys are designed to achieve two objectives:

■ To create space and passing angles where neither existed.
■ To mislead the defenders into thinking the ball will be played in one direction so that the ball can be played in a different direction.

Timing the release of the ball. If the ball is released too soon, it will be for one of two possible reasons:

■ The pass was made before the space or the passing angle was created.
■ The pass was made before the team-mate was available to receive the pass.

If the ball is released too late, it will be for one of three possible reasons:

■ The player did not observe that a pass was on.
■ The player delayed and gave the defenders time to seal off space and passing angles.
■ The player delayed and the team-mate ran off-side or into a position of disadvantage.

The pass released at the right time places the passer's team-mate in a position of maximum advantage and the defender in a position of maximum disadvantage. In Diagram 11, X_2 is in possession of the ball. O is defending and is last in the line of the defence. X_1 makes an overlap run. At position 1, the ball is released too soon and O will be first to the ball because the pass was made before X_1 was available to receive the pass. At position 3, the ball is released too late and X_1 is off-side. At position 2, the ball is released at the correct time, placing X_1 in a position of maximum advantage and placing O in a position of maximum disadvantage.

The pace or power of the pass. If passes are too soft they will either be intercepted or they will fail to reach the target. If passes are too strong, they will either go out of play or to an opponent; or they will create control problems for the receiver; or they will give insufficient time to create space. It can be seen, therefore, that a pass must be delivered at a pace which enables the ball to reach its target with the minimum of control problems and at a pace which creates or maintains necessary space.

In Diagram 12a, X_1 has made a pass overpaced and direct to X_2. X_2 has a control problem and the pass fails to create space. In Diagram 12b, X_1 has played a pass of less pace and at a wider angle to draw X_2 towards the ball. O does not follow and space is created in front of O. In Diagram 12c, X_1 makes a similar pass and X_2 is drawn towards the ball. This time O follows but space is created behind O.

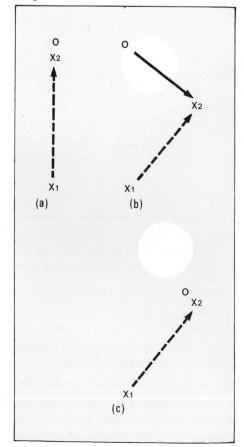

Diagram 11

Diagram 12

ORGANISATION FOR PRACTICE

The practice takes place in a 10-yard square, starting with four attackers against one defender (Diagram 13). The aim of the attackers is to make ten consecutive passes, after which the players rotate. The defender must try to win the ball and he should be rewarded for success by returning him to the attackers. Coaches sometimes make the player who was dispossessed become the defender as a form of punishment, but they should exercise care in this respect. If a player is poor at passing, he needs more practice; but under the punishment arrangement he gets less practice. The temptation should also be resisted to encourage the attackers to make 40 or 50 consecutive passes. This places an unfair burden on the defender and leads to unrealistic practice.

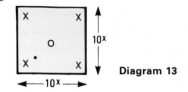

Diagram 13

In this practice the players should be conditioned to practise various techniques such as passing with the inside, the outside, or the instep of the foot. Players may be further conditioned to pass with the right foot, or the left foot only, or to feint at the ball before passing. These conditions may also be applied, for short periods, as the practices develop.

DEVELOPMENT OF THE PRACTICE

1. Once the players are reaching their target of ten consecutive passes with reasonable frequency, the degree of difficulty in the practice should be increased. This can be achieved, in the first place, by conditioning one of the attacking players to play the ball on the first touch. It is helpful if the player nominated wears a distinctive shirt or bib. It is also important that each of the players in turn should be conditioned to passing on the first touch.
2. The practice can be further developed, and the degree of difficulty increased, by reducing the number of attackers from four to three. The one-touch condition for one of the players should continue to be applied.
3. Further development can take place by imposing the one-touch condition on all three attacking players.
4. The next development should involve an increase in the number of defenders and the size of the grid area so that there are three attackers against two defenders in a grid measuring 20 yards by 10 yards (Diagram 15).
5. The practice should be developed by again imposing a one-touch condition on one of the attacking players.
6. A further increase in numbers in the same area, four attackers against three defenders, is the next progression.
7. A further development of the small-grid practices is for two of the four attackers to be conditioned to passing on the first touch.

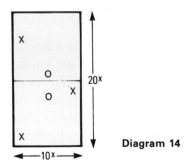

Diagram 14

POINTS FOR THE COACH TO OBSERVE

1. The defending players should always make a full effort to challenge and put pressure on the attacking players.
2. The conditions which are imposed should be adhered to by the attacking players.
3. Players should be comfortable when receiving the pass. This will be reflected in the quality of the first touch and the ability to create a new angle for safe passes.
4. Passes should be accurate. The majority of passes in these practices will be played to the feet without any difficulty, but players should be more precise and aim specifically for either the right foot or the left foot.
5. Players should time the release of the ball correctly. If the defender is not nearer to the passer than the receiver when the ball is released, then the ball has almost certainly been released too soon.

6. Players should pass the ball at the correct pace so that the receiver is given time to control the ball with ease.

7. Players should disguise their intentions when passing so that passing angles are opened up or widened and defenders are wrong-footed.

8. Players without the ball should be in good positions to receive the ball.

9. The player who has just passed the ball should move into a position of advantage.

WIDE-ANGLED SUPPORT

All the basic practices in the grids emphasise possession but are non-directional as the attackers do not attack a particular goal or target. Having established the techniques and attitude essential to retaining possession of the ball, it is important to place emphasis on directional play and introduce targets.

Players now have to be educated to understand that sometimes it is necessary to go backwards before progressing forwards. The reason for this is that once the play becomes directional, defenders will try to stop the play progressing in that direction. The requirement, therefore, is that attacking players, who are prevented by good defenders from passing the ball forward, should have team-mates in support of them who can achieve three things:

■ Position at an angle to receive the ball.
■ Position at an angle which makes a forward pass possible.
■ Position at a distance which gives time to make the pass.

The angle of support to receive the ball

A player is not in a supporting position if he is not available to receive a pass. In Diagram 15a, X_1 is in possession of the ball and is challenged by O_1 who is covered by O_3. X_2 is positioned behind the ball but cannot receive a pass because O_2 is in the line between X_1 and X_2. In Diagram 15b, X_1 is again challenged by O_1 who is covered by O_3. X_2, however, has moved to an angle where he can receive a pass from X_1.

The angle of support to pass the ball forward

A supporting player should not only be in a position where he can relieve the pressure on the man with the ball by receiving a pass. He should also be in a position where he can exert pressure on his opponent. His best position will enable him to observe the passing possibilities through as wide a range as possible and will allow him to pass the ball forward and past as many opponents as possible. It will also allow him to make an easy pass, with minimum control problems, to the receiver. Generally speaking, the best supporting angles are at roughly 45 degrees from the player with the ball.

In Diagram 16a, X_1 has passed the ball to X_2 who has played the ball over the head of O into the space behind him for X_3 to collect. This is not an easy pass for X_2 to make, nor an easy pass for X_2 to control. In Diagram 16b, X_2 has moved into a square supporting position and O_2 has intercepted the pass from X_1. Square supporting is dangerous because the pass may be intercepted. This may result in two players being put out of the game. In Diagram 16c, X_2 has supported at an angle of 45 degrees. X_2 can play an easy pass on the ground into the space behind O. X_3 also has a much easier task in collecting and controlling the ball as he moves into the space behind O.

Position at a distance which gives time to make the pass

Supporting distances can and do vary in accordance with the area of the field. If supporting players position too near to the player with the ball, they may not give

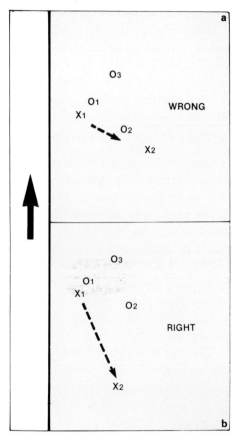

Diagram 15

Diagram 16a

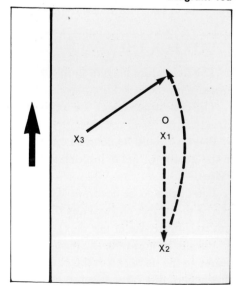

themselves sufficient time to make the forward pass. If, on the other hand, they position too far away from the player with the ball, they may take too much time and defenders may be able to recover. Time usually favours the defender, something that is specially important for attackers to remember in the attacking third of the field. The distance of support, therefore, may vary from 25 or 30 yards in the defending or middle thirds of the field, to 4 or 5 yards in the attacking third of the field.

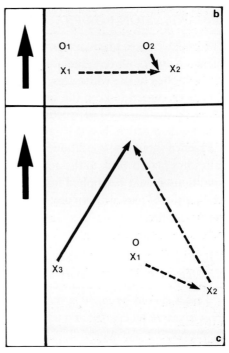

ORGANISATION FOR PRACTICE

The practice takes place in a grid measuring 30 yards by 20 yards. There is a server at one end of the grid and a target man at the other end of the grid. In the centre it is one against one.

In Diagram 17, X_1 plays a soft pass at an angle between X_2 and the touch line. This draws X_2 towards the pass. X_1, having made the pass to his left, moves to his right to produce a wide-angled support position for X_2. What X_2 does depends almost entirely on the movements of O_2. There are two possibilities:

- If O_2 does not follow X_2, then X_2 can turn and pass the ball past O_2 to the feet of O_1.
- If O_2 does follow X_2, then X_2 can pass the ball to X_1 who, from his wide-angled support position, is in a good position to pass the ball past O_2 to the feet of O_1.

The practice is then repeated from the other end with O_1 serving the ball to O_2 who is marked by X_2. X_1 is positioned as the target.

Diagram 16b, c

DEVELOPMENT OF THE PRACTICE

1. The practice is developed by reducing the width of the grid to 10 yards. This increases the degree of difficulty in producing the wide-angled support necessary to beat the defending player. The practice is performed in exactly the same way as before.

2. A further development of the practice can take place in the original grid area. A semi-circle, radius 5 yards, is marked at each end of the grid (Diagram 18). Inside each semi-circle there is a target player, T_1 and T_2, who is confined to that space. Outside the semi-circles, there are five X players against two O players. No outplayer is allowed in the semi-circle and the off-side law applies in the last two squares at each end.

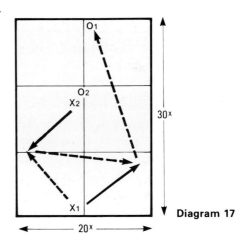

Diagram 17

The X players must combine to hit T_2 with a pass. T_2 must then pass the ball to an X player and the X team then combine to hit T_1. The X team must play all its passes on the ground and the ball cannot be played back to either of the target players. The condition that the ball must be played on the ground will ensure that the supporting angles are wide and that there are quick changes in the angle of the ball. The condition that the ball cannot be played back to either target player will ensure that the X players do support each other.

In the development of this practice there are three phases: first, two of the X team are conditioned to playing the ball on the first touch – so increasing the speed with which players move into supporting positions; second, the one-touch condition is imposed on the whole of the X team; third, the whole play becomes unrestricted.

Development of short passing and wide-angled support into a small-sided game

The temptation to leap from a small grid practice into eleven-a-side game must be resisted. The practices on short passing and support should be developed into a small-sided game.

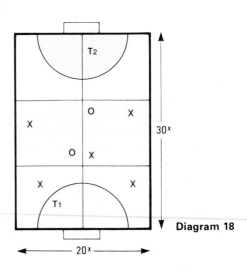

Diagram 18

ORGANISATION FOR PRACTICE

The practice takes place in a grid measuring 40 yards by 30 yards. In Diagram 19, there are six players, including a goalkeeper, on each side. The off-side law is applied in the white area. The overall area and the number of players have been chosen to keep the situation tight – thus keeping the passing short and necessitating good supporting positions. If the players cannot match up to a six-a-side practice then the numbers should be reduced to five-a-side.

Practice should be conditioned so that passes are played on the ground and the ball is not played back to the goalkeeper. In addition, one- and two-touch conditions should be applied for short periods. Practice should conclude with a final period of play without any restrictions. The off-side law, however, should still be applied.

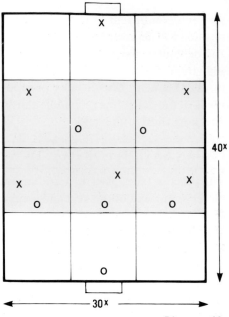

Diagram 19

POINTS FOR THE COACH TO OBSERVE

1. Passes should be made at the correct pace and at the correct angle in order to allow space to be created and exploited.
2. Supporting players should adopt a good position to receive the ball from a player under pressure.
3. The position adopted by a supporting player should be such that all forward passing possibilities can be observed and a forward pass can be made between defenders.
4. The distance between the player with the ball and the supporting player should be great enough to give the supporting player time to make a forward pass, but not so great that the defenders have time to recover.

COMBINING PLAY IN PASSING AND MOVEMENT

Eventually the various types of passes and movements have to be combined – short passes, long passes, passes on the ground and lofted passes. The understanding of players, the selection and quality of their techniques, the ability to make the correct decision at the correct time, the ability to be in the right place at the right time, must all be put to the test. Ultimately that test has to be applied in the eleven-a-side game. In terms of advantage, however, to both coach and player, it is best to progress gradually from small units of players to the eleven-a-side game. There are three phases to go through when developing towards the full game.

Phase One

ORGANISATION FOR PRACTICE

The practice takes place in a grid measuring 40 yards by 30 yards. In Diagram 20, three X players are opposing three O players and at each corner of the grid there is a target player. On each side of the grid, but outside the playing area, there is an extra player, Y, who can combine with whichever team is in possession of the ball by receiving the ball and playing it to their advantage. The Y players can move along the touch-line but they cannot move into the grid.

In the practice, the X players are in possession of the ball and their objective is to reach either T_1 or T_2. In order to prevent two of the defending players from retreating and marking the two target players, it is sensible to debar both defenders and attackers from entering the white areas.

Once the ball has reached, for example, T_1, he passes the ball across the pitch to T_2. The players position themselves in order to continue the practice in the opposite direction. If the X players have succeeded in playing to the T players, then the T player will play the ball to an O player.

The practice is physically demanding and short but intensive periods of practice are recommended. It will be noted, however, that there are six players on the pitch and six players off the pitch. Periods of rest are achieved, therefore, by the groups changing over.

The value of the practice is that it can be conditioned to achieve any type of pass or movement, for example:

■ Play is conditioned to two touches.
■ Play is conditioned to one touch.
■ All passes must be on the ground.
■ The target must be hit from passes made inside the attackers' defending half of the pitch. If the passes are lofted, they must pitch in the target player's square.
■ Passes must be followed by a diagonal run.
■ Passes must be followed by an overlap run.
■ Attackers must respond to man-to-man marking by making cross-over plays.

Any one condition should only be enforced for a short period of time and the practice should end, as usual, with a period of unrestricted play.

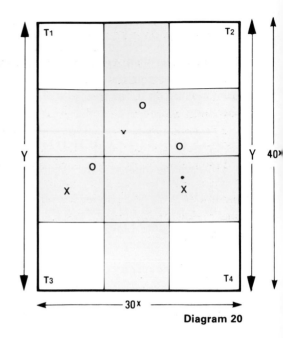

Diagram 20

Phase Two: Coaching a small-sided game

ORGANISATION FOR PRACTICE

The practice takes place inside a grid measuring 60 yards by 40 yards, a suitable size for a six-a-side practice. The off-side law is operative. To develop the practice, various conditions should be imposed to place an emphasis on specific techniques or movements, as in the previous practice. In particular, players should be encouraged to look for opportunities to change the direction of play.

Three relevant factors should be understood:

■ Defenders will try to make play predictable by forcing it to continue in one direction.
■ Defenders will react to the movement of attacking players.
■ Attackers moving forward from deep positions will frequently be unmarked.

If there is no satisfactory route forward, it means that the defenders have gained the upper hand. One way of regaining the initiative is to transfer the ball to the opposite side of the field, presuming, of course, that space and attacking players are available there. Although ground may not be gained, this method can be particularly effective, even if the ball is only transferred 15 or 20 yards.

In Diagram 21, X_1 has the ball and is marked by O_1. X_2 has made a diagonal run and is tracked by O_2, thus creating space (the white area). X_1 passes the ball into the space created and X_3 moves forward from a deep position to receive the pass. The movement of an attacking player has been made in one direction and the ball has been played in the opposite direction. As well as reacting to the movement of players, defenders will also react, of course, to the movement of the ball. When the ball, and one or more attackers, move in opposite directions, defending becomes a little more complex.

Changing the direction of play presupposes that the player in possession of the ball is comfortable with the ball and is patient enough to wait for the space to be created. Although he will sometimes pass the ball direct to the feet of his team-mate, there are distinct advantages to be gained from playing the ball to the

Diagram 21

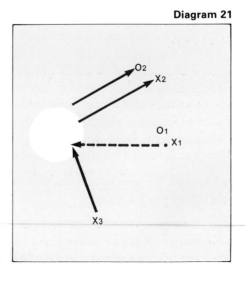

space for the team-mate to move on to. In this case, the team-mate moving forward should allow the ball to be delivered into the space and then move on to the pass, rather than wait in the space for the pass. By moving into the space late there is a greater probability of being unmarked; of having a better field of vision when moving on to the pass; and of being able to pass the ball on the first touch if necessary.

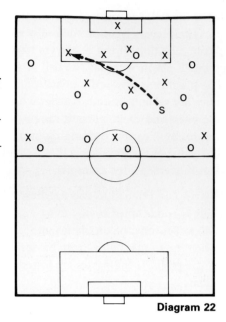

Diagram 22

POINTS FOR THE COACH TO OBSERVE

1. Observe the quality of the passing:

    (i) Disguise.
    (ii) Timing of the release of the ball.
    (iii) The pace of the pass.
    (iv) The accuracy of the pass.

2. Observe the quality of the support:

    (i) The angle for receiving the ball.
    (ii) The angle for passing the ball forward.
    (iii) The distance to give time to pass the ball forward.

3. Observe the selection of passes, especially:

    (i) Passes which penetrate.
    (ii) Passes which change the direction of play.

4. Observe the movement of players without the ball to create passing angles.

Phase Three: Coaching the eleven-a-side game

The final realisation of all that has gone before in terms of developing the techniques and understanding of passing and support can only be achieved by coaching in the eleven-a-side game. Achievement depends upon a patient and systematic approach and the task is basically twofold:

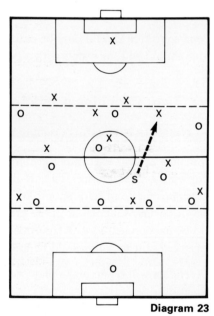

Diagram 23

- To develop team understanding of how to calculate between safety and risk in each of the thirds of the field.
- To combine the techniques of passing with movement to create and exploit space.

The coach should control and concentrate the practice by coaching in three stages:

Stage One

It is important that players have practice in switching their concentration from defending to attacking. In Diagram 22, based in the defending third of the field, there are two progressions to the practice:

    (i) S, the coach, makes a variety of services to the X players. The objective for the X team is to get one of the X players over the half-way line in full control of the ball and facing the opponent's goal.
    (ii) S plays the ball to the O team so that the X team must first win the ball and then attack from its defending third of the field. Once again, the object is to get an X player over the half-way line in full control of the ball and facing the opponent's goal.

Stage Two

In Diagram 23, based in the middle third of the field, there are again two progressions to the practice:

    (i) S makes a variety of services to the X players. The X players attack the O team with the objective of getting an X player inside the attacking third of the field in full control of the ball and facing the opponent's goal.

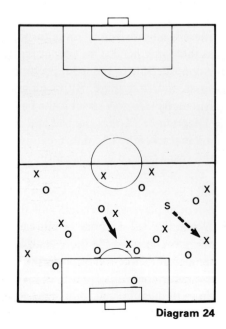

Diagram 24

(ii) S plays the ball to the O team so that the X team must win the ball back before attacking to achieve the same objective as before.

Stage Three

In Diagram 24, based in the attacking third of the field, there are again two progressions to the practices.

(i) S makes a variety of services to the X players. The X players attack the O team with the objective of creating a clear shooting opportunity and, hopefully, scoring a goal.

(ii) S plays the ball to the O players so that the X team must win back the ball before attacking and trying to score.

During each of the three stages, the coach should work to increase the understanding of individuals and the team in the following respects:

When to play behind the ball and when to move in advance of the ball. There is an element of risk involved in moving in advance of the ball. The risk is greatest for players moving from rear positions, so they should understand that it is not wise to move forward in advance of the ball if they are leaving behind team-mates who are outnumbered. At the same time, it is unwise to continue playing behind the ball when there is no opponent to mark and when the player in possession of the ball does not require support.

When to play the ball forward and when to play the ball back. Players should always be encouraged to look first to see if the ball can be played forward. If there are doubts in a player's mind, the nearer he is to his own goal the quicker he must decide to play safe. The nearer he is to the opponent's goal, the more he must regard playing the ball back as a last resort – unless, of course, he is playing the ball back from the goal-line to create a clear scoring chance.

When to pass across the field. The only reason for passing the ball across the field is that there is not a good opportunity to pass the ball forward. Passes across the field do involve risk, especially in heavily populated areas of the field and near to one's own goal. The defending third of the field, therefore, is the area in which the calculation must be made very carefully. Crossfield passes are more likely to pay dividends in the middle and attacking thirds of the field.

When to pass and when to run with the ball. Players should understand that there are two distinct disadvantages to running with the ball: it is slower than passing the ball; and it is difficult to run with the ball and retain a good field of vision. There are, however, two distinct advantages: by running at an opponent, or into a space between opponents, with the ball the defenders can be committed; and by dribbling past an opponent a numerical advantage can be created.

It can be seen that it is usually a disadvantage to run with the ball in the defending third of the field but the dividends can be high when in the attacking third of the field.

When to play to feet and when to play to space. The majority of passes, especially safe passes, are played to the feet. Playing to space requires a finer sense of judgment and touch and usually involves a greater element of risk, although judgment and touch and fine technique will always be rewarded, particularly in the attacking third of the field.

When to pass long and when to pass short. It should be clear that long passes incur the greatest risk, for there is a possibility that the pass will be inaccurate or that the team will become stretched. However, there are two distinct advantages to be gained from long passing: the maximum ground can be gained in the minimum time as one pass is more than twice as quick as two passes; and long passing offers the possibility for the most incisive penetration of the defence by putting the most opponents out of the game. Effective teamwork, based on playing the percentage game, will be based on short passing. There will be more than 75 per cent of passes of 30 yards or less, and less than 25 per cent of passes of 30 yards or more.

Increasing the range of vision. When players progress to playing eleven-a-side soccer, it is important to understand that there is a bigger field to look at and that there are more players on the field to observe. There is, therefore, more information to absorb than in the small practices, in roughly the same amount of time. Players must be encouraged to do three things:

- Play with their heads up.
- Observe the situation in advance of them.
- Observe the situation on the opposite flank.

In order to encourage players to increase their range of vision, the condition of concentrated one-touch football should be applied in each of the thirds of the field. This process should be regarded by coaches as standard procedure. Players sometimes play with their heads up but fail to survey the state of play. They are, as it were, one-eyed players who only see play on their side of the field. Constant verbal reminders from the coach will be required to encourage players to observe play on the opposite side of the field to themselves.

Increasing the speed and accuracy of making decisions. The amount of information that has to be absorbed in the eleven-a-side game can sometimes result in decisions being made more slowly than in the smaller games. Concentrated practice, however, for the team in the different thirds of the field will help to combine the players' awareness of the state of play. From the basis of that awareness, players will begin to synchronise their movements as a team. The more purposeful and concentrated the practice, the quicker the players will combine their awareness of the game, recognise possibilities and synchronise their movements.

Improving the quality of play. Whether it is a pass or a movement, play should be precise. Both runs and passes should be made at the correct time, the correct speed and the correct angle. Precision play depends on precise techniques and, more important, a desire, by the individual players and the players as a team, to be precise. Such an attitude cannot be achieved without concentrated and repeated practice in the eleven-a-side situation in the various thirds of the field.

POINTS FOR THE COACH TO OBSERVE

1. Observe that the players always position realistically to start the practice.
2. Observe that players abide by any conditions that are applied.
3. Observe the players' attitude to safety and risk in each of the thirds of the field.
4. Observe the quality and range of short, long, forward and cross-field passes.
5. Observe the quality of the supporting play and the players' understanding of when to move forward from support positions.

6

ATTACKING (1)
FLANK AND DIAGONAL CROSSES

Attacking in the attacking third of the field can be roughly divided into two areas: flank attacks and central attacks. Central attacks are considered in the next chapter. Flank attacks, in the form of wing crosses and diagonal passes, are considered in this chapter.

Defences will try to deflect attacks to the flanks. The two flanks are also the areas where a team can expect to find most space in the attacking third of the field. It therefore follows that crossing the ball, from a wing or flank position, is one of the most important techniques in attack. There are three potential target spaces: the near post; the middle of the goal; and the far post. In addition to these, there are diagonal passes to the back of the defence, passes which exploit the space between the rearmost defender and the goalkeeper.

NEAR-POST CROSSES

Near-post crosses are delivered from the flank in an area lying roughly between the penalty area and the touch-line. They should be aimed at a point on the edge of the six-yard area level with the near post, although anywhere within a radius of two to three yards of that point would normally be satisfactory (Diagram 1).

Diagram 1

It is important to remember that crosses made to the near post should be played to the back of the defence to be effective. This becomes more difficult to achieve the nearer one gets to the goal-line, for defenders will have had more time to recover into the near-post area.

Three things should be considered before making the decision to play to the near post: the space available; the position of the defending players; and the position of the attacking players.

The space available. Players should ensure that they have enough space available on the flank in which to play the ball. They should also ensure that there is enough space available at the near post to play the ball into.

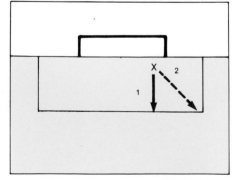

Diagram 2

The position of the defending players. The position of the goalkeeper is all important. Because he can use his hands, he has an immense advantage over all other players. It is essential, therefore, for the player crossing the ball to avoid playing it to where the goalkeeper is positioned.

It should be remembered that the nearer the ball is to the touch-line, the more likely it is that the goalkeeper will be in the back half of his goal. In Diagram 2, it can be seen that when the ball is with X_1 on the flank, goalkeeper O_1 will be in the back half of his goal. When the ball is with X_2, goalkeeper O_2 will be in the front half of his goal. If the goalkeeper is in the front half of his goal, the ball should be played a little farther out and away from the goal.

It is worth remembering that few goalkeepers come beyond the near post to attack near-post crosses (Diagram 3, route 2). The majority are more likely to come out on a route almost at right angles to the goal-line (Diagram 3, route 1).

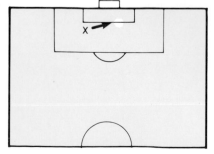

Diagram 3

The position of the attacking players. It should be understood that the ball is played into the space at the near-post area so that the receiver can move to attack the ball in the space at speed. The crosser of the ball is *not* looking for the receiver to be waiting for the ball in the space itself. The attacker will normally move from a position well out from the six-yard area and often wide of the goal (Diagram 4).

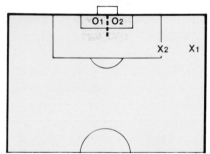

Diagram 4

Technique for crossing the ball

Having established that he is going to cross the ball to the near-post area, the player must now effect that cross in the best possible way. Sometimes sufficient space will be created on the flanks to ensure that when a player is crossing the

1 Attacker heading at the target area of the near post
A flying header from Keegan with the ball entering the net at the near post. The goalkeeper is completely taken by surprise and is caught well out of position. This is not unusual with near-post headers: the goalkeeper often prepares to take the cross in the mid-goal area and fails to adjust in time.

2 Position of the goalkeeper for a near-post cross
The goalkeeper, plus a defender just inside the six-yard area, positioned for a near-post cross.

ball he is not closely challenged by a defender. In these circumstances, the player crossing the ball need only concentrate upon striking it in such a way that it is played accurately, and at the right pace, into the required space. Against good teams, however, one should expect a defender to be challenging. The defender will try to block the cross and is likely to succeed if the attacker does not alter the angle of the ball (Diagram 5a).

In Diagram 5b, X has moved the ball nearer to the touch-line. From that position, X will have a wider angle to play the ball past O and, because of his angled approach to the ball, will be able to impart more spin and swerve to the ball, thereby bending it past O.

Once the correct position for crossing has been adopted, the final contact with the ball is made. This should be slightly below the horizontal mid-line, using the front part of the inside of the kicking foot. The action of the kicking leg should be across the ball from inside to outside. The ideal height for the ball to arrive in the target area is head height or below.

Attacking the crossed ball

There are three factors to be considered by the player moving to attack the ball: the angle of his run; the timing of his run; and his final contact with the ball.

Players score goals at the near post having made runs to it through almost 90 degrees. The angle which gives the best chance of a good contact on the ball is the angle which comes closest into, rather than across, the line of flight. In Diagram 6, route 1 takes the attacker across the line of flight. Route 2 gives the attacker a better chance of making a good contact with the ball.

Diagram 5a

Diagram 5b

Diagram 6

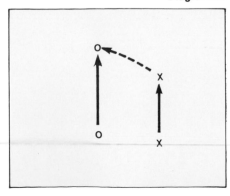

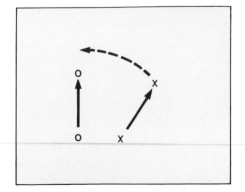

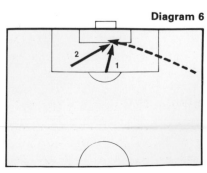

The player should time his run so that it comes late but at speed. The major fault in timing is to be in the target area too early, waiting for the arrival of the ball. At the same time, the player must make absolutely certain that he is the first to reach the ball. It can be seen therefore that once the run is started, no attempt should be made to slow down in order to make a good contact on the ball in the target area.

Contact with the ball should be through its top half, so that it is played downwards. The action is one of deflecting or steering the ball into goal. If the attacker is moving quickly, then his body momentum, allied to the speed of the ball, will generate all the power needed to beat the goalkeeper. The easiest contact is usually with the head, since such a contact requires little or no adjustment to the running action.

It is not always advantageous to play the ball towards the goal. Sometimes the attacker will be making contact with the ball well beyond the near post and sometimes the contact will be close to the goal-line beyond the near post. On these occasions there are two possibilities for the attacking player. The first is to play the ball back towards the penalty spot or the edge of the penalty area. The second is to flick the ball on towards the far post. There is one further possibility for the attacking player when making a run to the near-post area. If he is certain

3a

3b

3 Technique of crossing the ball to the near post

3a Brooking screwing the ball into the near-post area (front view).

3b Side view of Brooking playing the ball, with swerve, past Wilkins into the near-post area.

3c Keegan standing at the target point at the near post to indicate to Brooking where to aim the ball.

3c

4 Angle of run to attack the ball at the near post

4a Keegan starting his run to the near post. He is just in the back half of the penalty area and about 15 yards out from goal.

4b He runs directly to the near post at something like 45 degrees.

4c A lovely controlled header to the far post.

5 Being first to the ball at the near post
Keegan leaps to meet a high cross at the near post. He is easily first to the ball – his opponent has still got both feet on the ground.

6 Contact on the ball at the near post
Keegan first to the ball again and about to steer the ball into the goal. A good contact is more important than power.

that he is being supported by a team-mate moving into the space behind him, he can feint to play the ball and let the ball run through. This play can be especially effective if the player running to the near-post area is closely marked.

ORGANISATION FOR PRACTICE

The practice is organised on one of the flanks in the attacking third of the field. It is most important that the appropriate area of the field is used for this practice. The reason for this is that the angles and distances are much easier to calculate when the practice takes place within the normal field markings.

In Diagram 7, X_1 crosses a moving ball to X_2 who has positioned himself as a target man in the target area.

Squad practice

Squad practice can be achieved by placing a portable goal on the half-way line (Diagram 8) with cones to indicate precisely the corners of the penalty area and the six-yard area. The goalkeepers, X and O, have a supply of balls. X throws the ball to X_1, who crosses for X_2 to strike for goal. O then serves the ball to O_1, who

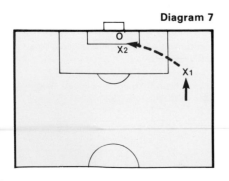

Diagram 7

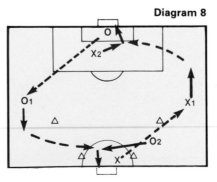

Diagram 8

crosses the ball for O_2 to strike for goal. The service should be reversed to give practice in crosses from the left flank. The only difference is that X throws the ball to O_1.

The same basic organisation for squad-practice can be used for practising crosses to the near post, the middle of the goal and the far post. It has the advantage that there is a realistic start to the practice. Also, as play develops at one end, the players at the other end have time to reposition and prepare to repeat the practice.

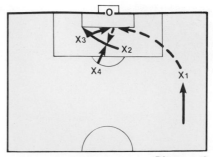

Diagram 9

DEVELOPMENT OF THE PRACTICE

1. The practice is developed by bringing in two attacking players. While the cross is being made, the players, X_2 and X_3, cross over (Diagram 9). X_3 moves to attack the near post and X_2 moves into the space towards the far post. X_1 plays a moving ball into the near-post area and X_3 attempts to score. X_3 can vary his play by sometimes feinting to play the ball but allowing the ball to run through for X_2. When X_3 does this, the feint play must eliminate the goalkeeper. It is also important that X_2 should attack the ball in the space behind X_3. It is a mistake for X_2 to go too wide or to wait for the ball.

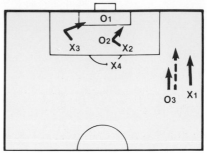

Diagram 10

2. Sometimes it will be necessary for the player at the near post to play the ball back towards the edge of the penalty area. For this purpose the practice is progressed to include a further player, X_4. X_3 now has three possible plays at the near post: he can play for goal; he can feint to play, but allow the ball to run across the goal; and he can play the ball back towards the edge of the penalty area.

3. The next progression is to bring opponents into the practice. The attackers now vary their movements and the defender, O_2, can elect to mark X_2 or X_3 (Diagram 10). The practice starts by O_3 passing the ball to X_1 and then chasing after him in order to pressurise him as he crosses the ball. X_2 and X_3 can vary their movements, making either cross-over runs or the zig-zag runs shown in Diagram 10. The ball should still be played into the near-post area.

Whether it is X_2 or X_3 who moves into the near-post area, two points already discussed should be remembered – the attacker must move as late as possible into the target area and he must beat the defender to the ball. The player attacking the far-post area should move in such a way that he can always see the movements of the ball, the goalkeeper and his team-mate moving to the near post. He must *never* have his back to the play.

7 Feint to play but allow the ball to run

7a Keegan moving to the near post to a ball played in low.

7b Keegan feints to play the ball but allows it to run through to Blissett who shoots for goal.

8 Play the ball back to the edge of the penalty area

8a Keegan turns Brooking's cross back for Wilkins to shoot.

8b Wilkins shoots past and almost through Keegan!

MID-GOAL CROSSES

The mid-goal area is an area 6 to 9 yards out from goal and almost the width of the goal (Diagram 11). It is not the easiest place on the field to achieve space. It is, however, the most lethal, given that the ball and attacker meet at the same time. The space can be created in two ways:

1. By drawing a central defender beyond the near post, creating space behind him. In Diagram 12, O_2 has followed X_2 into and beyond the near-post area, so giving away space. X_1 delivers the ball into the mid-goal area for X_3 to attack.

2. By taking defenders away from the mid-goal area. It is probable that there will be, not one, but two central defenders. It is therefore necessary that each of them should be drawn out of the central area. This is achieved by the two central attackers making split runs, one running into the near-post area and the other running into an area well beyond the far post (*see photograph on page 91*). A third attacker then moves from a deeper position, outside the penalty area, to attack the space in the mid-goal area.

In Diagram 13, X_2 and X_3 have made split runs to create the central space. X_1 has played the ball into that space and X_4 has moved, as late as possible, from a position outside the penalty area to attack the ball in the space and strike for goal. It is imperative that the player crossing the ball, X_1, should look up and observe the space available and then clip the ball into that space. If the ball is floated into the space it will give defenders, especially the goalkeeper, time to recover their positions and intercept the ball. A floated ball will also cause more problems for the attackers when timing their runs and striking for goal.

ORGANISATION FOR PRACTICE

The practice again takes place in the attacking third of the field, as in Diagram 10. Apart from the goalkeeper there is only one defender in the penalty area, O_2. X_1 must observe the situation and select whether to play to the near post or the mid-goal area. X_2 and X_3 should be encouraged to vary their runs and O_3 to vary his challenge. At first he should give X_1 plenty of time to observe and make his selection. Later, more pressure should be exerted on X_1 to give him less time.

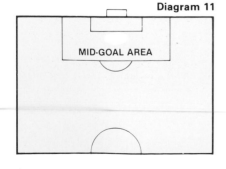

Diagram 11

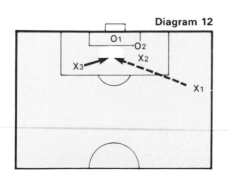

Diagram 12

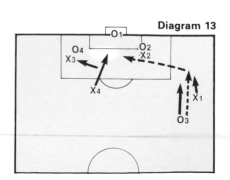

Diagram 13

9 Mid-goal crosses – target area

9a The mid-goal area opening up.

9b The mid-goal area opened up.

9c The ball played into the vacant space.

9d A devastating finish.

DEVELOPMENT OF THE PRACTICE

Progress is made by introducing into the practice a second defender, O_4. The starting positions are as in Diagram 14.

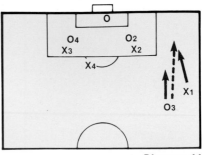

Diagram 14

FAR-POST CROSSES

The first requirement in far-post crosses, as with all types of crosses, is to eliminate the goalkeeper. The actual target area will largely depend, therefore, on his position; and his position will largely depend on the area from which the ball is crossed.

In Diagram 15, if the cross is made from any point in the shaded area, C, the goalkeeper will certainly be in the back half of his goal. To eliminate the goalkeeper, the target area will need to be outside the six-yard area and towards the side of the penalty area.

If the cross is made from a position much nearer the goal, then the goalkeeper will position in the front half of the goal. In Diagram 16, the cross is made from the shaded area, C. In these circumstances the target area, T, is the area most likely to achieve the best results.

It is not only the crosser of the ball who should observe the position of the goalkeeper: any attacking player positioning in the far-post area should also observe the position of the goalkeeper – and, of course, the position of the crosser of the ball.

Technique for crossing the ball

The two types of crosses to the far post are different in terms of technique.

10 Split runs and cross-over runs to create mid-goal space

Keegan and Blissett crossing over as they make split runs, Keegan to the near post and Blissett to the far post. Space will be created in the mid-goal area, 6 or 8 yards either side of the penalty spot. The defender is not sure what is going on or whom he should mark.

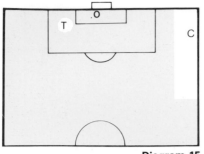

Diagram 15

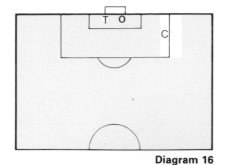

Diagram 16

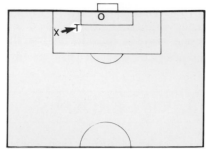

Diagram 17

Target area beyond the six-yard area. It is unlikely that this cross will be much less than 40 yards, and it may even be as much as 50 yards. It is likely that the ball will also have to clear numerous defenders en route. The technique which will best serve the purpose is the lofted drive with the wide-angled approach (*see page 67*).

Target area inside the six-yard area. This cross will be played over a much shorter distance, probably 20 to 30 yards. The ball needs enough height to clear the defenders, especially the goalkeeper, and enough pace to reach the target area before the goalkeeper can recover across his goal. The technique is similar to the lofted drive with the wide-angled approach, but the ball is 'clipped' rather than driven.

Attacking the crossed ball

The positioning of attackers in the far-post area should always provide for the attacker to run in to meet the ball. In this way it is easy for the attacker to gain height if he has to leap to head the ball. The attacker must adopt a very wide position near to the side of the penalty area if the cross is expected beyond the six-yard area (Diagram 17). If he adopts this position it will give the attack a further advantage. The defender is most unlikely to be drawn into such a wide position so he is likely to find himself moving backwards to deal with the cross. It is extremely difficult to jump whilst moving backwards. If the defender positions quickly he may find that he can make a standing jump, but he will be at a severe disadvantage against an attacker who is positioned to run in to attack the ball. It should be emphasised that the attacker must never turn his back on the ball or the goalkeeper.

11

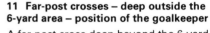

11 Far-post crosses – deep outside the 6-yard area – position of the goalkeeper

A far-post cross deep beyond the 6-yard area. Note the position of the goalkeeper – he would have taken easily any ball played into the back half of the 6-yard area.

12 Far-post crosses – inside the 6-yard area – position of the goalkeeper

12a The ball crossed to the far post and the goalkeeper trying to get across his goal.

12b Blissett wins the ball at the far post inside the 6-yard area. Note that the goalkeeper has not got across his goal into the correct position.

12c The ball has been squeezed into the net at the near post.

12a

12b

12c

If the ball is crossed deep beyond the six-yard area, it is likely that the goalkeeper will have had sufficient time to get across his goal to reposition. The attacker, striking for goal, is therefore unlikely to score at the near post. Faced with a blocked near post, the attacker is presented with two good alternatives: he can either aim the ball towards the far post into the position from which the goalkeeper has just moved (Diagram 18); or he can play the ball back or across the face of the goal (Diagram 19).

Which of these possibilities the attacker selects will depend on his precise position and on the position of opponents and team-mates. If the crosser of the ball is moving in towards goal or the goalkeeper moves into the front half of his goal, then the attacker, at the far-post area, must adjust his position and be ready to attack the target space inside the six-yard area (Diagram 20).

ORGANISATION FOR PRACTICE

The practice again takes place in the attacking third of the field. On this occasion, however, the crosser of the ball, X_1, crosses the ball from a variety of positions (Diagram 21), constantly observing the position of the goalkeeper and selecting the appropriate cross and target area.

DEVELOPMENT OF THE PRACTICE

1. The practice is developed by introducing a second attacking player to the penalty area against one defender. One of the attacking players attacks the near post and the other attacks the far post. The defender can elect to mark either player and the crosser must play to the unmarked attacker.
2. The next development is to bring a second defender into the penalty area. The situation therefore becomes two-v-two in the penalty area. A third attacker is positioned on the edge of the penalty area. He is available to receive balls played back or to attack the mid-goal area if sufficient space is created. The crosser of the ball is also chased by a defending player as in previous practices.

POINTS FOR THE COACH TO OBSERVE

1. Observe the technique of the player crossing the ball:

   (i) Head up in order to assess the state of play.
   (ii) Positioning of the ball prior to crossing.
   (iii) Contact on the ball.
   (iv) Correct selection of the target area.
   (v) Accuracy of delivery.

2. Observe the movements of the attackers at the near post:

   (i) The angle of the run.
   (ii) The timing of the run.
   (iii) Being first to the ball.
   (iv) Selection – to feint, play the ball for goal, back from goal or across goal.
   (v) Contact on the ball.

13a

13b

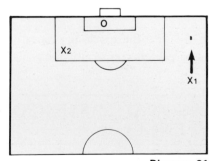
13c

13 Far-post crosses – attacking the ball

13a A good run in by Blissett takes him higher than the defender to attack the ball.

13b Blissett heads the ball high over the goalkeeper towards the far post.

13c The goalkeeper is caught out of position and the ball goes over the line near to the far post.

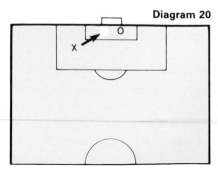
Diagram 21

Diagram 18

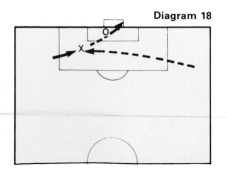

Diagram 19

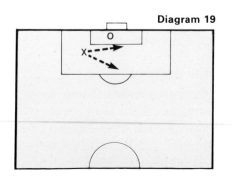

Diagram 20

14a

14b

14c

**14 Far-post crosses – attacking the ball –
heading back across goal to score**

14a The ball is crossed to the far post
with the goalkeeper at the near post and
Blissett outside the 6-yard area at the far
post.

14b The goalkeeper has moved across his
goal and Blissett attacks the ball.

14c Blissett heads the ball back where the
goalkeeper has just come from and scores
at what is now the far post.

3. Observe the attacking of the mid-goal area:

   (i) Moving in behind the attacker at the near post.
   (ii) Moving in from the edge of the penalty area between split runs to the
   near and far posts.

4. Observe the positions of the attackers at the far post:

   (i) With the goalkeeper in the front half of his goal.
   (ii) With the goalkeeper in the back half of his goal.

5. Observe that the attacking players observe the position of the ball and the key
defending players – especially the goalkeeper.

DIAGONAL PASSES TO THE BACK OF THE DEFENCE

Not all effective crosses are played from advanced positions on a flank. There are
considerable advantages to be gained from playing diagonal passes from deep
positions, and positions sometimes well in from the touch-line.

Playing the ball into the space behind the defence

There are considerable advantages to be gained from playing the ball into the
space behind the defence before the defence has retreated fully. Diagram 22
shows the space available between the rearmost defender and the goalkeeper (the
shaded area). The more the attack is delayed, the more likely it is that the defence
will retreat into that space. The attacking players can, however, affect the retreat

Diagram 22

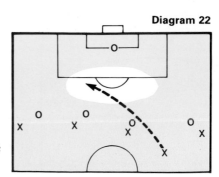

15 Far-post crosses – heading the ball back for a team-mate to shoot

15a Blissett leaps high at the far post and heads the ball back to his team-mate on the edge of the penalty area.

15b A volley shot at goal results.

16 Diagonal passes – attacking the central area behind the defence

16a Keegan, marked, on the left of the picture, and Blissett, marked, on the right of the picture, make split runs to open up a central space. Wilkins attacks the space by passing the ball into the space. Brooking attacks the space by running into the space from a deep position.

16b Brooking, clear of the defence with only the goalkeeper to beat.

17 Movement from the opposite side of the field from the ball

17a Keegan taking his opponent No 11 towards the ball. Blissett taking his opponent No 2 away from the ball. Brooking, top of the picture on the right, makes a run towards the penalty area to receive the ball from Wilkins who is wide on the opposite flank.

17b A vast space is created by Keegan and Blissett, and Brooking goes into that space.

17c Brooking gets to the back of the defence and attempts a diving header. Note that both Keegan and Blissett are now moving in towards the goal.

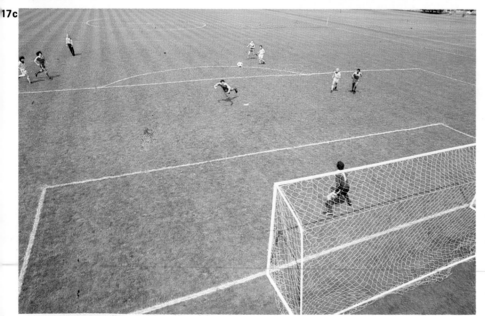

of the defence by making diagonal runs. This particularly applies to central attacking players. The effects of such runs are likely to be threefold:

- The retreat will be slowed.
- The central defenders will be taken out of their normal line of retreat.
- A space will be created between the two central defenders.

In Diagram 23, the two central attackers, X_1 and X_2, have made diagonal runs in opposite directions simultaneously and have opened up a central space.

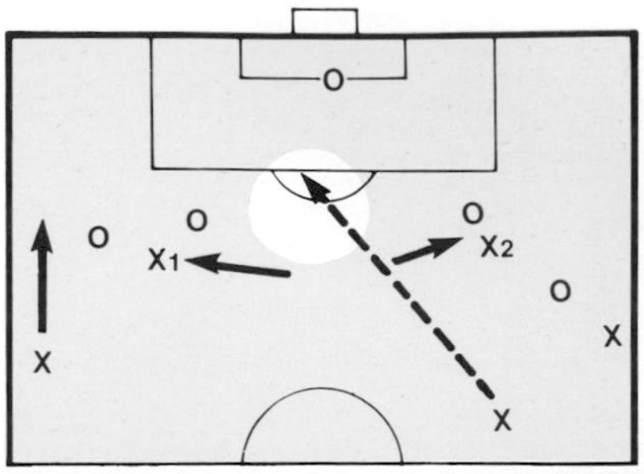

Diagram 23

Exploiting the space created

Final exploitation of the space created can only be achieved by an attacking player moving into the space, unmarked or improperly marked – often a difficult task. The best chance of success is for the attacker to move from the opposite side of the field to the ball, and preferably from a deep position. There are two reasons for this:

- Attacking players on the opposite side of the field to the ball are less likely to be marked, particularly if they come from deep positions.
- Many defenders on the opposite side of the field to the ball are inclined to watch the ball to the exclusion of their opponent. The opportunity is thereby presented for the attacking player to move behind his opponent on his blind side.

In Diagram 24, X_3 has moved forward on the blind side of O_1 into the space created by X_1 and X_2. In this situation the well-tried formula still applies: space is created, the ball is delivered, and the attacker then moves into the space.

It will not always be possible to create space or deliver a diagonal pass in the central position. It happens frequently, however, that defenders on the opposite flank from the ball are drawn into central positions. Space is then available round the back of the defence, on the opposite side of the field to the ball. That space can be exploited by a diagonal pass to an attacking player moving into the space from a deep position.

In Diagram 25, X_1, X_2 and X_4 have made diagonal runs and created space on the attacking left flank. X_5 plays a diagonal pass into that space and X_3 moves forward, on the blind side of O_1, to receive the pass in an advanced position.

ORGANISATION FOR PRACTICE

The practice takes place on the edge of the attacking third of the field. The practice starts with five defenders, including the goalkeeper, against six attackers. In Diagram 26, X_4 passes the ball to X_2 who passes back to X_4. X_1 and X_2 then make split runs to create the central space, X_4 makes a diagonal pass into the space, and X_3 moves into the space to receive the ball and strike at goal.

The same practice organisation is used to create space on a flank.

DEVELOPMENT OF THE PRACTICE

The practice is developed by introducing an extra defending player. The extra defender should be instructed to challenge the player with the ball and threaten the line of pass. Without this condition, the defender will retreat into the space and defeat the object of the practice.

POINTS FOR THE COACH TO OBSERVE

1. The forward players should create space either in central positions, or on the opposite flank to the ball.
2. Observe the quality of the diagonal runs.

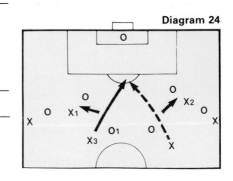

Diagram 24

18a

18b

18c

18 Attacking the space on the outside of the defence on the opposite flank to the ball

18a Keegan and Blissett have brought the two central defenders on to the same side as the ball. Top right of the picture also shows the full-back being brought into a central position. Brooking is moving into the space they have created on the far side of the defence. Wilkins plays the ball.

18b Both the ball and Brooking are now in the space.

18c Brooking receiving the ball with an excellent scoring chance.

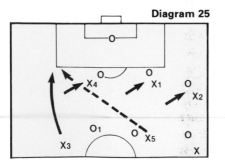

Diagram 25

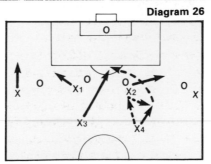

Diagram 26

3. Once the space is created, the ball should be played as early as possible. Observe the quality of the pass.

4. The player moving into the space should arrive as late as possible.

5. Observe the quality of the strike at goal.

Coaching in the game – concentrated practice on all types of flank crosses and diagonal passes

All the examples of crosses in this chapter have been from the right flank of the field. It should be emphasised that the quality of crosses from the left flank is usually not as good as that from the right, the reason for this being that most teams contain more right-footed than left-footed players.

The coach must ensure, when coaching crosses in the game, that substantial amounts of practice are given on each of the flanks – hence the value of the squad practice. Two points are of particular importance:

■ To achieve the concentrated practice required, play should be contained in the attacking half of the field.

■ In order to ensure that the attacking team creates sufficient space to make the cross, or the diagonal pass, the starting position of certain defenders should be conditioned.

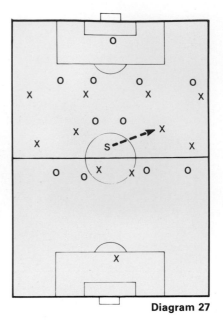

Diagram 27

In Diagram 27, there are eight attackers against six defenders plus a goalkeeper in the attacking half of the field. S, who should be the coach, plays the ball to any of the X players who should be encouraged to look for situations in which to play crosses or diagonal passes. The organisation of the practice ensures that they have space and a numerical advantage on the flanks in order to do so. The four O players and two X players who are positioned behind the half-way line are brought into play at the discretion of the coach who will eventually allow all six players to move into the practice when he serves the ball.

When the X team can perform satisfactorily under the previous conditions, one of the defenders starting behind the half-way line is moved goal-side of the ball at the start of the practice, so putting the X team under more pressure.

ATTACKING (2)
CENTRAL POSITIONS

Central attacks can be considered to take place in an area rather less than the width of the penalty area – the shaded area in Diagram 1. Defenders will recognise the importance of this area by attempting to deflect the attack to the flanks. They will do this by denying space, and therefore time, to the attacking players in the central area. It follows that in order to increase the momentum of a team's attack in the attacking third of the field, space must first have been created in front of the defence.

Once space has been created, two things should be remembered:

- Any delay in increasing the momentum of the attack will assist the defence.
- The attitude of attackers, with and without the ball, must be to calculate on the side of risk.

Thinking time is minimal and, unless players have the correct attitude to the taking of risks, the team's initiative will almost certainly be lost. The momentum of the attack is increased in one of two ways, or by a combination of both: players can attack at speed with the ball; and they can attack at speed without the ball.

There are three possible choices for the player in possession of the ball: a pass; a dribble; or a shot at goal. Shooting is considered in the next two chapters. It should be stated here, though, that if a player is in doubt, he should shoot. Attackers should be encouraged to shoot as often as they can for their chance of success is usually better than they imagine. If the attacker decides to pass the ball, his top priority should be to play to the space at the back of the defence. If he decides to dribble with the ball, this will always involve committing a defender by running straight at him with the ball, and then doing one of four things:

- Pass the ball past the defender.
- Pass the ball to a team-mate and run into space behind the defender for a possible return pass.
- Dribble the ball past the defender.
- Shoot for goal past the defender.

Players without the ball should give first priority to attacking the space at the back of the defence. Of all the possibilities which confront defences, the worst, short of the ball ending up in the net, is for the ball and an attacker to end up in the space behind the defence. The essence of sound tactics is to give the opposition what they least desire – this is particularly important in the attacking third of the field. It can be seen therefore that the attitude of attacking players in the attacking third of the field must be characterised by boldness and risk taking,

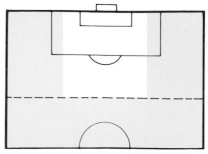

Diagram 1

1 Attacking at speed with the ball

1a Blissett makes a run behind the defender, into the space where the defender is trying to force Keegan.

1b Keegan used Blissett as a decoy, attacking the inside of the defender at speed and turning the defender through 180 degrees.

1c & d Keegan is now well clear of the defender and shoots before the defender has any chance of recovery. Note that Keegan has kept the ball on the foot farthest from the defender.

2 Attacking at speed without the ball

2a Keegan, just in picture, making a determined run at speed without the ball.

2b Receiving the pass from Brooking and just beating the defender to the ball.

qualities that coaches must work hard to instil and encourage.

A major part of the work of coaches is to help players appreciate that high risk is consistent with a low success rate. A ton of practice may be needed to bring about an ounce of improvement; but when the scales are evenly poised, it only needs an ounce to tilt the balance. So it is that while the difference between winning and losing is enormous, the line which divides them is often so very small.

Games are sometimes won in a moment of inspiration. But inspiration is what is condensed from hours of hard work on the practice ground. Good coaching will make that hard work as purposeful and enjoyable as possible.

There are six basic movements or plays which are especially effective in increasing the momentum of the attack and/or attacking space at the back of the defence in the attacking third of the field. They are: blind-side runs; overlap runs; cross-over plays; wall passes; dribbling; and improvised or inventive play.

3 Top priority – play to the back of the defence

3a Keegan passes the ball to Blissett in a very tight situation.

3b Keegan moves at speed to attack the back of the defence and Blissett attacks the back of the defence with a first-time pass, chipped a few feet off the ground.

3c Keegan volleys the ball into the net.

BLIND-SIDE RUNS, OVERLAP RUNS AND CROSS-OVER PLAYS

ORGANISATION FOR PRACTICE

The practice takes place in a grid measuring 30 yards by 10 yards. Using a portable goal, there are two attackers, one defender and a goalkeeper. The off-side law applies.

4a

4b

4 Attacking the back of the defence without the ball

4a Brooking, extreme right of the picture, attacking the back of defence without the ball. Wilkins, extreme left of the picture, about to attack the back of the defence with the ball.

4b Brooking, at the back of the defence, heading Wilkins's pass towards the goal.

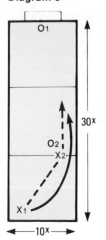

Diagram 2

Blind-side runs

In Diagram 2, X_1 passes the ball to X_2, who is challenged by O_2. X_1 then makes a run to the back of the defence on the blind side of O_2. X_2 must try to pass to X_1 or beat O_2 on the inside if O_2 has elected to mark X_1. If X_2 decides to pass the ball, he may have to lift the ball over the outstretched leg of O_2. X_2 should also try to bend the ball round O_2 into the path of X_1.

The space and angles are very tight and, even with the numerical advantage being on the attackers' side, the practice is demanding.

Overlap runs

In Diagram 3, X_1 has passed the ball to X_2, who is again marked by O_2. X_1 has made an overlap run outside X_2. X_2 can either pass the ball into the space beyond O_2 for X_1 to run on to, or dribble past O_2 on the inside if O_2 has marked X_1.

Cross-over plays

In Diagram 4, X_1 has passed the ball to X_2. X_1 follows the pass. X_2 controls the ball and dribbles the ball across the face of X_1. X_2 can either stop the ball and sprint away marked by O_2, leaving the ball for X_1 to shoot first time; or he can feint to stop the ball, but take the ball on to the side of O_2 to shoot for goal.

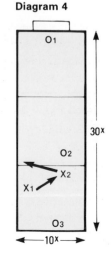

Diagram 3   **Diagram 4**

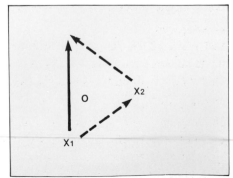

5 Blind-side runs

5a Blissett passes the ball to Keegan.

5b Blissett then makes a run on the blind side of the defender. (The defender has opened up the space outside him for Keegan, but it is Blissett who is going into that space.)

5c Keegan's pass beats the desperate lunge of the defender.

DEVELOPMENT OF THE PRACTICE

1. Once the attackers are adept at performing the three basic movements, the practice can be developed by allowing the attacking players to play whichever movement is most appropriate. The players at this stage should be encouraged to improvise and, most of all, to attempt difficult techniques.

2. The practice can be further developed by bringing in an extra defending player, O_3 (Diagram 4). O_3 is allowed to start his recovery run when X_1 has passed the ball to X_2. The effect of the recovering player is to inject into the attacking players a greater sense of urgency and willingness to take risks.

POINTS FOR THE COACH TO OBSERVE

1. The momentum of the attack should be increased. When the recovering player is brought in, he should not be able to recover on to the goal-side of the ball if the momentum is increased.

2. The players should be decisive in their movements.

3. The players should play with their heads up, watching each other's movements.

4. The players should be willing to try difficult techniques.

WALL-PASSING

Wall-passing can be one of the most devastating methods of beating defenders in any part of the field. In most parts of the field, however, a defender, by retreating, can prevent a wall-pass from succeeding. Wall-passing, therefore, is most effective in situations where the defender cannot or does not retreat – usually in the attacking third of the field. Although space is likely to be more restricted in the attacking third of the field, wall-passing should be considered an essential part of the armoury of any attacking team.

The basic concept of the wall-pass is extremely simple. It is based on the idea of playing a ball against a wall at an angle and receiving the ball back at roughly the same angle. With a player replacing the wall, the technique is now used to beat a defender. In Diagram 5, X_1 passes the ball to X_2 (the wall) who redirects the ball behind O. Having made the pass, X_1 runs into space behind O to receive the pass from X_2.

There are a number of simple points for both the dribbling player and the wall player to observe.

Diagram 5

The dribbling player

Angle of run. The dribbling player should commit the defending player by running straight at him with the ball. In Diagram 6, routes 1 and 2 are wrong and will give the defender the opportunity to adjust his position. In Diagram 7, the movement of X_1 is correct and will commit O.

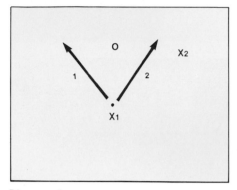

Diagram 6

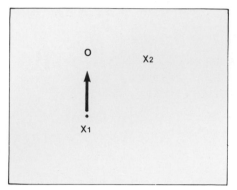

Diagram 7

The point of release. The ideal point at which to release the ball is just outside tackling range, two yards from the defender. If the ball is released too early, the defender will have time to adjust his position. If the ball is released too late, the defender will block the pass.

The method of release. The ball is best played with the instep (the laces) at the point of release. This allows the pass to be disguised and the player passing the ball to remain in his normal stride pattern. The ball should, of course, be passed to the wall player's feet.

Change of pace. It is important for the dribbling player to remain in his normal stride pattern. Once the ball has been released, he should accelerate and sprint into the space behind the defender to receive the ball back from the wall.

The wall-player

The angle from the defending player. This should be either square, or slightly forward of square of the defending player. It should be remembered that wall-passing will sometimes be used against a defender who is the last line of

6 Wall-passing

6a Keegan dribbling at the defender. Note the defender's sideways position. Keegan is about to release the ball, from well outside dribbling range, to play a wall-pass with Brooking. Note that Brooking, who is the wall, is moving in.

6b The pass is made and the defender is turned through 180 degrees. Note that Brooking plays the ball first time with the inside of his left foot. This makes the angle as wide as possible and the pass as safe as possible. Keegan, having made the pass, makes a determined run into the space behind the defender.

6c Keegan receiving the ball yards clear of the defender.

6a

6b

6c

defence. Where the off-side law is a consideration, the wall must, of course, be forward of square.

The distance from the defending player. If the wall is too close to the defending player, the ball will be intercepted. If the wall is too far away from the defending player, he will have time to adjust his position. Generally speaking, the tighter the situation, the more devastating the wall-pass will be. The ideal position is for the wall to be four or five yards away from the defending player at the moment the ball is played.

Moving into line. Unlike a brick wall, the wall-player can move into line from a wide position so that the wall is presented as late as possible. In Diagram 8, X_1 moves directly towards O and X_2 moves into line from a wide position, so creating the correct angles for a wall-pass.

The pass. The pass must be played on the first touch and should be directed into the space behind the defender and in front of the attacker moving into the space (Diagram 5). The pass can be made effectively with either foot. If, however, the pass is made with the outside foot, the foot farthest from the passer, the angle for playing the ball behind the defender will be made as wide as possible.

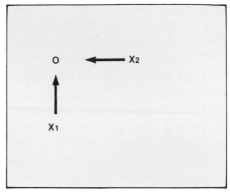

Diagram 8

Wall-passes need not always involve a player dribbling at an opponent with the ball. Nor is it always necessary to have a two-v-one situation in favour of the attackers. Sometimes it is possible to execute a wall-pass in a position where there is little space in front of the defence and there is an extra defender. This is especially the case if the defenders are square.

In Diagram 9, X_1 passes the ball to X_2 who moves to meet the pass and plays the ball between O_1 and O_2. X_1 moves into the space behind O_1 to receive the pass. It should be noted that the pass from X_1 to X_2 was nearly square and that the pass into space from X_2 was at an angle of 45 degrees. This, however, is still regarded technically as a wall-pass.

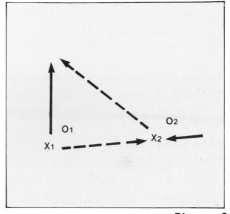

Diagram 9

ORGANISATION FOR PRACTICE

The practice takes place in a 10-yard square. In Diagram 10, X_1 plays a wall-pass with X_2 without any opposition. The players should be allowed to practise wall-passing freely inside the 10-yard grid alternating the roles of dribbler and wall.

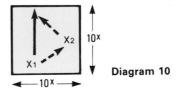

Diagram 10

DEVELOPMENT OF THE PRACTICE

1. The practice area is extended to 20 yards by 10 yards and an opponent is introduced. O is conditioned to make a challenge in the first square (Diagram 11, the white area). If this condition is not imposed, O is likely to retreat to the 20-yard line, thus preventing any chance of a wall-pass being played. X_1 and X_2 must make a wall-pass and reach the 20-yard line in full control of the ball.
2. The practice is developed further by introducing a second defender. A two-sided game can now take place, the object being to reach the opponent's goal-line in full control of the ball. The players should be encouraged to be as inventive as possible and only play the wall-pass when they recognise that it is likely to succeed. In this practice, the real skill of wall-passing comes out – the simultaneous recognition of the suitable circumstances, and the execution of the technique, by two co-operating players.

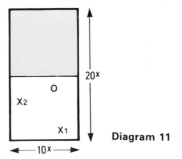

Diagram 11

POINTS FOR THE COACH TO OBSERVE

1. The dribbling player should commit the defender by running at him with the ball.

2. The dribbling player should release the ball just before he is tackled.

3. The pass should be made with maximum disguise and without interrupting the stride pattern.

4. The pass should be played to the wall-player's feet.

5. The wall-player should be positioned at the correct angle and distance from the defending player.

6. The wall-player should move into line as late as possible.

7. The pass should be directed into the space behind the defender and in front of the attacker. Observe which foot is used.

8. Observe, when the practice becomes free and inventive, that the attacking players recognise when it is suitable to make a wall-pass.

DRIBBLING

It is not just a coincidence that almost all the exciting players are good dribblers of the ball. It is also a fact that all the best teams contain several players who can beat opponents by dribbling. All dribbling, however, involves a risk – a risk of being dispossessed. The point should be made, however, that a high risk for one player may be a low risk for another.

It should be appreciated that the dividends for dribbling in the defending third of the field are low, while the risk element is high. In the attacking third of the field, however, the reverse is the case. Players who can dribble, and who do so in the attacking third of the field, are invaluable to a team.

The attitude of players to dribbling is an important factor, particularly when crowds are involved. Crowds can undermine the confidence of a player by dismissing a failed dribble as selfish – yet they would be the first to greet him as a hero if it succeeded. Players should always remember that dribbling is a matter of percentages and that even the best dribblers are likely to fail more often than they succeed. Adopting the correct attitude to failure and criticism, therefore, is very much part of the match skill of dribbling.

There is a significant difference between running with the ball and dribbling. Most players run with the ball too frequently but dribble less frequently than they could. Running with the ball involves covering ground without trying to dribble past opponents. When running with the ball, it is often a disadvantage to

7 Dribbling – close control

7a Keegan showing close dribbling control. Note Brooking moving away from the space Keegan wants to use.

7b Keegan has dribbled past the defender on his outside foot, the foot farthest from the defender. Note that Brooking has created the space for Keegan by attracting the covering defender away from the space.

8 Dribbling – feinting and changing direction

8a Keegan, having feinted to go outside the defender, changes direction and comes inside, turning the defender through 180 degrees.

8b He loses no time in taking his shot which he hits with ferocious power.

9a

9b

9c

9 Dribbling – change of pace

9a Blissett prepares to beat the challenging player.

9b He beats the challenging player by an explosive change of pace.

9c His pace also beats the covering player.

maintain close control. The reasons for this are that there is not usually an opponent in close proximity and the fewer the touches required on the ball, the easier it is for a player to get his head up and observe the general state of the game.

All effective dribbling is based on combining four qualities:

- Close control.
- Ability to feint and dummy.
- Ability to change direction.
- Ability to change pace.

ORGANISATION FOR PRACTICE

The practice takes place in a 10-yard square (Diagram 12). Five players, each with a ball, dribble the ball anywhere inside the square's boundaries. They must avoid bumping into other players or balls. The coach should control the practice by giving commands to stop, start, turn, change direction and change pace, and by conditioning the practice as follows:

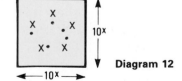

Diagram 12

- Dribbling and turning only with the outside of the foot.
- Dribbling and turning only with the inside of the foot.
- Turning with the ball by using the sole of the boot.
- Dribbling only with the right foot.
- Dribbling only with the left foot.
- Dribbling with either foot.

A combination of the commands and the conditions will soon place a premium on close control. The players should also be encouraged to look up and find space. This particular practice can be made more difficult and enjoyable by:

ATTACKING (2)

- Introducing more players, each with a ball, into the same amount of space.
- Encouraging the players to keep their ball out of the playing distance of other players at the same time as trying to kick the ball of any other player out of the area.

Once the players are composed and comfortable in dribbling the ball with close control, the practice can be developed.

DEVELOPMENT OF THE PRACTICE

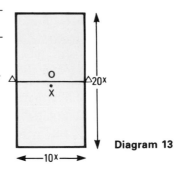

Diagram 13

1. The practice is developed by combining the technique of close control with feinting and dummying. Feinting is frequently referred to as 'selling the dummy'. In essence, it is pretending to move in one direction, in order to unbalance one's opponent, before moving away in the opposite direction.

The practice takes place in a grid measuring 20 yards by 10 yards. There is a cone on each touch-line at the 10-yard line. In Diagram 13, X is in possession of the ball, one yard from the centre line, and O is positioned opposite him. Neither player is allowed to cross the line.

X must feint to unbalance O and then move to either of the cones with the ball before O can stop him. The players then change over so that each one benefits from the practice. Emphasis should be placed on the following:

- Moving the ball from side to side.
- Feinting to play the ball, but taking the foot over the ball.
- Feinting with the upper body while remaining balanced on the soles of the feet.

2. The practice is developed further by adding a cone to the centre of each of the goal-lines. X has two choices this time: either he can feint and move off to either cone on the half-way line; or he can feint and try to dribble the ball to the cone on the goal-line behind O. X should be encouraged to unbalance O and then dribble past him.

The players again change over so that each gains practice in attacking.

3. Further development of the practice takes place in the same grid area with the introduction of an extra attacker. In Diagram 14, X_1 is in possession of the ball. He can pass to X_2 if he wishes, or he can use him as a decoy. X_1 must try to dribble past O and through the cones on the goal-line behind O. O is conditioned to challenge in the first 10-yard grid.

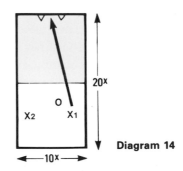

Diagram 14

It is a good coaching method to give the dribbling player a team-mate with whom to co-ordinate if necessary as it introduces game reality into the practice. Sometimes the dribbler can play a wall-pass to his team-mate, sometimes he can feint to play a wall-pass and dribble through. The dribbling player, however, should be encouraged to dribble most of the time and to use his team-mate, X_2, as a decoy for feint plays.

At this stage, great emphasis must be placed on combining the techniques of close control and feinting with the other two important qualities in dribbling, change of direction and change of pace. There are three phases in the dribble:

The approach. This should be to commit the defender by moving straight at him at a moderate or slow speed.

Unbalancing the opponent. This must take place just outside tackling range and will involve a change of direction, or a change of pace, or both.

Exploding into the space behind the opponent. This involves a rapid change of pace once the opponent is off balance and the player can follow one of two options:

- He can play the ball past the opponent. This will apply when there is plenty of space behind the opponent with no other opponents in close proximity.
- He can dribble the ball past the opponent under close control. This will apply when the space behind the opponent is restricted and there is an opponent in close proximity.

4. To give the attacker a considerable test of dribbling ability, the practice can be developed so that there is one attacker against two defenders. In Diagram 15, the server, S, passes the ball to X. As the ball is travelling, O_1 and O_2 move in, one to challenge and the other to cover. X must try to dribble past both the challenging and the covering player and reach the 20-yard line in full control of the ball.

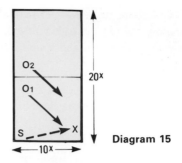

Diagram 15

POINTS FOR THE COACH TO OBSERVE

1. Players should have the ability to dribble the ball under close control.
2. Players should have the ability to disguise their intentions and unbalance their opponent by moving the ball, and by making feinting movements without playing the ball.
3. Players should have the ability to make sudden changes of direction.
4. Players should have the ability to change pace by explosive movement past the opponent.
5. Players should appreciate when to play the ball, and when to take the ball past an opponent.
6. Players should adopt the correct attitude to success and failure in dribbling.

ENCOURAGING IMPROVISATION AND INVENTIVE PLAY

The techniques, movements and combined play discussed so far in this chapter provide a sound basis for attacking in the attacking third of the field. Players should be encouraged to use that basis to become even more inventive and to develop individual flair.

Coaches should remember that 'necessity is the mother of invention'. If players are not placed in tight situations, they will not produce inventive play – for there will be no need to do so. Frequently, inventive play is an instinctive response to a difficult situation, usually posed by opponents.

It is a mistake to believe that inventive and instinctive play cannot be coached. Coaching this quality will reap rich rewards in four respects:

- The attitude of players to taking risks in the attacking third of the field will be strengthened in favour of risk.
- There will be a recognition of, and familiarity with, tight and difficult situations.
- The difficult will become accepted as the norm – not something to be feared or avoided.
- Confidence, which can only accrue from successful performance, will be developed.

ORGANISATION FOR PRACTICE

The practice takes place in a grid measuring 30 yards by 10 yards. There are two attackers, two defenders, a goalkeeper and a server. In Diagram 16, S passes the ball to either X_1 or X_2, each of whom is marked respectively by O_2 and O_3. The attacking players can use any method of attack, either combined or individual, but must shoot at goal as quickly as possible. The degree of difficulty can be

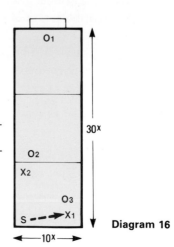

Diagram 16

10 Inventive play

10a and 10b Keegan changes direction and moves inside the defender.

10c Blissett makes an overlap run round the back of Keegan.

10d Keegan back-heels the ball to Blissett – note that he does it on the foot farthest from the defender, thereby screening the ball.

10e and 10f Blissett moves on to the ball and shoots for goal.

11a

11b

11c

13a

increased by bringing into the practice a further defender who can recover from behind the server once the ball is played to the attackers.

The attitude of the coach during this practice is especially important. It must be one of constant encouragement so that the attacking players achieve quick and inventive play with a high element of risk taking.

DEVELOPMENT OF THE PRACTICE

1. The practice is developed so that the importance of the role of the player without the ball is emphasised. His role is to destroy the covering position of the defender who is covering the challenging player. The width of the practice area is now increased to 20 yards, but the number of players remains the same.

In Diagram 17, S passes the ball to X_1, who is challenged by O_3. X_2 then makes a movement to destroy the covering position of O_2. He will do this by destroying the angle, or the distance, or both, between O_2 and O_3. Once X_2 has destroyed the covering position of O_2, he can try to combine with X_1, if X_1 has not already beaten O_3. The degree of difficulty can again be increased by introducing a further defending player who will position himself behind the server. The timing of his recovery should be controlled by the coach.

2. The practice is further developed in the attacking third of the field, but at an angle moving in from the flank (Diagram 18, shaded area). While the basic attacking methods and the number of players remain the same, it should be appreciated that angles and spaces are different when moving in from a flank rather than from in front of goal.

S passes the ball to X_1 who is marked by O_2. O_3 covers X_2. The players should practise five basic methods of combining:

- If X_2 can bring O_3 into a square position, a wall-pass can be used.
- If X_2 can bring O_3 into a square position, X_1 can attack O_2 by feinting to make a wall-pass and then dribbling past O_2 on the outside.
- X_1 can pass to X_2 and follow the pass to perform a cross-over play.
- X_1 can pass to X_2 and then attack O_2 on the outside. X_2 can then feint to pass but turn inside to shoot.
- X_2 can make a diagonal run to take O_3 out of a central position. X_1 can then attack O_2 on the inside.

All the above movements should be practised individually, and then the practice should be allowed to go free and the players play what is most appropriate.

3. The practice is developed by using five attackers, five defenders and a goalkeeper in an area measuring 40 yards by 40 yards. In Diagram 19, S passes the ball to any one of the X players, each of whom is marked by an O player. The attackers must combine to produce a shot at goal. It should be noted that this is not a small-sided game. The ball is returned to the server after each attack and the players reform in tight marking positions to restart the practice, thus ensuring that the attackers are always under pressure. All the various methods of attacking should be encouraged both in terms of combined play and inventive individual play. When the practice is actually in progress, the play will be intense and

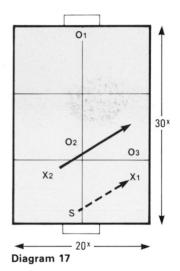
Diagram 17

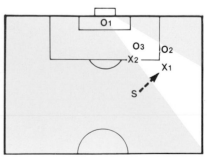
Diagram 18

12a

12b

12c

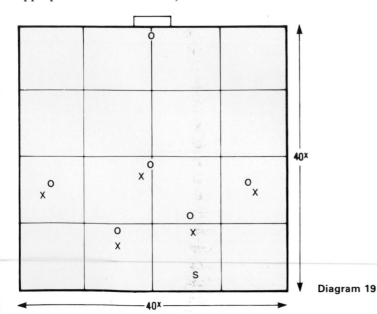

13b

11 Destroying the position of the covering and challenging players

11a Brooking and Keegan preparing to destroy the positions of the challenging and covering players.

11b They achieve this by a cross-over play.

11c Keegan moves in on goal clear of the defender.

12a This time Blissett runs past Keegan.

12b Keegan takes the ball and they completely destroy the defenders.

12c Keegan scores from close range.

13a Blissett taking the covering player away from the covering position.

13b Shaun Brooks exploits the space by beating the challenging player and shooting for goal.

physically demanding. It is advisable, therefore, to give the players frequent rest periods.

4. Further development of the practice should take place in the attacking third of the field, using the same number of players. In Diagram 20, S passes the ball to any one of the attackers, each of whom is marked by a defender. The players should be encouraged to deploy all their individual and combined attacking skills towards setting up a shot at goal. Emphasis should be placed on attacking through central positions, but if the attack is forced to a flank, and it becomes appropriate to cross the ball, then the ball should be crossed.

Diagram 19

40x

40x

Diagram 20

The degree of difficulty in this practice can be increased by introducing two further defending players who should be positioned, one on each flank, behind the server. The timing of their recovery on to the goal-side of the ball should be controlled by the coach. The effect of this development will be to produce a greater sense of urgency in the attacking players who will be keen to build their attack before the two extra defenders are able to recover.

5. Coaching in the game. The final development is to coach the various individual techniques and combined movements in the game itself. The attack should originate in the middle third of the field, so that the team is made to work patiently towards creating space, and thereby an attacking opportunity. Once the opportunity to attack arises, the team should exploit it as rapidly as possible.

In Diagram 21, S passes the ball to any one of the attackers in his own defending half of the field. The X players then develop their attack through the middle third of the field and into the attacking third of the field to create a shot at goal. The practice is developed by the server passing the ball to any O player in the middle third of the field. The X players, therefore, have to win the ball from the O team, play with composure as they build their attack, and then gather momentum for the final thrust for goal.

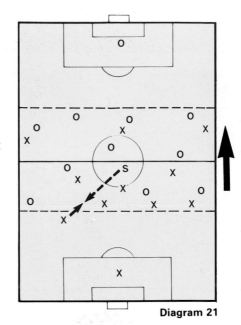

Diagram 21

The coach must encourage a positive attitude towards risk taking in the attacking third. To help achieve this, three conditions can be applied in the attacking third:

- Any X player receiving the ball must attack and try to dribble past his immediate opponent.
- The ball must always be played forward, except from a position on, or near, the goal-line.
- Players must attack the back of the defence, with and without the ball, using the various movements and techniques considered earlier in this chapter.

Crosses should not be emphasised in these sessions but, if they seem to be appropriate, the players must be encouraged to make the correct play.

POINTS FOR THE COACH TO OBSERVE

1. The players should always start the practices in realistic positions.
2. The players should be prepared to be inventive and take risks in tight situations.
3. Players without the ball should attack and destroy the positions of covering players.
4. Players, both as individuals and in combined play, should have the ability to attack when moving in from flank positions.
5. Observe the ability of the players to combine their attacking movements and techniques in:

    (i) A small-sided practice.
    (ii) A phase practice in the attacking third of the field.

6. Observe the ability of the players in the eleven-a-side practice in relation to:

    (i) Inventive play and risk taking.
    (ii) Increasing the momentum of the attack to exploit space.
    (iii) The ability to attack the back of the defence with and without the ball.

7. Observe the quality of the shooting.

SHOOTING (1)
ATTITUDE, TECHNIQUE AND SKILL

THE COACH'S ATTITUDE

The raw excitement of soccer, contained in even the most mediocre games, is embodied in shooting. There can be no doubt that shooting is the most important aspect of attacking play. Everything that an individual or team does is designed to contribute towards creating a shooting opportunity. It is surprising, therefore, that at every level of soccer a high percentage of opportunities to shoot are missed.

Some teachers and coaches are mystified by the fact that players often fail to shoot when they are in a position to do so. But it is the teachers and coaches themselves who, unwittingly, regularly contribute towards the downfall of their players. They can fail to maximise the shooting potential of their players in several ways:

By reducing shooting to a secondary consideration

It is easy when coaching passing, or some other aspect of attacking play, to lose sight of the main objective which is to score a goal. As a result, many coaches fall into the trap of being satisfied with the creation of a scoring opportunity. A poor shot, or indeed no shot at all, frequently passes without comment. We even hear managers, speaking after games, making observations such as: 'We played very well – we just did not take our chances.' But playing very well involves taking scoring chances. It can be seen therefore that, whatever aspect of attacking play one may be coaching, the emphasis should always be on the taking of scoring opportunities.

By praising unselfish play

As if the previous fault was not sufficient, it is often compounded by teachers and coaches who, far from criticising players for not taking shooting opportunities, praise them for unselfish play. Players who pass when they are in a position to shoot are more anxious to pass the responsibility than the ball. Where scoring goals is concerned, unselfish players do not win matches. Players should be educated to have an aggressive approach to shooting. Accepting personal responsibility for scoring, as well as missing, is fundamental to that aggressive approach.

By providing unrealistic practice goals

One of the less endearing features of five-a-side football is the size of goals used. Many teams use the five-a-side goals for a variety of training practices which are designed to end up with a shot at goal. The effect of these goals is to produce bad scoring habits for, if unrealistic goals are used, unrealistic shooting will result. Quite apart from any other consideration, realistic shooting must be tested against realistic goalkeeping, something that is impossible to achieve with five-a-side goals.

The best solution is to use portable goals. Not only do they encourage realistic shooting but they can also save goalmouth wear. If these are not available, the goal should, at least, always be the correct width, even if corner flags are used for goal-posts.

By failing to improve poor technique

None of us should seek to hide the fact that a large percentage of shots miss the target. This is largely due to poor technique, which frequently relates to incorrect practice. More will be written about this aspect later in the chapter.

By failing to encourage the correct attitude to shooting

All the points mentioned above underline the fact that a player's mental approach to the problem under consideration is of vital importance to shooting – as it is to all aspects of play. The attitude to shooting should be that it is the major factor in attacking play and that failure is failure to shoot – not failure to score. The attitude to practice should always be to practise as one intends to play. In the eleven-a-side game one does not play with five-a-side goals – so full-sized goals should be used in practice. The attitude to poor technique should be to analyse the fault and correct it through more practice, not less.

The importance of adopting the correct mental approach to shooting can be proved by the most simple analysis which will also prove to coaches that attitudes must be corrected first and techniques second. In preparing the films which were made in conjunction with this book, an analysis of the players' attitude to shooting was made in a small-sided game. The game was played for a set period of time, during which the number of opportunities to shoot were counted. The number of shots taken were also counted. At the end of the period of analysis, the players were made aware of the results and were told to inject a greater sense of urgency into their play. The game was then replayed for exactly the same period and the same analysis was made. The results of the second analysis showed a 40 per cent improvement in chances taken and a 50 per cent improvement in goals scored.

Similar analyses have been done by other coaches with many different groups of players. The results have always been comparable.

The results of the analyses exemplify two simple truths:

- Attitude is the factor of play with which coaches must deal first of all. All other factors are secondary in terms of priority.
- Improvement in attitude will bring about the biggest and quickest improvement in performance.

Coaches who feel that coaching is exclusively about communicating technical and tactical points should review their thinking and – dare one make the point? – adjust *their* attitude.

ANALYSIS OF SHOTS

Shots off Target

Analysis of shooting shows that of the shots which are taken, a large percentage miss the target.

It should be emphasised that it is a lesser sin to shoot wide than high. A shot going wide may have some chance of a deflection; a shot going high merely gives the opposition a goal-kick. Missed shots are not always entirely due to a fault in technique. The personal attitude of the player may well be a contributory factor, particularly when a player places a greater emphasis on power than accuracy – the correct attitude should always be accuracy before power.

Low Shots

Shots along the ground are more difficult for a goalkeeper to save than shots in the air. A player may like to see the roof of the net bulge, but in going for a high shot he is offering the goalkeeper a greater chance of stopping the ball. Diagram 1 shows that a goalkeeper will move more quickly to a ball at point B than he will at point A. Point A is actually farther away than point B, for the goalkeeper has to move the whole of his body to save at that point. At point B it may be possible to save by stretching out one arm.

One other consideration should persuade a player to shoot low: the flight of shots in the air is easier to assess than the path of shots along the ground. Shots along the ground, in addition to the possibility of them being deflected, are likely to stick, bump and skid – all of which makes the goalkeeper's task a little more difficult.

Diagram 1

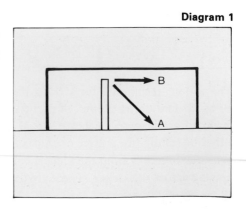

Shots going away from the goalkeeper

Shots going away from the goalkeeper to the far post are usually more difficult to save than shots to the near post (Diagram 2). Not only are they more difficult to hold, but they are also more difficult to knock away to safety.

Shots from bouncing or dropping balls in the penalty area

An analysis of shooting in matches reveals that a high percentage of shooting chances occur from bouncing or dropping balls in the penalty area. There is evidence that a low percentage of practice time is devoted to practising these types of shots. In the advanced levels of the game, the skill of defenders has increased so much that it is extremely difficult for attackers to find a ground route into the penalty area. Added to this, a high percentage of goals are scored from corners and free kicks, the ball from these kicks almost invariably being delivered in the air. Attacking players in the penalty area do need, therefore, good techniques for taking the ball on the volley.

SHOOTING TECHNIQUES

The various techniques for kicking the ball are described in detail on pages 60 to 72. Only brief points, of particular reference to shooting, will therefore be made in this chapter. Goals are scored from three types of shot, all of which can either be rolling (for a drive or chip) or bouncing (for a volley or half-volley): balls moving away from the kicker; balls moving towards the kicker; and balls moving across the kicker. There are five principal technical points which apply to all six permutations:

1 Low Shot
Low shots are difficult to save. Steve McKenzie passes the ball into goal, low and wide of the goalkeeper.

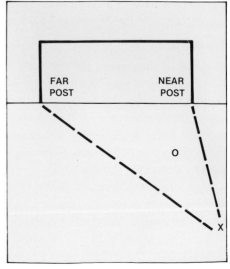

Diagram 2

2a

3a

2b

2 Bouncing Ball

2a Blissett into the hitting stride for a volley shot. Head and non-kicking foot are perfectly positioned.

2b Airborne follow through – a performance of composure and power.

3 Rolling ball for kicker

3a Keegan striking a rolling ball. His non-kicking foot and his head are perfectly positioned.

3b A lovely follow through showing that considerable power has gone into the shot.

3b

4 Ball bouncing away from kicker
Keegan, perfectly composed, with his head down and steady, about to make contact through the middle or top half of a ball bouncing away from him.

- Observe the position of the goalkeeper. (*Photograph 5, page 121*)
- Select the most vulnerable area of the goal to aim at. (*Photograph 6, page 121*)
- Concentrate on accuracy. (*Photograph 7, page 122*)
- Keep the head down and steady for contact on the ball. (*Photograph 8, page 122*)
- Strike through the middle or top half of the ball. (*Photograph 9, page 123*)

Balls moving away from the kicker

ORGANISATION FOR PRACTICE

Practice takes place in a grid measuring 40 yards by 10 yards. Corner flags, placed 8 yards apart, are used as goal-posts to enable the practice to flow from either side. This gives more practice to more players and eliminates the need for fielders. In Diagram 3, S_1 serves the ball for X_1 to run forward to and shoot for goal, ideally from 15 yards. At this stage of the practice there is no requirement for the shooting player to strike the ball first time. The practice is then repeated by S_2 serving for X_2. The players should, of course, rotate so that each one gains practice in shooting and the ball should be served from either side of the grid so that each foot is used. It should be stressed that the player in goal must try his best as a goalkeeper. Although few of the players will be goalkeepers, they should still try to narrow the angle and make an effort to stop the shot. Passive goalkeeping detracts from all shooting practice.

DEVELOPMENT OF THE PRACTICE

1. Once the shooting player is confident and accurate, the pressure on him should be increased. This is done by the server chasing the shooting player once

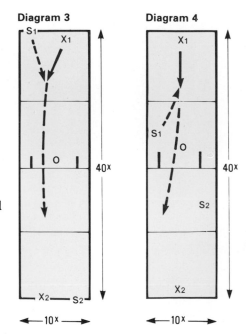

the ball has been served. The ball should be served from either side of the practice area so that the attacking player is made to shoot with his weaker foot. This practice is designed to help shooting players to appreciate the following:

- They usually have more time than they imagine.
- If the challenging player is not within tackling range when the shot is made, his presence should not influence the performance.
- Composure and steadiness are prerequisites of a successful technical performance.
- The more a player worries about missing, the less likely he is to score next time.
- The skill of shooting is that of passing the ball past the goalkeeper, just like passing the ball past any other opponent.

2. The practice is developed by changing the service so that the attacking player has to deal with bouncing balls. The attacker, therefore, has to use the volley and half-volley techniques for shooting. The practice has three phases: practice without the server chasing; practice with the server chasing from either side; and practice with a variety of rolling and bouncing serves, from either side, always with the server chasing.

Balls moving towards the kicker

The great danger, with this type of service, is that the player will make contact through the bottom half of the ball and send it over the bar. It is, therefore, most important that the attacker should observe three particular technical points:

- Get the non-kicking foot well up to the ball.
- Keep the head steady and down over the ball.
- Make contact either through the middle or slightly above the mid-line of the ball.

ORGANISATION FOR PRACTICE

In Diagram 4, S_1 plays a ball on the ground for X_1 to shoot for goal. The practice is then repeated from the other side of the grid. It should be noted that S_1 and S_2 are positioned some five yards from the goal-line. This provides a more realistic angle for the service than would be the case if the ball were served from the corner.

5 Observe the goalkeeper

5a McKenzie has his head down watching the control. The goalkeeper starts his advance from goal.

5b He now observes the goalkeeper as the ball rolls forward within comfortable distance.

5c and 5d The end result is testimony to good observation and technical application.

6 Select the most vulnerable area of goal
The goalkeeper has not covered his near post. Brooks selects the most vulnerable area and punishes the goalkeeper's mistake.

7a

7b

7 Concentrate on accuracy

7a McKenzie sets himself to concentrate on accuracy rather than power.

7b The ball is beautifully slotted inside the post with the goalkeeper going the wrong way.

8a

8b

8 Head down for contact on the ball

8a Keegan's head is steady and he is watching the ball as he prepares to shoot.

8b Into the hitting stride with his non-kicking foot and his head well positioned.

8c A spectacular follow through demonstrating that his body momentum has gone into the shot.

8c

9a

9b

9 Strike through the middle or top half of the ball

9a Wilkins approaching the hitting stride for a power shot.

9b Contact is made through the middle of the ball. The non-kicking foot and head are perfectly in position.

9c Airborne in the follow through – an excellent finish for power shooting.

9c

10 Shooting past a defender

10a This is a good shooting opportunity and the decision to shoot is taken quickly.

10b As the defender closes in, the chances of scoring increase, since the goalkeeper's view may be obstructed or there may be a deflection.

DEVELOPMENT OF THE PRACTICE

1. The practice is developed by the server following his service and challenging the attacker. The practice is not altogether popular with servers since they may be struck a painful blow. It is, however, important that attackers have practice in shooting when challenged. There are two reasons for this:

- The attacker must be quick to take the shot, but must not be panicked by the challenge into snatching the shot.
- The attacker must aim to hit gaps, not defenders.

Indeed, it is possible that a defender may be used as a screen for the shot, thereby obscuring the vision of the goalkeeper.

2. The practice is repeated with a bouncing ball served from the same position. The development of the practice has three phases: practice without any challenge; practice with challenge from either side; and practice with a variety of rolling and bouncing serves from either side, always with challenge.

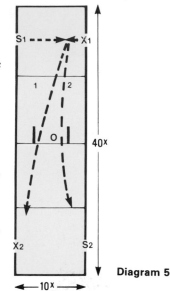

Diagram 5

Balls moving across the kicker

ORGANISATION FOR PRACTICE

The technique adopted in this type of kick is for the attacker to move towards the ball and strike it with a sweeping action of the kicking foot. The kicking foot is the foot nearest to the ball – if the ball comes from the player's right-hand side, he will strike the ball with his right foot. There are two types of shot from this position:

  (i) In Diagram 5, X_1 takes shot 1 and places the ball inside the goalkeeper's left-hand post. For this shot the non-kicking foot is well to the side of the ball but the body is closed to the target with the chest sideways on. The kicking foot can either go through or across the ball, inside to out, to swerve the ball in at the left-hand post.

  (ii) X_1 takes shot 2 and places the ball inside the goalkeeper's right-hand post. The non-kicking foot is well to the side of the ball and the chest is open to the target. The kicking foot wraps round the ball and 'pulls' the ball into the area of the right-hand post. Which of the two shots is used, largely depends on the position of the goalkeeper.

Practice takes place in isolation and the service is repeated from each side.

DEVELOPMENT OF THE PRACTICE

1. The practice is developed to bring in opposition. It is the server who should provide the challenge by following his serve. The practice is repeated from each side.

2. Once again the practice is repeated with a bouncing ball served from the same position. The development of the practice has three phases: practice without challenge; practice from either side, with challenge; and practice from a variety of rolling and bouncing serves from either side, always with challenge.

11 Ball rolling across the kicker

11a A sweeping action before contact from Blissett to a ball rolling across him.

11b A similar sweeping action, but after contact, from Keegan to a ball also rolling across him.

2a

12b

12 Ball bouncing across the kicker

12a Keegan about to strike a ball bouncing across him.

12b His head is steady and his eyes are watching the ball. His body is already leaning towards the target.

12c The body lean is even more marked now. This helps the kicking foot to sweep through and make contact through the top half of the ball.

2c

Pressure training

Pressure training for shooting can be highly beneficial and also tremendous fun. The main proviso, as with all types of pressure training, is that the player must be technically competent, otherwise the practice has no value. There are different practices which can be used for pressure shooting, but one of the best and most enjoyable is shown in Diagram 6. The practice area measures 20 yards by 20 yards. There is a portable goal and a goalkeeper, and a server is positioned at each corner with a good supply of footballs, thus ensuring a full service through 360 degrees. It is advisable to have two fielders behind the goal.

X is the player under pressure and he is positioned in the centre of the square. The coach nominates a server who has the choice of serving either a rolling or bouncing ball. The servers should vary their services as much as possible. In every case, the ball should be played towards X to give him the minimum amount of running. The coach should time each period of pressure – one minute is ideal – and a server should be nominated to count the number of shots. The scores should be kept so that the practice has a competitive element. At the end, an overall winner is declared. It is important that the practice is controlled by the coach – if the organisation is slick, five players can have a session of pressure in ten minutes.

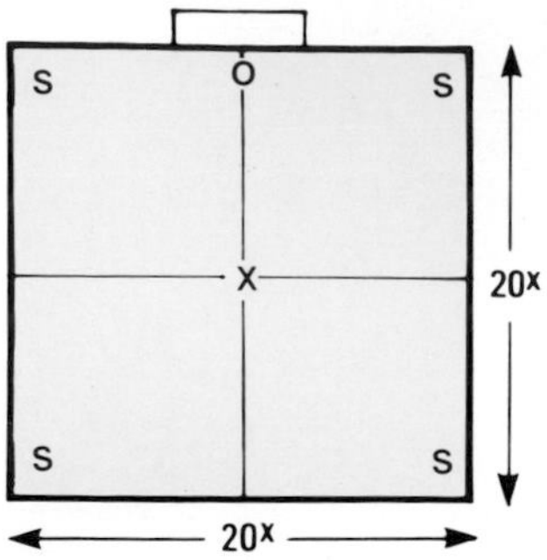

Diagram 6

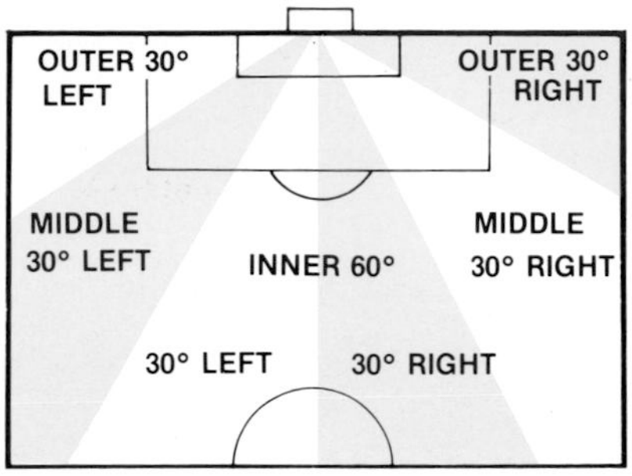

Diagram 7

Related practices in the penalty area

All the practices so far have been in grids where they have taken place in front of the goal. In matches, chances frequently occur at an angle. It is important, therefore, that players are given practice in shooting at an angle and in playing in the environment of the penalty area.

Shooting in and around the penalty area inevitably takes place through 180 degrees. It is convenient to divide the area into six angles of roughly 30 degrees each, as shown in Diagram 7. The previous shooting practices have all been concentrated in the inner 60 degrees.

ORGANISATION FOR PRACTICE

Practice takes place in the middle 30 degrees. In Diagram 8, S plays a rolling ball, inside the shaded area, so that X_1 can run forward and shoot for goal. The goalkeeper, O, must narrow the shooting angle. X_2 is positioned for any rebound or knock down by the goalkeeper. Much emphasis should be placed on X_1 observing the position of the goalkeeper. The use of swerving shots or lobs over the head of the goalkeeper is also important. Practice should be given from both the right- and left-hand sides.

DEVELOPMENT OF THE PRACTICE

1. The practice is repeated, but this time S chases X_1 after having played the ball.
2. The next development is for S to play a high bouncing ball for X_1 to run on to and shoot on the volley or half-volley.
3. A further development is for S to play a high bouncing service and then chase after X_1. All these practices should be undertaken in the middle 30 degrees on each side.
4. Having gained practice in volleying balls going away from the attacker, practice should now be given in volleying balls crossed from the opposite goal-line into the middle 30 degree area. In Diagram 9, S crosses the ball from inside the penalty area on the left-hand side. The ball is crossed over the head of O_2 into the middle 30 degrees for X_1 to head, volley or half-volley into goal. X_2 is once again positioned for rebounds. The practice should be repeated from the opposite side.

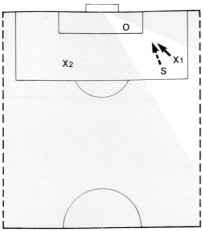

Diagram 8

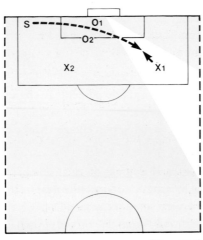

Diagram 9

13 Playing across goal and beating the goalkeeper at the near post

The goalkeeper has been tempted to try to cut out the ground cross inside the 6-yard area. He is, however, beaten by the pace of the pass and Blissett has an easy scoring chance.

When not to shoot

Part of the skill of shooting is to know when not to shoot. There are three situations in which a player should refrain from shooting:

■ When an opponent is so close as to be certain to block the shot.
■ When the distance is so great that it gives an unacceptable percentage chance of scoring. (This factor will be dealt with in the next chapter on shooting.)
■ When the angle is so small that it gives an unacceptable percentage chance of scoring.

The angles which are unacceptable are in the outer 30 degrees on each side of the penalty area (Diagram 7). When an attacker is moving in towards the goal in the outer 30 degrees, the chances of scoring will be very small if the goalkeeper has narrowed the angle correctly. If he has not narrowed the angle correctly, then there may indeed be an easy scoring opportunity, so attackers must always ensure that they observe the position of the goalkeeper. In normal circumstances, however, there are better possibilities for the attacker than shooting when in the outer 30 degrees. These possibilities are largely dictated by, first of all and most important, the goalkeeper; and second, the relative positions of other attackers and defenders.

In Diagram 10, X_1 is positioned on the inside of the outer 30 degrees and inside the penalty area. In this position we would expect the goalkeeper to be positioned at the near post. The task for X_1 is to eliminate the goalkeeper by playing the ball across the face of the goal. He must play the ball firmly and give the goalkeeper no chance of either interception or recovery from the near post. X_2 is positioned to attack the back half of the goal. The task for X_2 is relatively easy.

In Diagram 11, X_1 is nearer to the goal-line. O is at his near post and X_2 is positioned to attack the back half of the goal. X_1 can still eliminate O by playing the ball across the face of the goal – about five yards out from the near post. The angle of the pass makes the task for X_2 a little more difficult.

In Diagram 12, X_1 is in position on the goal-line inside the penalty area. O_1, the goalkeeper, is at the near post and O_2, a defender, has recovered into the near-post area and is blocking the ground route across the face of the goal. X_2 is again positioned to attack the back half of the goal. X_1 elects to play the ball over O_1 and O_2 into the space in the far-post area for X_2 to attack.

In Diagram 13, X_1 is on the goal-line. O_1, the goalkeeper, is at the near post, O_2 is defending the near-post area and O_3 is defending the far-post area. X_2 is in position to attack the back half of the goal. X_3 is in position to shoot a pass turned back from the goal-line and, in this case, the ball turned back to X_3 is the best available play.

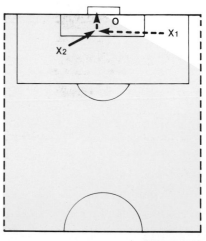

Diagram 10

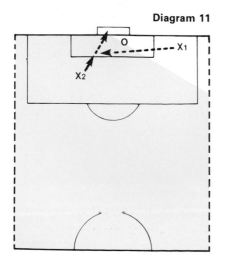

Diagram 11

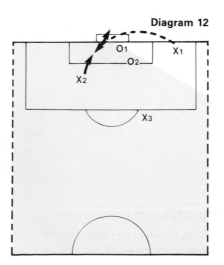

Diagram 12

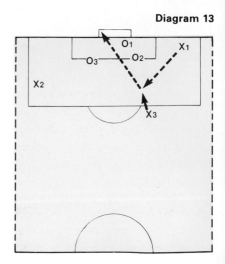

Diagram 13

14 Playing over the top of the goalkeeper at the near post

14a A recovering defender intercepts the ball in the ground route across goal.

14b The ball over the top to the far-post area is a far better way of beating the defender and the goalkeeper.

14c The goalkeeper has moved across his goal, but Blissett's diving header is directed to where he has just been.

14d The goalkeeper well beaten by a header inside what is now his far post.

ORGANISATION FOR PRACTICE

Practice takes place in the penalty area (Diagram 14). S passes the ball to X_1 at various angles. X_1 has four choices:

(i) Shoot if O_1 is badly positioned.
(ii) Pass on the ground for X_2.
(iii) Pass in the air for X_2.
(iv) Pass on the ground to X_3.

DEVELOPMENT OF THE PRACTICE

1. The practice takes place as in Diagram 14, but this time S follows his pass and puts X_1 under pressure.
2. The next development of the practice is to bring in an extra defending player, O_2, who has the choice to mark X_2, X_3 or space in the near-post area. X_1 must observe the position of O_1 and O_2 and make the correct selection.
3. The practice is developed further by bringing in a third defending player, O_3, who must combine in defence with O_2. Together they can achieve two of the three choices mentioned in the previous practice. All the above practices should take place first from the right-hand side, and then from the left-hand side of the penalty area.

Coaching shooting in a small-sided game

Small-sided games are always useful for practising shooting, provided that they are well organised. The following points should be built into the organisation:

Diagram 14

■ Full-sized portable goals should be used. Anything less than the full-sized goal will detract from the value of the practice.

■ The area should be relatively small in relation to the number of players. An area measuring 40 yards by 40 yards, roughly the area of two penalty areas, is ideal.

■ The number of players in that area should be six-v-six, including two goalkeepers.

■ A good supply of footballs is necessary in order to maintain the momentum of the session.

The coach should encourage the players to understand that of the three possibilities – passing, dribbling or shooting – shooting will bring the highest percentage success in and around the penalty area. In the small-sided game, therefore, the coach should discourage the players from making interpassing movements and encourage them to accept responsibility for shooting.

POINTS FOR THE COACH TO OBSERVE

1. The organisation for practice should be correct – especially in relation to the size of the goals.
2. Players should accept responsibility for shooting.
3. The shooter, prior to shooting, should observe the position of the goalkeeper.
4. Observe the selection of the target area of goal.
5. Observe the technique of striking the ball in relation to:

    (i) The position of the head.
    (ii) The position of the non-kicking foot.
    (iii) The contact of the kicking foot on the ball.

6. Players should concentrate on accuracy before power.
7. Players should appreciate when, and when not, to shoot.
8. Observe the skill of the players in selecting alternatives when deciding not to shoot.

9

SHOOTING (2)
SPEED, SKILL AND
COMBINED PLAY

QUICK SHOTS IN AND AROUND THE PENALTY AREA

The skill of shooting is concerned with combining techniques at the correct time and in the correct place. Forward players, for example, have to accept the fact that they will often receive the ball in and around the penalty area with their backs to the opponent. The techniques of checking, to create a yard or so of space, and turning become all important; so does the first touch on the ball, for the slightest error in ball control will result in a lost opportunity for a shot at goal. Players in these situations must also accept that difficulties will often be compounded by a less than perfect service, or by the unexpected, such as a ricochet.

It can be seen that it will not always be possible to get the body into the ideal position, but two technical factors must remain constant in all shooting:

■ The head must be steady.
■ Contact with the ball must be through the middle or top half of the ball.

Players, therefore, who are quick, who can combine techniques, who can adjust and improvise, and who can retain the above essential elements in their performance, are not only extremely skilful but also invaluable.

Throughout this book, repeated emphasis has been laid on the attitude adopted by players to a given situation. Again, the players' mental approach becomes an integral part of the skill needed in and around the penalty area and it should be characterised by the following:

■ Players who play safe in the opponent's penalty area cannot win matches. They should therefore calculate on the side of risk.
■ Passing in the opponent's penalty area and involving other team-mates should always be a second choice. The first choice must be to accept the responsibility in total and shoot.
■ Performing difficult techniques in difficult circumstances should be accepted as normal in the penalty area.
■ Missing the target must not put players off shooting – in order to score once, it may be necessary to miss ten times.
■ Players should not be afraid of physical challenge. Coaches, through encouragement and realistic practice, can help players to appreciate that the only thing they have to fear is fear itself.
■ Missing the opportunity to shoot is much worse than missing the target. This is, perhaps, the most important single factor in shooting, for no defender likes playing against an opponent who seizes every conceivable chance to shoot.

In a situation where most players are naturally lacking in confidence and are, frankly, uncomfortable, skilful coaching, which includes lots of encouragement and practice, can make players more confident, more comfortable, and more successful. Players need to have practice at the following:

■ Moving in one direction, before checking and moving away from the defender. (*Photograph 1, pages 134 and 135*)
■ Receiving the ball and turning in one movement. (*Photograph 2, page 136*)
■ Shooting on the half turn. (*Photograph 3, page 136*)
■ Shooting round opponents. (*Photograph 4, page 137*)
■ Letting the ball run through the legs before turning and shooting. (This is not effective if the opponent is directly behind the line of the ball.)
■ Feinting to shoot, in order to unbalance the opponent, before moving the ball to one side to create an angle for the shot. (*Photograph 5, page 137*)

SHOOTING (2)

ORGANISATION FOR PRACTICE

The practice takes place in a grid measuring 30 yards by 20 yards (Diagram 1). There are two portable, full-sized goals with a goalkeeper in each goal. Each of the goalkeepers has a good supply of soccer balls at the side of the goal. The basic practice is between two attackers and two defenders.

X_1 serves the ball to either X_2 or X_3. The first priority of the X player receiving the ball should be to attempt a shot at goal, only passing if absolutely necessary. The O players should mark as tight as possible. The practice is repeated with the O players attacking and the X players defending.

The practice can be very tiring for the players if it is continuous. It is therefore advisable to give the players rest periods, when coaching points can be discussed and demonstrated, between bouts of activity.

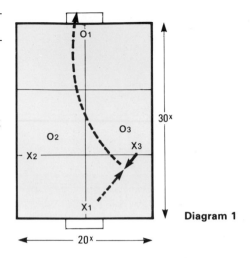

Diagram 1

Pressure training on the theme of quick shooting

It is almost impossible to coach players to improvise in isolated practices, for players will only improvise when the situation demands it. On page 126, the pressure-training practice was directed towards developing technique. This practice involves opponents and a co-operating player. The situation is extremely tight and competitive and will demand improvisation from the players.

Diagram 2

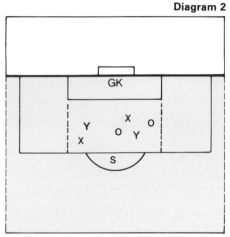

ORGANISATION FOR PRACTICE

The practice takes place in an area measuring 20 yards by 18 yards, reflecting the width of the six-yard area and the distance from the goal-line to the edge of the penalty area (Diagram 2). Inside the area there are seven players, consisting of a goalkeeper, GK, and three pairs of players, X, Y, and O. There is also a server, who should be the coach, positioned in the 'D' outside the penalty area, with a large supply of soccer balls. Each pair of players can combine together so that there are always two attackers against four defenders and a goalkeeper. The ball is only dead when the ball goes out of the area, or when a goal is scored.

The coach varies the service in terms of angle, flight, and pace. He can also vary the speed at which the ball is served in. It is sometimes an advantage to let the players recover to their starting positions after the ball has gone dead. This will ensure that the players get a rest between services. It will also ensure that the player receiving the ball is challenged.

It is beneficial, exciting, and enjoyable to organise a competition between the three pairs of players for a period of one minute. During this period, the coach will serve a ball in rapidly each time a ball goes dead. In these circumstances it is an advantage to use fielders, however large the supply of balls. If six fielders are used, then the players can change over, six performing while six are fielding. The goalkeepers should also be changed. An overall winning pair can be established on a knock-out basis. Every opportunity to have competitions of this nature should be taken. They make the practices more worthwhile, more enjoyable and therefore more beneficial.

POINTS FOR THE COACH TO OBSERVE

1. Players should have the correct attitude to the following: taking risks; accepting sole responsibility for shooting; attempting difficult techniques and improvising; missing the target or failing to score; and physical challenge.
2. Players should be able to create space for a shot.
3. Players should be able to shoot past opponents, using them as a screen.
4. Players should be able to control the ball and turn in one movement.
5. Players should be able to disguise their intentions or do the unexpected.
6. Players should make the correct contact with the ball.

133

1a

1b

1c

1g

1h

1i

1m

1n

1 Checking away from opponents

1a Keegan in front of goal marked tight.

1b The defender trying to get in front of Keegan.

1c Keegan makes a movement to his right.

1d He now checks his movement and moves off to his left.

1e Keegan is into his running stride. The defender, both feet on the ground, has not yet started to run.

1f Both players now running, but the defender is not on the goal-side of Keegan.

1g Keegan prepares to receive the ball.

1h He is now in position to receive the ball and screen the ball from the defender.

1i Keegan now in control of the ball and the defender in a hopeless position.

1j and 1k Keegan turns and the defender tries to challenge.

1l Keegan is now turned towards goal with a chance to shoot.

1m He elects to beat the defender on the inside.

1n and o He beats the defender comprehensively and shoots for goal.

2a

2b

2 Receiving the ball and turning

2a Shaun Brooks receives and takes the pace off the ball with his right foot.

2b He turns and screens the ball away from the defender.

3a

3b

3 Shooting on the half-turn

3a A high cross from the right flank is played to Blissett positioned beyond the far post.

3b Blissett plays the ball down to Keegan who is positioned near to the penalty spot.

3c and 3d Keegan shoots first time on the half-turn and pivots round as the ball rockets towards the net.

3c

3d

4 Shooting round opponents

4a Keegan has just taken the ball in a cross over with Wilkins.

4b He turns towards goal and prepares to shoot.

4c He shoots for goal round the defending player.

5 Feinting to unbalance the opponent before altering the angle of the shot

Blissett has made a feint play to go outside and has unbalanced the defender. Blissett alters the angle of the ball as he moves inside the defender for a shot at goal.

SHOOTING FROM OUTSIDE THE PENALTY AREA

If the players are only prepared to shoot when they are in the penalty area, they will reduce their shooting chances by as much as 50 per cent. When a player decides to beat that extra man, or make that extra pass, his intention is to create a better scoring chance – but most of the extra dribbles and passes result in no shot at all.

Give a player ten shots with a rolling ball from inside the 'D', without any opposition except the goalkeeper, and the chances are that he will score once or twice. Put several players between the kicker and the goalkeeper and the chances are that the scoring rate will increase. This will be for two reasons:

- The goalkeeper will not have such a clear view of the ball since players will inevitably obstruct his vision on occasions.
- There is a possibility of a deflection off one of the players – completely wrong-footing the goalkeeper.

It is probable that a number of shots will be blocked if there are players between the kicker and goalkeeper, but blocked shots are likely to produce a mêlée which could very well favour the attacking players. Such situations are evidence of a disorganised defence, so they will never favour the defence. These are good reasons why teams should not only take many more shots from outside the penalty area, but should also try to get as many players as possible forward into the penalty area.

Why then do players not shoot as frequently as they could from outside the penalty area? There are three basic reasons:

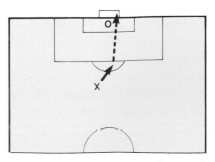

- They do not appreciate that their chances of scoring, or of producing a scoring chance, are good.
- They persuade themselves that they do not have a powerful enough shot.
- They are afraid of missing and being criticised for shooting from too far out.

The first two factors are linked and are a matter of individual and team education. Coaches should encourage players to appreciate that taking shooting opportunities from outside the penalty area is part of effective teamwork. If players are inaccurate from such distances, that can be rectified by practice. The greater problem belongs to the player who believes his shot is not sufficiently powerful and therefore will not shoot. Once again we are largely out of the area of technique and into the area of attitude, for there are very few senior players who would not be confident of taking a goal-kick and reaching the half-way line. One is only asking for more accuracy, not more power, and this can be brought about by practice.

6 Shot past crowd of players
6a Wilkins on the ball prepares to shoot.
6b Keegan runs across the path of the ball obstructing the goalkeeper's view of the ball.
6c Wilkins shoots past the crowd of players.

ORGANISATION FOR PRACTICE

Practice takes place in and near the penalty area (Diagram 3). X plays a rolling ball into the 'D' and runs forward to strike the ball first time into goal. As X moves to strike the ball, so O, the goalkeeper, will narrow the angle. It is therefore important that X should look up to observe the position of O before he selects his shot. Depending on the goalkeeper's position, he may choose a swerving shot, a lob over the goalkeeper's head, or a powerful ground shot.

The techniques of swerving, lofting and driving the ball are described on pages 60 to 72. Only two further points need to be made here about shooting from long range:

- Get well up to the ball to avoid overreaching. Reaching for the ball will result in the body weight not being transferred into the shot, resulting in a loss of power to the shot. Overreaching is often the result of the player trying to exert too much power.
- The attitude towards striking the ball must be aggressive – the player must be determined to score each time. The attitude of simply 'taking pot-luck' should be discouraged.

Once a player has the correct attitude to shooting from outside the penalty area and is aware of the necessity to look at the goalkeeper's position before selecting his shot, he is ready to be tested. He should take ten shots at goal with a rolling

Diagram 3

7 Getting well up to the ball to avoid overreaching

7a and 7b Keegan appears to be overreaching for the power volley but he is, in fact, beautifully positioned and composed for the shot.

7c A lovely action and an accurate finish.

7d Wilkins moving forward to strike a rolling ball from outside the penalty area. Note the concentrated observation of the coach Bobby Robson.

7e The ball is struck and Wilkins's head is still down and steady as a rock.

7f The follow through shows that Wilkins is perfectly balanced and that his body weight was transferred into the shot.

ball from outside the penalty area. Two goals or more is a very good result. By practising in more realistic situations, when the goalkeeper may be unsighted and when there may be deflections and rebounds, the results could be even better.

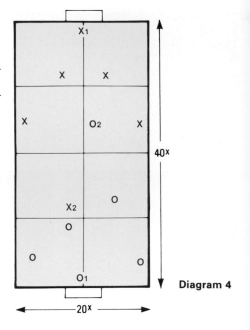

Diagram 4

DEVELOPMENT OF THE PRACTICE

1. The practice should be developed by introducing a greater sense of realism. This is achieved by practising with four attackers, a goalkeeper and a defender in each half of a grid measuring 40 yards by 20 yards. Full-sized portable goals are used.

In the top half of Diagram 4, X_1 serves the ball to one of the four X players. O_2 challenges the X players when they have possession of the ball and are trying to create a shooting opportunity at O_1's goal. Shots should be played from 20 yards or more and players should be encouraged to make few passes. If necessary, the X players may use X_2 to set up a shot for them, in which case one X player will pass to X_2 who will then pass back to another X player. However, the major role of X_2 should be to challenge for rebounds off the O players or the goal-posts once the X players have shot for goal. The practice should be repeated in each half of the grid in order to give all the players plenty of practice at shooting from more than 20 yards. It is important to remember that the players should not move out of their respective halves of the grid and that the emphasis of the practice is on shooting rather than passing.

2. The practice is further developed by introducing an extra X player and an extra O player to each half of the grid, making the situation four against two. The practice becomes even more realistic but it may reduce the number of shots – although it will increase the number of rebounds. The next development is best made in the eleven-a-side game, but this is considered on page 145.

POINTS FOR THE COACH TO OBSERVE

1. Observe the accuracy and power of the shots.
2. Players should observe the position of the goalkeeper and select their shots accordingly.
3. Players should vary their shots by using power, swerve and lob.
4. Players should be willing to shoot in the grid game.
5. Players should have the correct attitude to missing the target.
6. Observe the incidence of deflections, rebounds and direct goals.

BEATING THE GOALKEEPER WHEN CLEAR OF THE DEFENCE

The task for an attacking player who breaks clear of the defence and only has the goalkeeper to beat is never as easy as it appears. Perhaps it is the very fact that the chance appears to be easy, and everyone expects the player to score and is greatly excited by the prospect, that puts mental pressure on the player.

The attitude of the player is, therefore, of vital importance – he must be composed and keep his head when all those about him may be losing theirs. This is achieved by knowing what to do and by knowing one can do it.

There are four elements involved in beating the goalkeeper when clear of the defence.

The approach

An attacker will have broken clear of the defence either by running on to a ball which has been played by another player, or by dribbling the ball past the last

defender and on towards the goal at speed. Either way, there is usually substantial space between the attacker and the goalkeeper. There is, therefore, no need for close dribbling control – indeed, it is important to play the ball well forward of the feet in order to eliminate the need for close control so that the player can get his head up to observe the goalkeeper.

Observation

An attacker should observe closely the speed and angle of the goalkeeper's movements in order to determine the space available to the side, behind, and in front of the goalkeeper. When a player breaks clear of the defence, the task of a goalkeeper is to move out from goal and, by decreasing the space between himself and the ball, show as little of the goal as possible to the attacker. The goalkeeper will also wish to be on his feet and balanced at the moment the shot is taken. If he gets close enough to the attacker to eliminate the shot, he will go down at the feet of the attacker by spreading his body in a long barrier across the angle of the goal (Diagram 5a). Those goalkeepers who spread themselves *down* the angle make their goals vulnerable as they fail to narrow the angle (Diagram 5b). Goalkeepers who dash out from goal are also extremely vulnerable.

8 Beating the goalkeeper by shooting past him

8a McKenzie with his head down controlling the ball.

8b The approach – the ball well in advance of the feet and the head up observing the situation.

8c The decision is taken to shoot and the head is down for an accurate contact with the ball.

8d The ball is passed into the goal.

Decision

Having observed the speed and angle of the goalkeeper's movements, and the amount of space available, the player has enough information to decide how to play the ball. He has two possible choices: he can either shoot the ball past the goalkeeper; or he can dribble the ball past the goalkeeper.

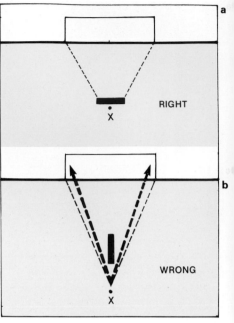

Diagram 5

Shooting the ball past the goalkeeper. Perhaps shooting is not quite the best word – passing the ball past the goalkeeper may be a more adequate description of the task. Balls passing close to the goalkeeper's feet are very difficult to save. If the player decides to pass the ball into the goal, he must be sure there is sufficient space available to play the ball past the goalkeeper. Sometimes the space available can be increased by moving the ball slightly off line and altering the angle immediately prior to the shot. Sometimes the space can be increased by feinting to shoot, in order to draw the goalkeeper to one side or at least unbalance him, and then passing the ball into the goal.

On other occasions, it may be suitable to loft the ball over the goalkeeper's head. If space is available in front of the goalkeeper, and if the ball is bouncing, this is often the easiest of all options. However, it should be noted that it is quite a difficult technique to loft a ball rolling away from a player when moving at speed. There is no reason why the technique should not be used; but players should make sure that they practise it.

Dribbling the ball past the goalkeeper. There are two important factors in dribbling the ball past the goalkeeper:

- The goalkeeper must be eliminated, i.e. the ball should be outside his reach.
- As a result of eliminating the goalkeeper, the space and angle for passing the ball into the goal should be increased, not decreased.

In order to eliminate the goalkeeper, the decision to dribble past him must be made when the ball is outside his playing distance but close enough to commit him and make it impossible for him to readjust his position. If a feint or disguise is to be used, this is the moment to do it – its use can be devastating. The ball should then be played outside the goalkeeper's long-barrier reach (Diagram 5a) and preferably past him.

The principal mistakes to occur are threefold:

- The attacker dribbles the ball too close to the goalkeeper and allows him to confiscate the ball.
- The ball is not played sufficiently wide of the goalkeeper to defeat the long barrier.
- The ball is played so far past and wide of the goalkeeper that the player has a terrific chase to the goal-line and ends up by hitting the ball into the side netting.

Execution

Whatever the decision, the execution of the pass or dribble should be characterised by two factors:

- A positive performance – no changing of the decision of doubts about what to do.
- A clinical and calm performance with accuracy the prime consideration.

As stated previously, composure in beating the goalkeeper is determined by knowing what to do and by knowing one can do it. Confidence is based on knowing one can give a performance – and good performance is a product of correct practice. The more players practise the four elements listed above, the more adept their performance will become and the more confident they will be in their performance.

9 Beating the goalkeeper by dribbling past him

9a McKenzie with his head down controlling the ball..

9b The approach towards goal. The ball is well in front of his feet and his head is up and observing the movements of the goalkeeper.

9c His decision is made to dribble past the goalkeeper and he prepares therefore to eliminate the goalkeeper.

9d and 9e The angle is widened and space is created for an easy pass into the goal.

10 4-v-2 Practice

10a Four attackers against two defenders plus a goalkeeper.

10b The attacking player is clear of the defence on the left flank.

10c The attacker elects to dribble past the goalkeeper.

10d and 10e The attacker, having eliminated the goalkeeper, is composed as he passes the ball past a recovering defender.

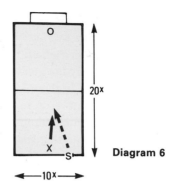

Diagram 6

ORGANISATION FOR PRACTICE

Practice takes place in a grid measuring 20 yards by 10 yards. In Diagram 6, there is a portable goal and a goalkeeper, O. A server, S, passes the ball on the ground for X to run on to and score.

DEVELOPMENT OF THE PRACTICE

1. The practice is developed by making S active, as a defender, once he has served the ball. By varying the distance from which the ball is served, X can be given more or less time to score.

2. The practice is further developed to help players who break clear of the defence in flank positions, for the task is much more difficult from these positions because of the narrow angle. Practice takes place in the attacking third of the field (Diagram 7). There is a goalkeeper, O_1, and a defender, O_2, who is positioned in a central area several yards outside the penalty area. The server, S, passes the ball to X_1, who can either dribble the ball forward or pass to X_2 or X_3, both of whom should start in wide positions outside the penalty area. The off-side law is not operative.

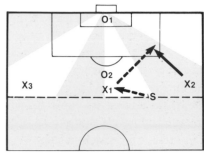

Diagram 7

3. The practice is developed by bringing in an extra defender and an extra attacker (Diagram 8). The server can pass to any one of the X players who should spread wide. Once the first pass is made, the off-side law is dispensed with. O_2 and O_3 must position several yards outside the penalty area and should challenge the player receiving the ball.

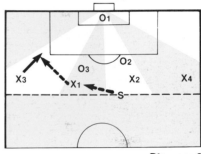

Diagram 8

POINTS FOR THE COACH TO OBSERVE

1. The attacking player should play the ball well forward of his feet when approaching the goal.

2. The attacking player should observe the movements of the goalkeeper and the space available to the side, behind, and in front of him.

3. Observe that the attacking player makes the correct decision when deciding whether to pass the ball, or dribble the ball, past the goalkeeper.

4. Observe that the execution of the pass or dribble of the ball into the goal is accurate.

5. Observe that the organisation is correct when practising angled approaches on goal.

6. Observe the variants in performance when a challenging defender is introduced and when the attacking player approaches goal at an angle.

COACHING IN THE GAME

Shooting is not the easiest aspect of soccer to coach in the game as a specific skill. The point has to be made, however, that all aspects of attacking play are designed to end in a shot at goal. The coach must not consider that he is departing from the theme if he emphasises shooting. The fact is that whatever the theme being coached, it cannot be truly effective without the correct emphasis being laid on shooting. However, to place a specific emphasis on shooting, play can be concentrated in the attacking third of the field. By starting the practice with the attacking players holding a slight numerical advantage, a large variety of shooting situations will occur in and around the penalty area. In Diagram 9, S passes the ball to an X player in an area where the X players have a numerical advantage. Other X players are moving forward and O players are recovering. The practice

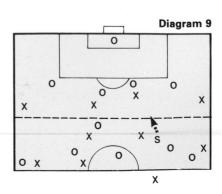

Diagram 9

can be started from the half-way line and back players can be encouraged to move forward into striking positions 25 or 30 yards out from goal.

Perhaps the hardest practice situation to produce is the one where the player is clear of the defence with only the goalkeeper to beat. To produce this situation, play should be concentrated in the middle third of the field and the defending players should be asked to move up to play the attacking players off-side. This will create space behind the defending players and the attacking players should be instructed to play the ball into that space. In Diagram 10, play is concentrated in the middle third of the field. S passes to an X player and the X players then inter-pass and play to the feet of one of the central attacking players, who must be supported quickly. As the ball is played back to the supporting player, so the O players move forward to play the X forwards off-side. The X supporting player plays a diagonal pass to the back of the defence and X players on the opposite flank move into the space, receive the pass and attack the goal. The X players must try to beat the off-side trap but, if they fail to do so, the attacking player should not be stopped from going through to score.

One final point should be made. In matches, players should always play to the whistle. If the referee has blown his whistle there is never any excuse for a player to continue and have a shot at goal. Conversely, if the referee has not blown his whistle, there is no reason to stop.

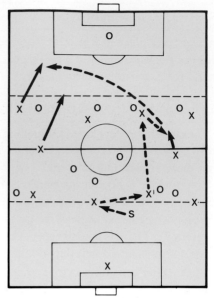

Diagram 10

GOALKEEPING (1)
SHOT STOPPING AND SUPPORTING THE DEFENCE

Of all the eleven individuals in a soccer team, the goalkeeper is the most important. If his performance is poor, he can and does lose matches on his own account. If his performance is good, he will give his team-mates confidence and often inspire them to play above themselves. It is, therefore, surprising that goalkeepers are so frequently neglected in coaching sessions. It is equally surprising that when they are given practice it is often in a goal marked by tracksuits or corner flags. Perhaps the most incongruous sight of all is a goalkeeper defending a small five-a-side goal.

The first and primary task of a goalkeeper is to stop shots which are fired at his goal. There is no magic to goalkeeping. Efficiency is based on correct technique.

THE STARTING POSITION

1 Starting position
Peter Shilton alert. His body weight is forward and his knees are slightly bent. He is in a composed and balanced position, ready to spring in any direction.

Feet: The feet should be shoulder width apart and the body weight should be forward on the soles of the feet.

Arms and hands: The arms should be slightly outside the line of the body and waist high. The palms of the hands should be facing each other or outwards towards the ball.

Head: The head should be steady and tilted slightly forward. This will assist in bringing the body weight on to the soles of the feet.

HANDLING

Ground Shots

There are two basic techniques for stopping ground shots when the goalkeeper has time to get the whole of his body behind the ball.

1 Stoop (Cup) technique
Feet: The feet should be close enough to prevent the ball from going between the legs.

Hands: The hands should be behind the ball with the palms facing outwards. The hands should then 'cup' the ball into the chest.

Head: The head should be steady and the eyes should watch the ball as long as possible.

2 Stoop technique

2a Shilton prepares to stop the ball using the stoop technique. Notice the position of his feet, hands and head.

2b Hands ready to receive the ball, head well down over the ball.

2c The ball being gathered into the body.

2d The ball about to be secured into the body.

It is not always possible to keep the eyes on the ball. The most important factor is to keep the head steady and watch the ball as long as possible.

In all ball games, it is a fact that it is not always possible to watch the ball into the hands, or on to whatever surface the player is using to play the ball. Because of this, it is absolutely essential that the head remains steady throughout in order to ensure that, having brought the controlling, catching, or hitting surface into line, that surface remains in line.

This is a fundamental truth that all players and coaches of ball games should understand. Needless to say, keeping the head steady is a vital element in the technique of goalkeeping.

2 Kneeling technique

Feet: The feet and lower body should be sideways-on to the path of the ball. The knee of the kneeling leg should be level with or just inside the heel of the other leg.

Hands: The palms of the hands should be facing outwards. The action of the hands is one of scooping the ball into the body.

Head: The head should be steady and the eyes should watch the ball as long as possible.

3 Kneeling technique

3a Shilton prepares to save a ground shot.

3b The first stage of the kneeling position. Notice Shilton's left foot already sideways-on and the right knee moving towards the kneel position.

3c The right knee almost in position. Notice the position of the hands and head.

3d The right knee in position and the hands ready to secure the ball.

3e The ball secured into the body by the hands and the chin.

4 The in-between position

This is the best position if the ball is bouncing. Note that the right knee is six to nine inches off the ground. Note also how carefully Shilton is watching the ball.

3 The in-between position

The ball will sometimes bounce a yard or so in front of the goalkeeper. On these occasions he may prefer not to go down into the full kneeling position, but to be, as it were, half-and-half, with the knee of the kneeling leg some six to nine inches from the ground.

Waist-high shots

Feet: The feet should be shoulder width apart in order to ensure a good balanced position. The body weight should be on the soles of the feet.

Hands: The palms of the hands should be facing outwards. The action of the hands is to cup the ball into the waist.

Head: The head should be steady and the eyes should watch the ball as long as possible.

Chest-high shots

Feet: The feet should again be shoulder width apart and the body weight should be on the soles of the feet.

Hands: The palms should be facing outwards and the action of the hands is to cup the ball into the chest. The chest should relax on impact and the ball must be trapped firmly between the hands, the chest and the chin.

Head: The head should be steady and the eyes should watch the ball as long as possible.

5 Waist-high shots

5a Shilton prepares to catch a ball waist high. Notice the position of the feet, hands and head.

5b The catch is made. The hands secure the ball and the upper body folds over the ball.

6 Chest-high shots

6a Shilton preparing to catch a ball chest high. Notice the position of his feet, hands and head.

6b The catch is made and the hands secure the ball to the chest. Note the rounding of the shoulders, evidence that the chest has relaxed on impact.

Head-high shots and above

Feet: The feet should be shoulder width apart and the body weight should be on the soles of the feet.

Hands: The hands and fingers should be to the side of the ball and also behind the ball. The fingers should be spread and relaxed. This is important, since the fingers must not be rigid on impact – rigid fingers would cause the ball to be dropped. Relaxed fingers help to secure the grip on the ball. Having caught the ball, the ball should be lowered quickly into the body in order to confiscate and secure the ball from the opponents.

Head: The head should be steady and the eyes should watch the ball as long as possible.

ORGANISATION FOR PRACTICE

Practice takes place in a grid measuring 20 yards by 10 yards (Diagram 1). There is a full-sized portable goal and a server on the 20-yard line. The server starts by rolling the ball towards the goalkeeper. He should then develop the practice by throwing the ball, in progression, at waist, chest and above-head height. The ball, at this stage, is thrown directly at the goalkeeper. The server should finally end up by kicking the ball at the goalkeeper at varying heights.

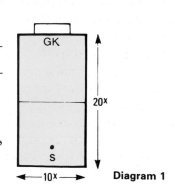

Diagram 1

7 Shots above the head

7a Shilton preparing to catch a ball above his head. Notice the position of the hands and fingers, and the head and the knee thrusting upwards. This not only helps to gain height but the knee gives some protection against the challenge of opponents.

7b The catch successfully made – hands to the side and behind the ball.

7c A back view of the position of the hands and fingers. Notice the thumbs close together.

7d The ball being secured into the body.

POINTS FOR THE COACH TO OBSERVE

1. Observe, before each serve, the starting position of the goalkeeper.
2. Observe the three techniques for dealing with ground shots: the stoop position; the kneeling position; and the in-between position.
3. Observe the technique for dealing with waist-high shots, especially that of 'cupping' the ball.
4. Observe the technique for dealing with chest-high shots, especially that of trapping the ball.
5. Observe the technique for dealing with shots above head height, especially the relaxed fingers and the securing of the ball after the catch.
6. Observe the ability of the goalkeeper throughout to keep his head steady.

MOVING INTO LINE

Each time the angle of the ball changes, the goalkeeper must adjust his position in order to achieve the correct position in relation to the position of the ball. He must always be positioned towards the mid-line of the triangle formed by lines joining the positions of the ball and the two goal-posts.

In Diagram 2, when the ball is in position 1, X is a few yards off his goal line but is positioned along the central line of the triangle. When the ball is in position 2, X is positioned to his right of the central line because his near post is a more vulnerable area than his far post. When the ball is in position 3, X is positioned to his left of the central line because his near post, now on the left-hand side, is a more vulnerable area than the far post.

It can be appreciated that if the ball were to be moved in two passing movements from position 2 to 1, and then from position 1 to 3, the goalkeeper

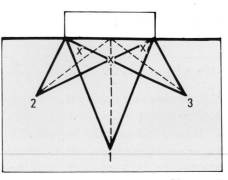

Diagram 2

151

8 Timing – when to hold

8a Shilton into line, but holding his position 4 or 5 yards out from goal as a shot is taken by No 9 from very close range. Notice the balance, composure and concentration.

8b Shilton moves to his left like lightning to save the shot. Notice how the legs have collapsed away to help him to get down quickly.

would have to adjust his position across his goal twice, in quick succession, in order to achieve a position in line between the ball and the goal.

The manner in which the goalkeeper moves is of importance. He should adopt a quick, sideways-skipping movement. The feet should glide across the ground. Jumping movements should be avoided, so should the crossing of the legs. The movement of the feet should be such that a steady, balanced position can be achieved very quickly if required.

The earlier the goalkeeper can get into the line of flight, the earlier he can move forward along the line of flight (Diagram 3), or balance and relax himself ready for the shot. This will be his starting position to save the shot. It can be seen therefore that the earlier the goalkeeper achieves a good position into line, and down the line, the more likely he is to deter the shot.

ORGANISATION FOR PRACTICE

Practice takes place in a grid measuring 20 yards by 30 yards (Diagram 4). There is a full-sized portable goal and a server. The server, S, plays the ball at any angle, left or right, inside the grid and then chases after the ball to shoot.

The goalkeeper, X, must adjust his position each time and move into line before the shot is taken. The server is only allowed two touches of the ball, shooting on the second touch. However, the goalkeeper is given plenty of time in which to move into line, since the server will have to move further than him.

DEVELOPMENT OF THE PRACTICE

The practice can be developed by introducing two further players, O_1 and O_2, in wide positions (Diagram 5). The server can pass the ball to either O_1 or O_2, or play the ball short and shoot himself. O_1 or O_2 can either play the ball first time or take two touches. The goalkeeper will now have to move much more quickly to achieve a position in line with the ball and the goal before the shot is taken.

POINTS FOR THE COACH TO OBSERVE

1. Observe the sideways-skipping movement of the goalkeeper – feet gliding across the turf.
2. Observe the speed of movement.
3. Observe the accuracy of the goalkeeper's movement into line. (The best position for the coach from which to observe is behind the goal.)
4. Observe how balanced and relaxed the goalkeeper is before the shot is taken.

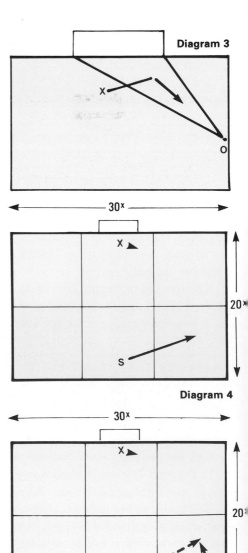

Diagram 3

Diagram 4

Diagram 5

ADVANCING AND DIVING

Timing

When not to advance: Having positioned in line, if the player in possession of the ball is in a position to strike the ball, the goalkeeper must hold his position and be balanced to save the shot.

When to advance: Having achieved a position in line with the ball and the goal, if the ball is outside the playing distance of the attacking player, then the goalkeeper should advance along the line, moving nearer to the ball.

How to advance: The goalkeeper should advance as fast as possible, consistent with the certainty of being able to achieve a balanced position before the ball can be shot at goal.

How far: If time permits, the goalkeeper must come all the way and take possession of the ball.

This technique, and the technique of spreading across the path of the ball, is considered further on pages 156 to 159.

Take-off

No matter how well a goalkeeper moves into line, or down the line, the probability is that the attacker will still shoot wide of him and on target for goal. Two types of shots may occur:

Shots near the body: These are more difficult to save than some people imagine, if the ball is on the ground. The main problem is that of getting the lower part of the body out of the way so that the upper part and hands can intercept the ball. Sometimes the feet have to be used as a matter of expediency, but it should be clearly understood that the hands should be used on all possible occasions.

Shots well away from the body: The correct technique is to move the body weight on to the leg nearest to the ball and then thrust off that leg to dive across to the ball.

Vision

It is important that the goalkeeper should avoid obstructing his vision by diving face down or by allowing his arms to move across his line of vision. His dive should be sideways-on and his arms should be positioned in such a way that they are outside the line of vision.

9 Take-off – shots near to the body

9a Shilton moving to save a shot near to his body on his right-hand side. The legs collapse away to enable him to get down quickly.

9b Shilton down very quickly with his upper body behind the ball.

10 Vision

Shilton in a perfect sideways-on position. Good retention of vision and excellent technique of catching the ball in an aerial position.

11 Ground shots (hold)

11a Shilton, balanced and composed as the shot is taken.

11b Moving to his left. Notice the position of his hands and head.

11c The ball stopped and held – notice one hand behind the back to stop the ball, one hand on top of the ball to hold the ball.

11d The ball is now secured. Notice how Shilton brings the ball into the body and also brings his knees up to help to protect and secure the ball.

12 Ground shots (deflect)

12a Shilton thrusting off his left leg to get across his goal to a low shot.

12b Deflecting the ball round the post and out of play. Notice the sideways-on position and the position of the head.

Handling

Ground shots (hold): The goalkeeper should think not only in terms of stopping the ball but also of holding the ball. The technique for holding ground shots is as follows:

- One hand behind the ball to stop the ball.
- One hand above the ball to still the ball and hold it.
- Having stopped and held the ball, the ball should be taken into the body quickly in order to secure possession. It is made even more secure if the legs are drawn up into the body simultaneously.

Ground shots (deflect): If there is any doubt about being able to hold the ball, it should be deflected away to safety. The wider the ball is deflected, the safer it will be. The best outcome is for the ball to be deflected out of play.

Aerial shots (hold): The hands should be to the side of the ball and behind the ball. If the ball cannot be gathered into the body in mid-air, the goalkeeper should twist and fall with the ball wedged between his hands and the ground. The ball should then be secured into the body as in a ground shot.

13 Aerial shots (hold)

A splendid picture of Shilton catching a shot which was destined for the top corner. Notice the position of the hands and the head.

14 Aerial shots (deflect)

Shilton deflects an aerial shot high and wide of the post. Notice the position of his right hand and his head.

Aerial shots (deflect): If the goalkeeper cannot hold the ball, he should deflect the ball high and wide. The best result is produced when the ball is deflected over the bar or round the post.

Deflecting the ball over the bar: Either one hand or two hands may be used. The one-handed technique is used primarily when the goalkeeper is recovering towards the goal to deal with a lob or dipping shot. The technique is one of palming or lifting the ball over the bar. The body is sideways-on and the hand which makes contact with the ball is the inside hand, the one which is nearest to the kicker. It is vital to keep the head steady and watch the ball throughout.

The two-handed technique is applied primarily to deflect powerful shots over the bar. The contact on the ball is made with the palms and fingers of both hands on the underneath part of the ball.

ORGANISATION FOR PRACTICE

The practice takes place in a grid measuring 30 yards by 20 yards. There are two portable goals and two goalkeepers. In Diagram 6, each of the goalkeepers has a supply of soccer balls. X_1 starts the practice by throwing the ball at the goal of X_2. X_2 repeats the practice by throwing the ball for X_1 to save. The players should be encouraged to throw varied services in order to bring about a variety of saves.

DEVELOPMENT OF THE PRACTICE

1. X_1 and X_2 kick the ball at each other instead of throwing it. The best results are usually achieved if the players half-volley the ball.
2. The second development is to introduce two challenging players who should threaten the goalkeeper and try to score if the goalkeeper fails to hold the ball or deflect the ball to safety. In Diagram 7, O_1 and O_2 challenge each service in turn. The practice is intended to simulate match conditions when the goalkeeper may be distracted by opposing forwards closing in while he is in the process of stopping a shot.

POINTS FOR THE COACH TO OBSERVE

1. Observe that the goalkeeper knows when to hold and when to advance along the line towards the ball.
2. Observe the technique of advancing – especially in relation to judging how far to advance and being balanced before the shot is taken.
3. Observe the technique of take-off in relation to:
   (i) Shots near to the body.
   (ii) Shots well away from the body.
4. Observe the technique of diving in relation to retaining good vision of the ball.
5. Observe the judgement and the technique for holding and deflecting ground shots.
6. Observe the judgement and the technique for holding and deflecting aerial shots.
7. Observe both the two-handed and one-handed techniques for deflecting the ball over the bar.

NARROWING THE ANGLE

Even in the best teams, there are times when opponents will break clear of the defence and an attacking player finds himself with only the goalkeeper to beat. On these occasions, the salvation of the goalkeeper, and his team, rests on his skill at narrowing the angle.

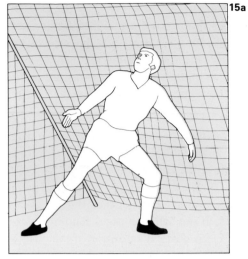

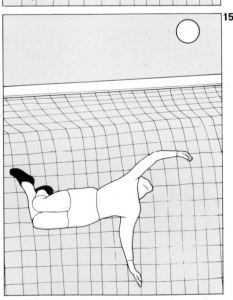

15 Deflection over the bar – one-handed

15a The position is sideways-on, the head is steady, eyes watching the ball.

15b The ball is played by the hand nearest to the ball. The palm and fingers lift the ball over the bar.

15c The eyes continue to watch the ball, as the ball goes over the bar.

Starting position. The starting position of the goalkeeper should be at such a distance from the goal-line that it gives him a chance to move further out from goal for an interception, but does not give the attacker a chance to lob the ball over his head and into the goal.

A guide to the correct starting position of the goalkeeper if the ball is in a central position is as follows:

- If the ball is in the attacking third of the field (roughly 70 to 100 yards distant from the goal the goalkeeper is defending), the position of the goalkeeper should be 12 to 18 yards out from goal in a line between the ball and his goal.
- If the ball is in the middle third of the field (roughly 40 to 70 yards distant from the goal), the position of the goalkeeper should be 6 to 12 yards out from goal in a line between the ball and his goal.
- If the ball is in the defending third of the field (a maximum of 40 yards from the goal), the position of the goalkeeper should be 3 to 6 yards out from goal.

If the ball is 30 to 40 yards out from the goal and wide on a flank, the goalkeeper will elect to position himself in the back half of his goal. This is his best position if he assesses that the major threat to his goal is a cross from the flank. If an attacker breaks clear of the defence in a flank position, then the goalkeeper must move into the front half of his goal. From that starting position he will narrow the angle.

Assess the position of the ball and the ground line. If the attacker has broken clear of the defence, the goalkeeper must narrow the shooting angle. He will rely on an assessment of the position of the attacker with the ball to determine his own position. This angle will be along a line from the ball to the front half of the goal if the ball is on a flank. It will be along a line from the ball to the centre of the goal if the ball is in a central position.

Approach. The goalkeeper's movement towards the ball should be as fast as possible while the ball is outside the playing distance of the attacker. He should be able to stop, and become balanced, before a shot or dribble can be made.

Stand up. It is vital for the goalkeeper to stand up and make himself as big as possible, as a deterrent to the attacker. It is also vital that the attacker should be made to make the first move – it is a bad mistake to anticipate any movement of the attacker. The goalkeeper should be composed and balanced and should adopt the position referred to earlier in relation to his feet, hands and head.

Going down to present a long-barrier block. If the goalkeeper assesses that he has time to cover the ground and get close enough to the ball to block a shot, or a dribble, he should do so. This technique involves going to ground and spreading the body in a long barrier across the angle between the ball and the goal.

The temptation to go down with one's feet towards the ball should be resisted as this means going down along the angle between the ball and the goal (Diagram 9) rather than across the angle (Diagram 8). As can be seen from the two

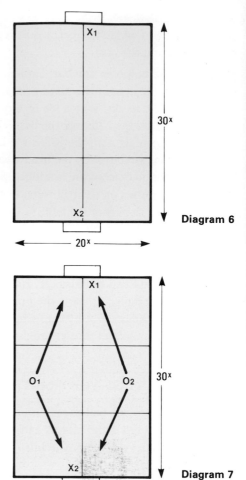

Diagram 6

Diagram 7

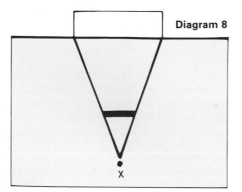

Diagram 8

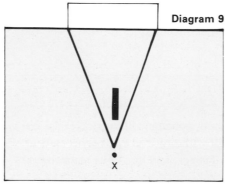

Diagram 9

16 Narrowing the angle – starting position

The ball is 30 to 35 yards out from goal and the goalkeeper is 4 to 5 yards off his goal-line. This starting position is correct.

17 Narrowing the angle – ground line

The ground line is correct, i.e. the goalkeeper is in line between the ball and the front half of the goal. The ball is also outside the playing distance of the attacker. The goalkeeper, therefore, is correct to make his approach towards the ball.

18 Narrowing the angle – stand up – composed and balanced

The goalkeeper is composed and balanced as Luther Blissett moves into the penalty area clear of the challenging defender.

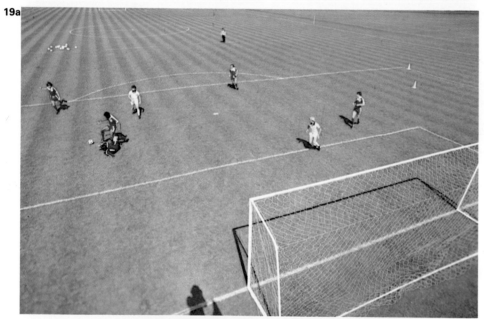

19 Narrowing the angle – the long barrier block

19a The goalkeeper going down at the forward's feet and presenting a long barrier to block the shot.

19b The ball rebounds away but the goalkeeper is quick to recover and stand up.

diagrams, going down across the angle blocks the route to goal; going to ground down the angle does not.

The point should be made that presenting a long-barrier block does involve courage on the part of the goalkeeper. However, courage alone will not suffice. The technique must be correct.

Decisions. The point has been made more than once elsewhere in this book that soccer is very much a game of decisions. In narrowing the angle, the goalkeeper has a number of decisions to make. The correctness of those decisions depends very much on the accuracy of the assessment that the goalkeeper will make in relation to the preceding five elements mentioned above.

ORGANISATION FOR PRACTICE

The practice takes place in the equivalent of two penalty areas, 44 yards by 36 yards. There are two full-sized goals and two goalkeepers, each of whom has a good supply of footballs.

In Diagram 10, X_1 serves a ball for B_1 to run on to. B_2 chases and gives challenge to B_1 as he closes in towards the goal of X_2.

B_1 and B_2, having completed the attack at the goal, reposition either side of X_2's goal. As they reposition, X_2 serves a ball for C_2 to run on to chased by C_1. Having attacked, they reposition at the side of X_1's goal.

X_1 then serves a ball for A_1 who is chased by A_2. The practice is continuous with each pair of players working once every three runs.

Each of the goalkeepers can be instructed to serve the ball to alternate sides in order to give them practice at defending against attacks from both the right and the left flanks. When the service is alternated left and right, the attacking player will always be the player who is on the side on which the ball is served. The chaser will always be the player on the opposite side.

It is helpful if the practice takes place in a penalty area as the markings assist the goalkeeper. The practice, therefore, simulates match conditions. However, as the goalkeeper at one end will not have the benefit of penalty-area markings, the goalkeepers should change over at suitable intervals.

Diagram 10

POINTS FOR THE COACH TO OBSERVE

1. Observe that the goalkeeper is in the correct starting position on every occasion in relation to his position off the goal-line.
2. Observe the ability of the goalkeeper to assess correctly the ground line: the line between the ball and the front half of the goal, if the ball is on a flank; and the line between the ball and the centre of the goal, if the ball is in a central position.
3. Observe the ability of the goalkeeper in making his approach. Observe that the goalkeeper moves quickly when the ball is outside the playing distance of the attacker, and that he is composed and balanced when the ball is within playing distance of the attacker.
4. Observe the technique of the goalkeeper in standing up in a composed and balanced position.
5. Observe the technique of the goalkeeper in going down to present a long-barrier block. Observe that this is across the angle, *not* down the angle.
6. Observe the speed and accuracy with which the goalkeeper makes his various decisions.

COMBINING SHOT STOPPING WITH SUPPORTING THE DEFENCE

It has to be understood that the goalkeeper is an integral part of the team. As such, he has a major part to play in supporting the players who play in front of him. His task of supporting players is, fundamentally, no different to that of any other player. There are three elements in supporting the defence: distance; angle; and communication.

Distance

The distance of the goalkeeper from his goal-line. The point has already been made that the position of the goalkeeper from the goal-line is determined by the position of the ball. If the ball is in the attacking third of the field, the goalkeeper should be 12 to 18 yards off his goal-line. If the ball is in the middle third of the field, the goalkeeper should be 6 to 12 yards off his goal-line. If the ball is in the defending third of the field, the goalkeeper should be 3 to 6 yards off his goal-line.

The distance of the goalkeeper from his rearmost defender. This space should be large enough to achieve compactness. This is especially true when a team is moving forward and the rearmost players are pushing up to the half-way line.

The space should also be small enough to make it extremely difficult for opponents to send the ball, and a player, into the space, and get him there before the goalkeeper or one of the other rear defenders. This is the objective of all support play. Thus, if the rearmost players were on the half-way line, and the goalkeeper were on his goal-line, the space between the two would be too large to ensure that the objective of support play could be achieved. If, however, in those circumstances the goalkeeper were to be positioned 18 yards out from his goal, the space between the two would be much smaller and the objective of support play would be much more likely to be achieved.

The angle

If the goalkeeper is not at the correct angle, then the probability is that the space between himself and his rearmost player will be increased. Furthermore, if the goalkeeper is not at the correct angle, his starting position must also be wrong.

The exception to all this is where the ball is on a flank in the defending third of the field and the goalkeeper positions himself, for the ball being crossed, in the back half of his goal.

Communication

Communication is an important factor in teamwork. Mistakes often occur because of confusion arising from misunderstanding. Of all the players, the goalkeeper cannot afford to be involved in any misunderstanding with his team-mates. There are two essential elements in good communication:

What to communicate. Goalkeepers are in a privileged position. For the most part they only have to observe through 180 degrees. All other players have to observe through 360 degrees – a much more difficult task. The goalkeeper, therefore, will see many situations more clearly and more quickly than his team-mates. He must make that count for the benefit of his team through good communication. What the goalkeeper communicates must be information and encouragement. This will fall in five main areas:
1. It is invaluable for the goalkeeper to convey information on the blind-side situation on the opposite side of the field to the ball. For example, when the ball

is in the left flank position, the goalkeeper should observe the marking on the right flank to ensure that all opponents are marked. The goalkeeper must also ensure that his defenders are made aware of opponents who are trying to sneak in behind them.

2. When the play is in and around the penalty area, and particularly when opponents play the ball backwards, defenders very often fail to close on the ball to prevent or block a shot at goal. In these circumstances, the goalkeeper should encourage the appropriate player to close in quickly to stop the shot.

3. Sometimes a defender is facing his own goal in possession of the ball and is not precisely aware of the situation behind him. The goalkeeper is in a much better position to assess that situation. It may be that it will allow him to support the player and receive the ball; it may be that the player will be best advised to play the ball into touch. The goalkeeper, by clear communication, can help the player to make the correct decision early.

4. It will happen, on occasions, that, while the goalkeeper is moving out for a ball, a defender is moving back to play the same ball. This situation has all the ingredients for an own goal. If, however, the goalkeeper communicates his intentions early, the problem of possible confusion, or collision, is solved.

5. When a team clears the ball from in and around the penalty area and begins to attack, the players should move quickly up-field. The goalkeeper, by good communication, can cause this to happen with beneficial results. In the first place, almost certainly two or three opponents will be caught off-side. This will mean that the attack, by moving out quickly, will gain a numerical advantage in the middle of the field. It will also mean, of course, that the team retains its compactness.

Even when play is in the opponents' half of the field, the goalkeeper must still observe and communicate relevant information to his team-mates.

How to communicate. There are four factors in effective communication, or 'calling', for goalkeepers:

1. The call from the goalkeeper must be early. The purpose of calling is to give information in time for effective action to be taken. Late calls do not permit effective action.

2. Clarity of voice and information is essential. The call must be loud enough for the players to hear. Goalkeepers must not be afraid of 'turning up the volume' – it may be necessary to compete with the noise of the crowd. The information must also be clear and must not violate the laws. If information is being given to a particular player, then his name should be called. If the goalkeeper intends to play the ball he should call early, 'goalkeeper's ball'.

3. The call should be decisive and should be in a voice of command. The circumstances in which the goalkeeper will have to communicate on the field is not one for confidential asides!

4. The voice, whilst being loud, decisive and authoritative, must also be calm. The worst thing which could happen would be to panic team-mates into action.

ORGANISATION FOR PRACTICE

The practice takes place in a grid measuring 30 yards by 20 yards (Diagram 11). There are two full-sized portable goals and a goalkeeper is in each goal. The situation, excluding the goalkeepers, is two against two.

Attention is focused on the goalkeepers in this small-sided game. Emphasis is placed on their positional play, both in adopting the correct angles to stop shots and also to support their team-mates. Emphasis is also placed on the communication by each of the goalkeepers.

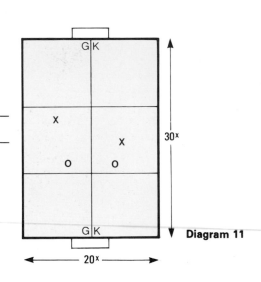

Diagram 11

DEVELOPMENT OF THE PRACTICE

The practice should be developed into a full eleven-a-side game. The game need not be conditioned to thirds of the field as it is best for the goalkeeper to practise in the rapid ebb and flow of the game.

The position of the goalkeeper, and the quality of his communication, becomes more critical in the defending third of the field. If he has problems in that area with either positioning or communication, then concentrated practice can be given in the defending third. It should be appreciated, however, that part of the problem for a goalkeeper is retaining his concentration when he has not had a touch of the ball for several minutes.

It is important for the goalkeeper to concentrate all the time, constantly adjusting his position in accordance with the position of the ball, and always communicating relevant information to his team-mates. However infrequently he may be called into action, his starting position must always be correct, and he must always be alert.

POINTS FOR THE COACH TO OBSERVE

1. Observe that the goalkeeper is the correct distance off his goal-line in relation to the ball.
2. Observe the distance of the goalkeeper in relation to his rearmost defender.
3. Observe that the goalkeeper is at the correct angle in relation to the ball.
4. Observe the information which the goalkeeper communicates to his team-mates and their reaction to that information.
5. Observe how the goalkeeper communicates the information and how his team-mates respond to it.

11

GOALKEEPING (2)
CROSSES AND DISTRIBUTION

TECHNIQUES FOR DEALING WITH CROSSES

On the face of it, shot stopping is the most important aspect of goalkeeping. It is, however, crosses which, effectively, sort out the men from the boys. High levels of performance require good technique, good judgement, good co-operation with co-defenders, and courage. Like all other aspects of soccer, sound technique is the foundation upon which to build.

There are six elements in the technique of dealing with crosses:

The starting position

The position of the goalkeeper in relation to the goal depends primarily on two factors:

■ The distance of the ball from the goal.
■ The angle between the ball and the goal.

In Diagram 1, the ball is in the shaded area, well in from the touch-line and some 30 yards out from goal. The goalkeeper, X, is three yards off his line and in the centre of his goal.

In Diagram 2, the ball is in the shaded area, near to the touch-line and some 12 to 15 yards from the goal-line. The goalkeeper, X, is between one and two yards off his goal-line and in the centre of his goal.

In Diagram 3, the ball is in the shaded area, near to the goal-line and near to the edge of the penalty area. The goalkeeper, X, is half a yard off his goal-line and approximately three yards from his near post.

In every case, the goalkeeper's position must enable him to observe through 180 degrees. Thus, his stance should be open and his body angle should be parallel with the goal-line. What the goalkeeper observes may also affect his position. For example, if an opponent makes a run to the area of the near post, the goalkeeper will almost certainly have to be prepared to adjust his position to deal with that threat to the goal. If the goalkeeper has not seen the run to the near post, then any adjustment of his position may be too late to avert the danger. Goalkeepers, therefore, like any other defender, must be careful not to be caught on the blind-side.

1 Stance and vision for crosses
Peter Shilton with a stance along the line giving him easy vision through 180°.

Assessing the flight of the ball

The most important factor in assessing the flight of the ball is to wait until the ball has been kicked before making a movement. The greatest mistake of all is to anticipate where the kicker is going to play the ball, for once the goalkeeper starts to move, assessing the flight becomes much more difficult.

The goalkeeper must assess three things before he moves:

■ The line along which the ball is travelling.
■ The pace at which the ball is travelling.
■ The trajectory of the ball, including the amount of swerve or dip expected.

Only when an assessment of these three factors has been made can the goalkeeper make an accurate decision and purposeful movement.

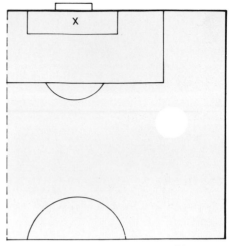
Diagram 1

Making an early decision

Once an assessment of the line, pace and trajectory of the ball has been made, the earlier the decision whether to move to attack the ball or to stay and defend the goal is made the better.

Before a decision is made to move to attack the ball, the goalkeeper must also assess the ground route to the ball. An early call will help to get his co-defenders out of his path to the ball, but he must be sure that his path is not impeded by attacking players.

If there is any doubt in the goalkeeper's mind about his ability to get to the ball, he must elect to stay and defend his goal. He should then adjust his position so that he is in the line between the ball and the goal and, if possible and necessary, down the line to narrow the angle of the shot. If the goalkeeper does decide to attack the ball, that decision is final and there must be no question of a change of mind.

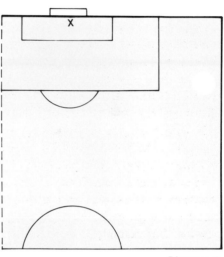
Diagram 2

Attacking the ball

When a goalkeeper decides to attack the ball, he will do so confident in the knowledge that he has an enormous advantage over all other players. That advantage is, of course, the use of his hands.

There are three instructions to remember when attacking the ball: move late; move quickly; and take the ball at the highest possible point in its trajectory. Having stressed the importance of making an early decision, it may appear paradoxical to advise goalkeepers to move late to attack the ball. There are, though, four advantages in delaying the movement to attack the ball:

■ More time is given to assess the trajectory of the ball.
■ More time is given for co-defenders to clear the route to the ball so that the goalkeeper is not impeded by opponents.
■ A later movement means that the goalkeeper must move more quickly. Greater height is achieved, therefore, when jumping for the ball.
■ Because greater height is achieved, the ball can in fact be taken earlier in flight than would be the case if the goalkeeper moved early, but slowly.

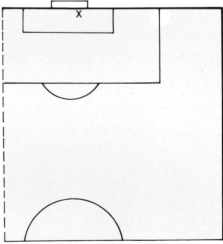
Diagram 3

What at first may appear a contradiction is in fact completely logical and sensible. The important factor is that this technique allows the goalkeeper to take the ball at the highest possible point in its trajectory.

Goalkeepers will take three types of crosses when attacking the ball:

When moving into line towards the ball. In this type of cross, the goalkeeper is in the line of the ball and moving towards it, as may be the case when a ball is hit diagonally towards the front half of the goal (Diagram 4).

When moving into line away from the ball. In this type of cross, the goalkeeper is in the line of the ball but has to move backwards to take it. In Diagram 5, the

2 One-footed take-off

Shilton showing a perfect example of a one-footed take-off to catch the ball.

3 Arms outstretched for a catch in front of the head

Shilton with arms outstretched about to catch the ball in front of the head. Note the position of his hands and fingers.

goalkeeper is in line, but under the flight of the ball. He has to move backwards in order to take the ball at the highest possible point in its trajectory. This is often the case with crosses hit well beyond the far post when a goalkeeper may have to take it even wider than the six-yard area.

When moving across the line of flight. In this type of cross, the goalkeeper is never in the line of flight until his hands make contact with the ball. In Diagram 6, the ball has been played back from the goal-line and the goalkeeper has moved across the line of flight to take the ball.

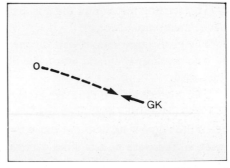

Diagram 4

Take-off

The greatest possible height will be achieved by a one-footed take-off. By adopting this technique, it will be easier to maintain balance and transfer the body momentum in an upwards direction. In a two-footed take-off, the body momentum must be stopped from moving forward before it is transferred in an upwards direction. Not only is less height achieved, but timing and balance become much more difficult.

Handling – catches

The arms should be outstretched in order to take the ball at the greatest possible height and the catch should be made in front of the head. The hands should be to the side and behind the ball and fingers should be spread and slightly flexed. The head, of course, should be steady throughout. Once the catch is made, it is important that the ball is brought into the body and secured as quickly as possible.

The goalkeeper may decide to punch or deflect the ball, rather than catch it. This aspect is considered on pages 168 and 169.

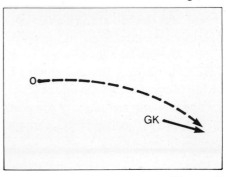

Diagram 5

ORGANISATION FOR PRACTICE

The practice takes place in one half of a full-sized pitch. It is important to practise on a full pitch so that the angles and distances are correct. A portable goal is placed in the centre circle on the half-way line in order to allow the practice to flow and to give practice to two goalkeepers rather than one. However, it should be noted that one goalkeeper will have the considerable advantage of the penalty area markings. The two goalkeepers, therefore, should change goals after a period of practice.

In Diagram 7, GK₁ starts the practice by throwing the ball to X who controls the ball, runs into a suitable position and crosses to the near post, far post or mid-goal area. GK₂ catches the ball and throws it to O who crosses for GK₁. X and O should be encouraged to cross the ball from a variety of positions and also to vary the target area.

In the practice indicated in Diagram 7, all the crosses are made from the right flank. Goalkeepers should, of course, also be given practice at taking crosses from their left flank. This can easily be achieved by the practice being reversed so that GK₁ throws to O who crosses from the left for GK₂. GK₂ throws in turn to X who crosses from the left for GK₁.

One final organisational point: each goalkeeper should have a good supply of soccer balls in the goal net. Inevitably, one or two crosses will escape the goalkeeper, but it is important that the continuity of the practice is preserved. A good supply of balls will ensure this happens.

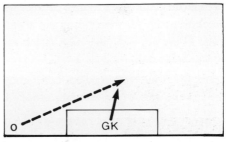

Diagram 6

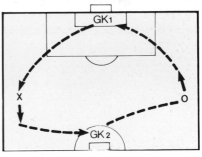

Diagram 7

POINTS FOR THE COACH TO OBSERVE

1. The starting position of the goalkeeper should be correct in relation to the ball's angle and the distance from the goal.

2. The starting position of the goalkeeper should be marked by an open stance to afford maximum vision.

3. The goalkeeper should wait for the ball to be kicked before assessing its flight.

4. The goalkeeper should assess the flight in relation to its line, pace and trajectory.

5. The goalkeeper should make an early decision to move to attack the ball or stay and defend the goal. The coach must insist that the goalkeeper positions to defend the goal if he does not move to attack the ball, even though, in this practice, there are no attacking players. The goalkeeper should be encouraged to develop good habits.

6. When the goalkeeper attacks the ball he should move late and quickly and should take the ball at the highest possible point in its trajectory.

7. Observe the technique of the goalkeeper when he is:
   (i) Moving into line towards the ball.
   (ii) Moving into line and moving backwards.
   (iii) Moving across the line of flight.

8. The jumping technique of the goalkeeper should be one-footed.

9. Observe the goalkeeper's technique of handling the ball in relation to arms, hands and fingers.

Handling – punches and deflections

When the goalkeeper makes contact with the cross his first priority will be to catch the ball. However, it is not always possible or wise to attempt to catch the ball. There are two particular circumstances in which the goalkeeper will elect not to catch the ball:

4 Deflecting the ball

4a Preparing to deal with a cross towards the far post.

4b The ball palmed over the bar by the arm nearest to the goal-line. The same technique is used to deflect crosses, beyond the far post, over the goal-line.

■ When he is not sufficiently sure of his balance. This may happen either because the cross is hit beyond the far post and, in addition to physical challenge, the ball may be too high to catch; or because the goalkeeper is moving backwards. On these occasions he should elect to deflect the ball out of play for a corner.

■ When there is a strong challenge from one or more opponents. On these occasions the goalkeeper should elect to punch the ball. Indeed, the golden rule for all occasions is, *if in doubt, punch the ball.*

Deflecting the ball
The action is with the arm nearest to the goal-line, thereby using the body as a screen from the opponents. Contact on the ball is made with the palm of the hand turned outwards to deflect or steer the ball out over the goal-line.

Punching the ball
Two-fisted technique. This is the best technique to use when attacking the ball along the line of flight. Contact on the ball is made with the surface of both fists. The fists strike through the bottom half of the ball, to propel the ball high, and the arms end in full extension.

One-fisted technique. This is normally the best technique to use when attacking the ball across the line of flight. The punch is made by the fist of the inside arm. Crosses from the goalkeeper's left, for example, should be punched by the goalkeeper's left fist. By using the goal-side arm, a greater swing of the arm is facilitated and thus more force can be exerted on the ball. Contact on the ball should be made through the bottom half.

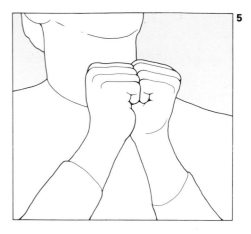

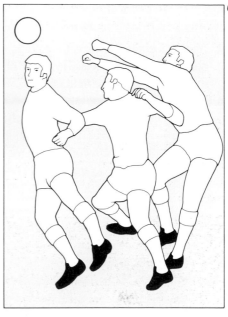

5 Double fist surface
Fists clenched and together to present a solid flat surface to the ball.

6 Double fist punch
A double fist punch after movement along the line to punch the ball at the highest possible point in trajectory.

7a

7b

7c

7 Single fist punch

7a Moving out from goal across the line to deal with a cross from the attacker's right flank to the far post.

7b A good leap to rise above the attacking player, and preparation to punch the ball with the left fist, i.e. the arm furthest from the attacker.

7c A successful execution of the punch with the left fist. The follow-through of the goalkeeper's position indicates clearly the amount of swing and power exerted by the left arm and fist.

CROSSES TO THE POSTS

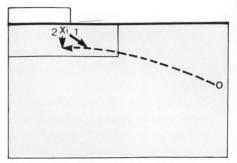

Diagram 8

Crosses to the near-post area

When the ball is crossed into the near-post area, the goalkeeper must position within touching distance of the near post. Should he decide not to come for the cross, he must hold that position. Should he decide to come for the cross he must ensure that he makes contact with the ball by either catching or punching it. The route he chooses must therefore give him the earliest possible contact on the ball.

In Diagram 8, the goalkeeper, X, has two possible routes to attack the ball. Route 1 is the correct route as it will give him the earliest contact on the ball.

Crosses to the far-post area

It will happen frequently that a goalkeeper will be drawn towards the near post and then the ball will be crossed to the far post. This necessitates the goalkeeper making a recovery run across his goal. Two points are of particular importance:

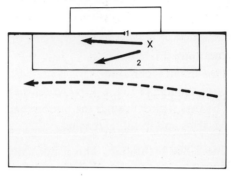

Diagram 9

■ As the goalkeeper turns to make his run across the goal he must turn into the field of play, never away from it. The goalkeeper is, of course, blind if he turns away from the field of play.
■ The goalkeeper must take the direct route to the far post, Route 1 in Diagram 9. In Route 2, the goalkeeper is following the path of the ball and is likely to leave a part to the right of his goal exposed. Although it is correct that he should think in terms of narrowing the angle, the procedure should be to move into the line as quickly as possible before moving down the line (Diagram 10).

It will be appreciated that, when a goalkeeper recovers across his goal to deal with a cross to the far post, he will complete that recovery run at the near post, by definition. His position, therefore, should be within touching distance of the post. A common fault in recovering to the far post is to follow the ball and go beyond the post. This must be avoided.

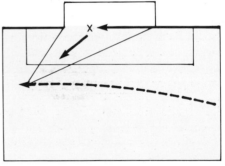

Diagram 10

Having achieved the position, the decision must be made whether to stay and defend the goal or move to attack the cross. If the decision is to stay, then the position near to the post should be held. If the decision is to come, then the goalkeeper should take the shortest possible route to the highest possible point of the ball's trajectory.

The final decision concerning all crosses is whether to catch, punch or deflect. If a catch is made, then the ball should be secured into the body and screened from opponents. If the ball is punched, the height, distance and angle of the clearance become crucial factors. If the ball is deflected, and this will only occur in crosses to the far post, the ball should be played to safety – preferably over the goal-line.

Communication with co-defenders

In the matter of crosses, co-defenders can either be a help or a hindrance to a goalkeeper. Defenders are, of course, a hindrance to the goalkeeper if they make his task more difficult in any way.

On most occasions, any hindrance will be due to a misunderstanding between the goalkeeper and his co-defenders. Calling, therefore, becomes an important part of a goalkeeper's skill. Where crosses are concerned, it is the prerogative of the goalkeeper to declare his intentions early. He should do so in a clear, firm and calm voice.

Co-defenders can help the goalkeeper in three important respects:

By clearing the ground route for the goalkeeper. Once the goalkeeper has declared his intention to move out from goal to attack the ball, defenders should get out of the ground route to the ball.

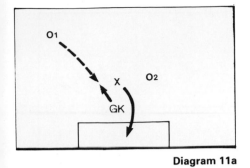

Diagram 11a

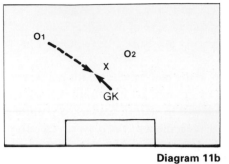

Diagram 11b

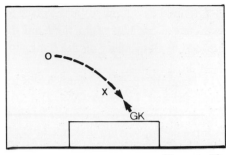

Diagram 12a

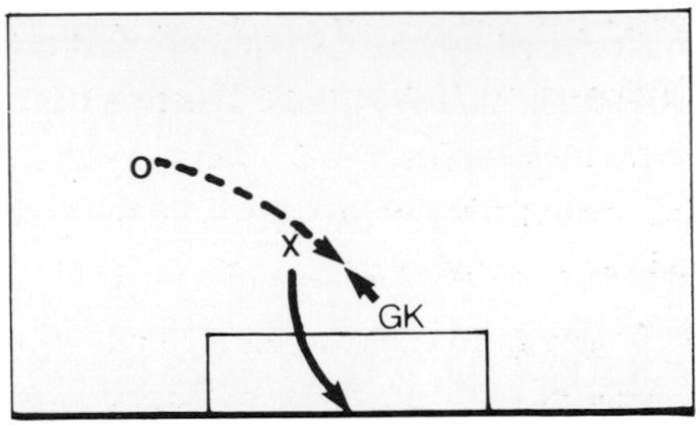

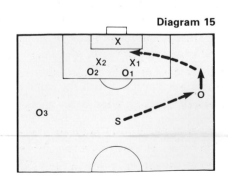

Diagram 12b

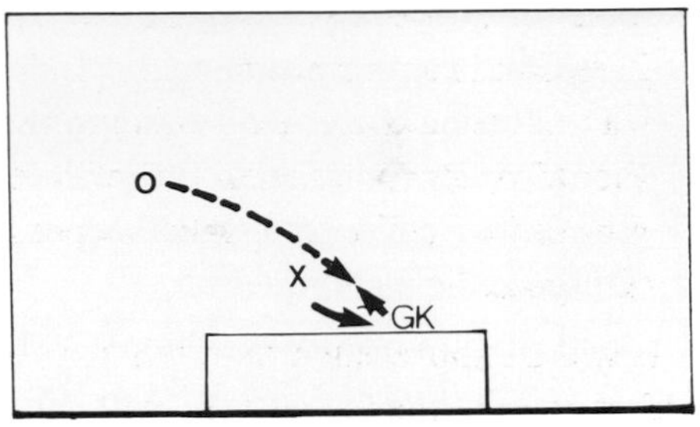

Diagram 12c

By giving protection to the goalkeeper. In Diagram 11a, O_1 has crossed the ball. GK has moved out from goal to attack the ball and X has dropped back into the goal to cover him. X has made the wrong decision as he has left GK to the challenge of O_2. In Diagram 11b, X has correctly stayed to protect the goalkeeper from the challenge of O_2.

By giving cover to the goalkeeper. In Diagram 12a, X is in the line of flight and is likely to hinder the goalkeeper if he remains in that position. There is, in this circumstance, no need to protect the goalkeeper so his position is wrong.

In Diagram 12b, X has moved back onto the goal-line to cover the goalkeeper. However, his position of cover is at the widest possible angle and he would find it extremely difficult to defend the goal from such a position on the goal-line.

The correct position to adopt is demonstrated in Diagram 12c. X has moved back into a position four or five yards out from goal to cover the goalkeeper. In that position he is nearer to the ball and has, therefore, effectively narrowed the angle and will be better placed to defend the goal.

ORGANISATION FOR PRACTICE

The practice takes place in the attacking third of the field (Diagram 13). There is a goalkeeper, X, with one co-defender, X_1, in the penalty area. A server in a central position passes the ball to an attacking player, O, on the left flank. The attacking player must cross the ball from a variety of distances and angles. The defending players must play the ball to a target player, T, on the right flank, who in turn will pass the ball back to the server. The same practice should be repeated from the left flank.

DEVELOPMENT OF THE PRACTICE

1. Once the goalkeeper and his co-defender have had practice in combining their play, an attacking player, O_1, is introduced to the penalty area (Diagram 14). The attacking players should now vary their play as much as possible and try, with the cross, to eliminate the goalkeeper.

2. Given a satisfactory performance from the right and the left flanks, the practice should be developed to include two central defenders, X_1 and X_2 (Diagram 15). O and O_3 are positioned on the flanks so that the crosses can be alternated . They also act as target players for X, X_1, and X_2.

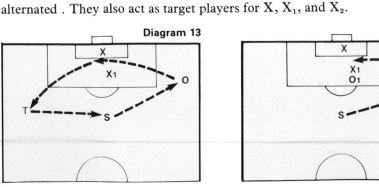

Diagram 13

Diagram 14

Diagram 15

3. The final development takes place in an eleven-a-side game. The game is restricted to one half of the field and the position of several defenders is conditioned to allow space on the flanks to be created to ensure a large number of crosses.

In Diagram 16, X_{11} is conditioned to stay on the half-way line until the server passes the ball. Likewise, X_6 is conditioned to a central position until the ball is played. O_4 and O_2, on the other hand, are allowed to start in unmarked positions within easy supporting distance of O_7. The arrangement of the players, therefore, whilst being slightly false, will guarantee a high percentage of crosses.

When the X players take possession of the ball, especially the goalkeeper, they must distribute the ball quickly and try to get an X player in possession of the ball on the half-way line. The practice, of course, must be repeated from the opposite flank.

Finally, the practice must be developed into a full, unconditioned eleven-a-side game.

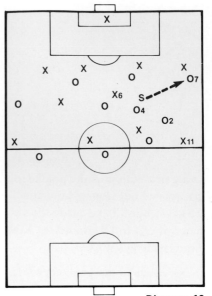

Diagram 16

POINTS FOR THE COACH TO OBSERVE

1. Observe the co-operation between the goalkeeper and his co-defenders with respect to:
    (i) Good communication.
    (ii) Clearing the ground route to the ball.
    (iii) Giving protection to the goalkeeper.
    (iv) Giving cover to the goalkeeper.
2. Observe the techniques of:
    (i) Catching, securing and screening the ball.
    (ii) Deflecting the ball away at the far post.
    (iii) Punching the ball two-fisted.
    (iv) Punching the ball one-fisted.
3. Observe the performance of the goalkeeper in dealing with near-post crosses with respect to:
    (i) Holding the position at the near post.
    (ii) Attacking the ball.
4. Observe the recovery run of the goalkeeper from the near post to the far post with respect to:
    (i) Turning into the field of play.
    (ii) The direct route across goal.
5. Observe the performance of the goalkeeper in dealing with far-post crosses with respect to:
    (i) The position at the post.
    (ii) Communication.
    (iii) Attacking the ball.
6. Observe the performance of the goalkeeper under strong physical challenge.
7. Observe the balance and composure of the goalkeeper in distributing the ball after having caught a cross from a flank.

DISTRIBUTION

At the lowest level at which the game of soccer is played, goalkeepers just get rid of the ball. At the highest level, goalkeepers pass the ball. There is, of course, a vast difference of attitude between the two.

The primary task is to persuade goalkeepers that, in the matter of passing the ball, they have great advantages over all other players. These advantages are fourfold:

- The goalkeeper only has to observe through 180 degrees.
- Once possession has been achieved, opponents will not challenge the goalkeeper from behind.
- Once possession has been achieved, it is almost impossible to dispossess the goalkeeper.
- The goalkeeper can pass the ball by using either his hands or his feet.

Goalkeepers have a tendency to equate distance of clearance with success. They should be educated to think in terms of initiating attacks rather than clearing the ball. That is not to say that there will not be occasions when a goalkeeper will initiate an attack by kicking the ball two-thirds of the length of the field. Indeed, such a pass to a team-mate could have the great merit of penetration.

Passing the ball for goalkeepers is no different to passing the ball for any other player: the greater the distance of the pass, the greater will be the tendency to inaccuracy, and the greater will be the likelihood of the opposition winning the ball. There is no special merit in territorial advantage without ball possession.

Once the goalkeeper has the ball in his possession, his priorities should be as follows:

Make a penetrative pass. This means playing the ball past as many opponents as possible to the advantage of a team-mate. If the opposition has been drawn forward, it may be possible to play the ball into the space behind the rear defenders for a forward player to run on to. That situation does not occur often but it does happen sometimes, even at the highest level. If goalkeepers can exploit such a situation, then that is marvellous attacking play.

Sometimes a central attacker will have the beating, in the air, of a central defender. Such a situation offers excellent possibilities for penetration provided that the goalkeeper is accurate enough to land the ball on the head of the attacker. In such a situation a goalkeeper should be encouraged to take the risk of being inaccurate as the dividends for accuracy are likely to be high.

For the most part, goalkeepers should realise that long clearances do not achieve penetration and ball possession is frequently sacrificed.

Change the direction of play. No player has better opportunities to change the direction of play than the goalkeeper. Not infrequently, the goalkeeper will take possession of the ball by intercepting a cross from a flank. Almost invariably on these occasions space, and an attacking numerical advantage, is available on the opposite flank.

Since the goalkeeper only has to play through 180 degrees, observing a situation where the direction of play can be changed should be very much easier than it is for an out-player.

Give time for the attacking players to spread out. If there are no passing possibilities, the goalkeeper should hold the ball and stand still while the attacking players spread out. Many goalkeepers elect to roll the ball instead.

There are two reasons why this should not be encouraged:

- It is less easy to observe the movement of players.
- Having observed a player in a position of advantage, vital time may be lost in fielding the ball prior to making the pass.

By working through the order of priorities, the goalkeeper will make a selection of where to pass the ball. For reasons which have already been explained, that selection will be based on safety rather than risk on most occasions.

Having considered where to pass, one now has to consider how to pass. This involves making the decision whether to kick or throw the ball.

Kicking the ball

There are two basic methods of kicking the ball from hand for a goalkeeper:

The volley kick

The hands. The ball should be held with both hands comfortably outstretched in front of the body at waist height. From that position the ball should be dropped.

The kicking foot. The kicking foot should strike the ball in front of the body, and contact on the ball should be made by the instep through the bottom half and through the vertical line of the ball. The ball should leave the boot at roughly 45 degrees.

The non-kicking foot. The non-kicking foot should be placed behind the ball to facilitate an easy flowing swing of the kicking leg.

The head. The head should be looking down at the ball and should be steady.

The half-volley kick

The main difference between the volley kick and the half-volley kick is that the kicking foot strikes the ball as the ball contacts the ground in the latter.

The half-volley will have a much lower and faster trajectory than the volley and therefore has the advantage of reaching the target more quickly.

If a half-volley along the ground is required, then the non-kicking foot must be placed much nearer to the ball and the kicking foot must strike the ball through both the horizontal and vertical mid-line.

Because of the lower trajectory of the ball, the half-volley is a particularly useful technique to employ when kicking into a strong wind. It is not advisable, however, to use the half-volley kick on very muddy grounds or on very hard bumpy grounds.

ORGANISATION FOR PRACTICE

Practice should take place in a grid measuring 40 yards by 10 yards (Diagram 17). X should volley the ball for O to catch below head height. O then repeats the practice by volleying the ball back to X. The accuracy over this distance should be very high, and the receiver should not have to move to catch the ball. The same practice should be repeated for the half-volley kick.

If the accuracy of either the volley or the half-volley is poor, then the distance should be reduced by 10 yards. Distance should only be increased consistent with accuracy.

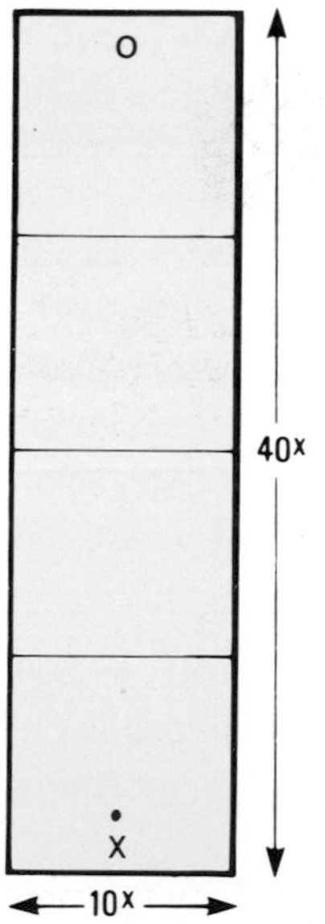

Diagram 17

DEVELOPMENT OF THE PRACTICE

Once accuracy to a high standard is achieved over a distance of 40 yards, the practice should be transferred to a playing pitch. In Diagram 18, X makes a volley or a half-volley kick to O on the half-way line. O can position in any one of three target areas: the centre circle; a gate, marked by cones 15 yards apart, on the right-hand flank; or a gate on the left-hand flank.

O, having caught the ball inside one of the target areas, will volley or half-volley the ball back to X. After a given number of kicks, X and O should change positions. It is, of course, a simple matter, and a good idea, to have a competition between the two players.

Further development from this stage should take place in the eleven-a-side practice game.

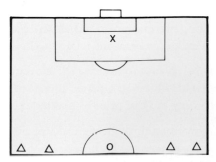

Diagram 18

8 Half-volley kick from hand

8a The ball is dropped from the hands.

8b The ball pitches just in front of the non-kicking foot as the kicking foot comes through to make contact through the bottom half of the ball. Note that the head is down and steady. The body is leaning slightly backwards.

8c The follow-through showing the body leaning backwards.

9a

9b

9 Volley kick from hand

9a The ball is dropped from about waist height, well in front of the body.

9b Contact is made with the instep through the bottom half of the ball. The eyes are looking down and the head is steady.

POINTS FOR THE COACH TO OBSERVE

1. Observe the position of the hands when holding the ball. Observe also that the ball is dropped from waist height and is not thrown up in the air to drop from chest or head height.
2. Observe the position of the kicking foot and the contact on the ball.
3. Observe the position of the non-kicking foot.
4. Observe the position and steadiness of the head.
5. Observe at all times that accuracy is achieved before power.
6. Observe the speed and trajectory of the kick.

Throwing the ball

Throwing the ball is usually more accurate than kicking the ball. The release of the ball can also be made more quickly, and therefore the delivery of the ball can be faster for distances up to 40 yards. It is not easy, however, to throw a ball accurately over a distance in excess of 40 yards.

Since the task of a goalkeeper is to be safe and accurate in his distribution, the various techniques for throwing the ball should be mastered. Those techniques should also, of course, be employed frequently during a game. There are three basic techniques for throwing the ball:

Rolling the ball. The action is similar to that used in bowls. One foot is placed well in front of the other and the ball is held in the palm of the hand. The ball is released along the ground from a position level with the front foot. This method of throwing the ball should only be used over short distances up to 20 to 25 yards. It is important, of course, that the ground route to the receiver should be clear.

The value of this throw is that the receiver has little or no control problem as it is easy to deliver the ball at the correct pace and along the ground. It is not wise to use this technique on muddy pitches.

Throwing the ball from the shoulder. The action of this throw is similar to that of putting the shot in athletics. For a right-handed thrower, the ball is held at shoulder height in the palm of the right hand. The palm is behind and under the ball and the elbow bent. The body is sideways-on and in line with the target.

The action in making the throw is to extend the throwing arm. The ball is released in front of the head and at head height, the head being steady throughout and the eyes looking at the target.

This method of throwing can be used for distances of up to 35 yards. The main advantage of the throw is the speed of release and also the speed of the ball through the air. The trajectory, of course, is low and therefore the ground route to the target should be clear.

The over-arm throw. The action of this technique is not unlike bowling in cricket. The ball is held with the fingers, palm and wrist of the throwing arm wrapped round the ball. The body is positioned sideways-on and in line with the target. The legs are wide apart to ensure good balance. The throwing arm moves upwards in an arc while the non-throwing arm moves downwards in a similar but opposite action. The ball is usually released from a straight arm just backwards of the vertical position. The actual point of release can be varied. The earlier the ball is released the higher will be the trajectory.

This technique allows the ball to be thrown over long distances, sometimes well in excess of 40 yards. The ball can also be thrown easily over the heads of opponents. However, the release of the ball is not quick and in very wet conditions the ball can prove difficult to hold and control.

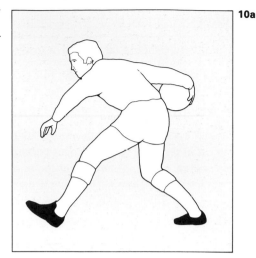

10a

10b

10 Rolling the ball

10a The ball is held in the palm of the right hand and supported by the wrist. The left foot is placed well forward and in line with the target.

10b The ball is released along the ground from a position level with the front foot.

11 Throw from the shoulder
The body is sideways-on and in line with the target. The ball is held in the palm of the right hand at shoulder height and the ball is released at the arm's full extension.

ORGANISATION FOR PRACTICE

The practice should take place in grids of the following dimensions:

- 20 yards by 10 yards for the roll technique.
- 30 yards by 10 yards for the throw from the shoulder.
- 40 yards by 10 yards for the over-arm throw.

Once the goalkeeper has mastered the techniques, and has established what he can do in terms of accuracy over certain distances, the problem is entirely one of the skill of selecting the correct technique at the correct time.

Special practices need not be set up to develop the techniques of throwing. The goalkeeper will best obtain the practice he needs in normal small-sided games, phase practices and eleven-a-side practice games.

POINTS FOR THE COACH TO OBSERVE

1. Observe the technique of rolling the ball in terms of:
   (i) Correct pace.
   (ii) Smoothness of roll. Observe that the ball is rolled along the ground and not bounced into the ground.
2. Observe the technique of throwing from the shoulder, especially the speed of release and the speed of flight.
3. Observe the technique of the over-arm throw, especially the sideways-on position and the windmill action of the arms.
4. Observe in every case the accuracy of the throw.

The quality of the pass

The quality required of a pass from a goalkeeper is no different to that expected from any other player. Goalkeepers should read carefully therefore Chapter 5 on *Passing and Support*.

Goalkeepers, as the first line of attack, will often start attacks. It should be understood that the quality of the first pass is crucial. On the quality of the first pass depends the ease of control and, therefore, the time and space for the receiver to make the second pass.

In simple terms, the goalkeeper must want to be a good passer of the ball. That attitude is a prerequisite for success.

12 Over-arm throw
The body is positioned sideways-on and in line with the target. The ball is held by the fingers, palm and wrist of the right hand. The right arm moves upwards in an arc and the ball is released near to the vertical position.

DEFENDING (1)
AS AN INDIVIDUAL

All defending is concerned with decreasing the time, the space, and the options an attacking player has to pass, dribble, or shoot for goal. To defend well as a team presupposes that players can defend well as individuals. In addition to technical and tactical qualities, defenders must display the mental qualities of concentration, patience, and self-discipline.

All players will find it necessary to challenge an opponent for the ball sometime during a game. There are three possible objectives in challenging for the ball: preventing opponents from turning with the ball; keeping play in front of the defenders; and forcing play in one direction.

PREVENTING OPPONENTS FROM TURNING WITH THE BALL

All players, especially those in rear defensive positions, should develop the technique of preventing opponents from turning with the ball. Defenders who allow opponents to turn with the ball give them the opportunity to pass the ball forward – thus the defender allows himself to be put out of the game.

Some defenders try too hard to win the ball when challenging opponents from behind. This will often result in an unnecessary free kick being given away or the defender being beaten comprehensively if the attacker evades the tackle. In making such ill-advised challenges, players will often fall over or deliberately go to ground by sliding in to challenge for the ball. The golden rule for defenders is *stay on your feet*. Players who go to ground unnecessarily, even though it may be for only three or four seconds, reduce their team to ten effective players. As with most rules, there are exceptions. A defending player can, with advantage, go to ground when challenging for the ball:

- When the opponent is clear of the defence and a last ditch effort is made by the defender to slide the ball away.
- When the opponent is near to the goal-line or the touch-line and the defender can play the ball dead.

Neither of these situations are likely to occur, however, when challenging an opponent from behind.

It is also a mistake for the defender to get too close to the attacker. The defender should be far enough away to see the ball and observe any movement by his opponent, and yet close enough to make an effective challenge for the ball should his opponent try to turn with it. The ideal position is two or three feet behind the opponent.

There are a number of considerations which defenders should bear in mind when learning the technique of preventing opponents from turning with the ball:

Watch the opponent with the ball. The opponent with the ball may not be the opponent whom the defender is marking. In Diagram 1a, O_1 is in possession of the ball. O_2 makes a quick movement towards O_1 and X_1 follows. O_1 does not play the ball to the feet of O_2 but into the space behind X_1. O_2 turns quickly on X_1 and receives the ball in the space behind X_1. The conclusion can be drawn that defenders must deny opponents the opportunity to play the ball behind them. Defenders should position themselves in such a way that opponents are forced to pass the ball in front of them.

Make up ground while the ball is travelling. In Diagram 1b, O_2 moves away from X_1 but X_1 denies the space behind O_2 until O_1 releases the ball. Once the ball is released, X_1 quickly closes up on O_2 while the ball is travelling. X_1 adopts a position three feet or so behind O_2 and prevents O_2 from turning with the ball.

Diagram 1

Watch the ball. Once the defending player is in a challenging position it is important that he should watch the ball, for he must react to the movement of the ball rather than the movement of his opponent. It is for this reason that the defender must give himself the space to see the ball. If he is too close, he can only react to the movement of the attacker, thus making himself vulnerable to feints by the attacker. Furthermore, if he is too close to the attacker, the attacker can turn past him with the ball and render his position ineffective.

Be patient. It is important for the defender to understand that, once he has adopted the ideal position of two or three feet behind the attacker and is watching the ball, the problems belong primarily to the attacker. Should he become impatient and attempt to win the ball from an unwinnable position, the problems for the attacker will be solved. The action by defenders who show such impatience is referred to as 'selling yourself'. Patience and concentration are essential qualities for defenders and are part and parcel of all the techniques of defending.

Select the correct moment to tackle. The correct moment to tackle is when the attacker attempts to turn and in fact is half-turned. It is at this moment that the attacking player ceases to screen the ball from the tackle and is most vulnerable in terms of his balance.

ORGANISATION FOR PRACTICE

The practice takes place in a grid measuring 30 yards by 10 yards with a server at each end (Diagram 2). The servers also act as targets. S_1 passes the ball to O who is challenged by X. X must try to prevent O from turning with the ball and passing it to S_2. The practice is repeated from the other end with S_2 passing the ball to X who is challenged by O. The challenging player must always start in a realistic position and should move to challenge while the ball is travelling.

1 Sliding the ball out of play
A well timed tackle on Blissett. The defender has gone to ground but the ball has been played over the touch-line, allowing the defender time to recover his position.

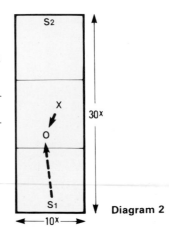

Diagram 2

2a

2b

2c

2d

2 Good defensive position to prevent the opponent turning with the ball

2a A defender in a good position to try to stop Keegan from turning with the ball.

2b Eyes on the ball and resisting the temptation to try to win the ball.

2c Keegan decides to play the ball to his supporting player.

2d The defender must now turn and run with Keegan to prevent him receiving the ball in the space behind the defender.

POINTS FOR THE COACH TO OBSERVE

1. The defender should make up ground while the ball is travelling.
2. The defender should be balanced, and in the correct challenging position, as the ball arrives at the feet of the attacker.
3. The defender should concentrate on watching the ball and reacting to its movement.
4. The defender should be patient and wait for the attacker to try to turn before challenging him for the ball.
5. Observe the timing of the tackle to win the ball.

KEEPING PLAY IN FRONT OF THE DEFENDERS

It is not always possible to prevent an opponent from turning with the ball, for attackers will sometimes receive the ball when facing their opponent's goal. On these occasions it is necessary to position in a way that will ensure that the opponent passes the ball backwards or square across the field. In Diagram 3a, X is preventing O from passing the ball forward. The position of X is a maximum of two yards from the ball. In Diagram 3b, X is too far away from O and allows O to play the ball past him – a common fault.

There are a number of factors to be considered in relation to the positioning of the challenging player:

The angle or line of approach to challenge. In order to adopt the correct challenging position (Diagram 3a), players must:

3 Tackling an opponent as he turns

A great moment for a young defender, dispossessing Kevin Keegan as he turns with the ball. The timing of the tackle is perfect. The one black mark against the defender is that he is going to ground without having played the ball dead.

3

- Make up ground while the ball is travelling.
- Get into line between the ball and the goal or target area. (The only reason for not being in this position would be if the player wanted to force the attacker to play on his weaker foot.)

In Diagram 4a, X makes a straight run to achieve a position in front of O_1 while the ball is travelling from O_2. The correct position has been adopted, but if X had been unable to make up the ground he would have failed to position himself between the ball and the goal. This has happened in Diagram 4b, with the result that O_1 is able to play the ball forward past X towards the goal. The first objective, therefore, must be for the defender to get into the line between the ball and the goal.

If there is any doubt about the defender achieving this objective in a straight run, he must elect to make a curved run. In Diagram 4c, X makes a curved run and adopts a position between the ball and the goal. Although he has not achieved a position two yards from the ball, his position is preferable to that of being close but outside the line to goal. It can be seen from the above how important it is for a defender to select the correct angle or line for his run when moving to challenge an opponent.

The speed of approach to challenge. The defender should approach his opponent as fast as he can while the ball is travelling in order to make up ground. It is important, however, for the defender to have slowed his approach by the time the ball has reached the opponent. If he continues at speed when the opponent has the ball under control he will find it difficult to change direction, so the attacker will be able to beat him by making a sudden sideways movement. It can be seen, therefore, that the approach by the defender should be slowed, and a balanced position adopted, just before the ball is brought under control.

Closing down the last few yards. If the defender is five or six yards away from the attacker when the ball is brought under control, his task is to close down the last three or four yards. Slightly crouching, he should adopt a sideways-on position and edge in slowly towards the attacker.

Gaining the initiative – feinting to tackle. The winner in all one-against-one contests is the player who gains the initiative. The defender can try to gain the initiative by feinting or pretending to tackle. Two possible effects from this play may result: either the attacker may look down at the ball to protect it from the tackle – once this happens the initiative is with the defender, since the attacker is now thinking in terms of defending the ball rather than attacking his opponent; or the attacker may attempt to move the ball away from the tackle and lose control of it.

Concentrating and watching the ball. The attacker will also be thinking in terms of feint plays in order to unbalance the defender and thereby gain the initiative. The defender will react against such feint plays more efficiently if he concentrates on watching the ball. It is the movement of the ball to which he must react and nothing else.

Being patient and staying on one's feet. Time, in these situations, always favours the defender. If the attacker has full control of the ball, the temptation to try to win the ball must be resisted by the defender. Remember, fools rush in, usually fall over, and present the opposition with a numerical advantage. Be patient and stay on your feet.

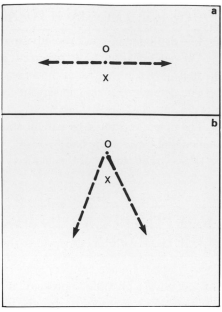

Diagram 3

Diagram 4

4 Keeping play in front of the defender

4a & 4b Two young defenders play very well against Wilkins and Brooking as they make a cross-over. The two young defenders hold their positions in relation to Wilkins and Brooking and succeed in keeping the play in front of them.

ORGANISATION FOR PRACTICE

Practice takes place in a grid measuring 20 yards by 10 yards. There is a server, S, who also acts as a target man, an attacker, O, and a defender, X. In Diagram 5, S and O are positioned at opposite ends of the grid and X is positioned to the side of the grid, 12 to 15 yards from O. S passes the ball to O who either controls the ball and passes it back to S, or passes it back to S with the first touch. S must remain stationary and X cannot move until S has passed the ball. X must then move to challenge O and prevent the ball from being played back to S. The position of X can be varied, thereby making his task easier or more difficult according to the proficiency of his technique. The players rotate positions so that each gains practice in challenging for the ball.

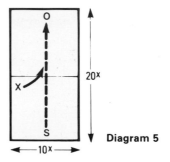

Diagram 5

POINTS FOR THE COACH TO OBSERVE

1. The players should be in the correct positions to practise.
2. The defender's angle or line of approach to challenge should be correct.
3. The defender should judge the speed of approach to challenge so that he slows, and adopts a balanced position, as the attacker controls the ball.
4. The defender should adopt the correct position and use the correct technique for closing down the last few yards.
5. The defender should feint to tackle in order to gain the initiative.
6. The defender should concentrate on watching the ball.
7. The defender should be patient and stay on his feet.

FORCING PLAY IN ONE DIRECTION

There will be occasions when it is not possible to keep play in front of the defence. There will also be occasions when it is desirable to force play to continue in one direction – as may occur when the ball is on a flank and the attacker, with the ball, is forced down the flank by a defending player. Defenders should remember that attackers will try to disguise their intentions and make the play unpredictable. Defenders should do the opposite and make the play of the attackers as easy to predict as possible.

There are two possible directions in which play can be forced: down the touch-line and across the field.

5

Forcing play down the touch-line

When the ball reaches an attacker in an advanced flank position, it is often advisable for defenders to force play down the touch-line. There are three reasons for this:

- The angle through which the attacker can pass the ball will be reduced.
- The number of players to whom the attacker can pass will be reduced to one or two.
- Play will become predictable.

When a defender challenges an opponent and tries to force play down the touch-line, he should adopt a position that eliminates the opponent's chance of playing inside. In Diagram 6, X is occupying the space inside O and is therefore denying O the possibility to utilise that space. Thus play is forced down the line.

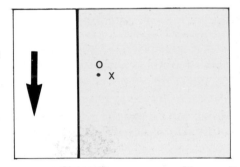

Diagram 6

ORGANISATION FOR PRACTICE

Practice takes place in a grid measuring 30 yards by 10 yards (Diagram 7). The server, S, passes the ball to O who is challenged by X. O must try to beat X on his inside and dribble the ball between the two cones set two yards apart on the 30-yard line. X must try to force O down the line and prevent him from coming inside between the cones. All the techniques for making an effective challenge should be employed by X. The practice should be repeated several times and then the players should rotate positions in order to give practice in defending to all three players.

DEVELOPMENT OF THE PRACTICE

The practice is developed by introducing a second defender to cover the player challenging for the ball. In Diagram 8, S serves the ball to O and X_1 moves into position to challenge O and force him down the line. At the same time, X_2 moves into a covering position so that he can challenge for the ball if X_1 is beaten. X_1 and X_2 must prevent O from reaching the 30-yard line, and must always force him down the line. At this stage, the situation should remain two against one in the defenders' favour.

The covering player's position is determined by three considerations: the angle and distance between the two players, and communication.

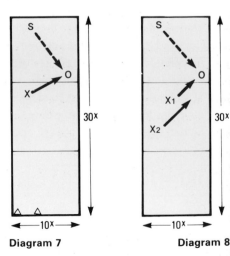

Diagram 7 **Diagram 8**

6 Forcing play down the line – challenge and cover

6a The challenging player closes in to force the attacker down the line. The covering player is already in position.

6b The challenging player, having closed in, and the covering player in a good position, make the attacker abandon the idea of going down the line.

6c The attacking player now tries to move inside but is prevented from doing so by the challenging player.

6d The challenging player tackles and wins the ball.

The angle. X_2 should be positioned at such an angle that he is just inside an imaginary line drawn through X_1 parallel to the touch-line (Diagram 9).

The distance. The distance between X_1 and X_2 is governed by four factors:
The area of the field. The distance between the challenging player and the covering player will vary according to the area of the field in which the ball is. If play is on the half-way line, there is likely to be a great deal of space behind the covering player. Should the covering player get too close to his team-mate, it is possible that a fast opponent could beat both the challenging and the covering player by speed alone. If play is on the edge of the penalty area, however, it would be dangerous for the covering player to be too far away from his team-mate. If he is, there is a danger that the challenging player will be beaten and that the attacker will shoot for goal before the covering player can challenge for the ball.
The compactness of the defence. The more compact the defence (i.e. the distance between the back defender and the front defender), the more assured covering players can be in adopting close covering positions. The more stretched a team becomes, the greater will be the space between and behind defending players, and the greater must be the caution of covering players in adopting close covering positions.
The type of opponent. Flank opponents will either use pace or tricks, or a combination of both, as a means of penetrating the defence. In dealing with pace, the covering player should position himself farther from the challenging player in order to give himself extra time for decision-making if the attacker breaks through. In dealing with a clever dribbler, the covering player needs to be closer to the challenging player in order to give the opponent less time and less opportunity to run at the covering player with the ball if his team-mate is beaten.
The speed of the defenders. If the defenders are faster than their opponents, the covering player can feel safe in adopting a close covering position. If the

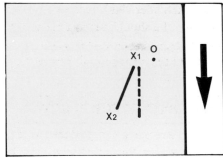

Diagram 9

defenders are slower than their opponents, the covering player should increase his distance from the challenging player.

It can be seen from all the points mentioned above that it is impossible to be specific regarding the distance of the covering player from the challenging player. A rough guide, however, would indicate the following:

- In the defending third of the field, 4 to 6 yards.
- In the middle and the attacking thirds of the field, 8 to 10 yards.

If the distance, in any part of the field, becomes more than 10 yards between the two players, then it is unlikely that the covering player can perform the task of challenging for the ball successfully if the challenging player is beaten.

Communication. The covering player should communicate with the challenging player. It should be understood that the covering player's position will be vulnerable if the challenging player is not in the correct position. The covering player should communicate information regarding the position of the challenging player and where to force the opponent by calling 'get closer', for instance, or 'force him down the line'. He should also give his team-mate encouragement as this will help the challenging player to be patient and concentrate on the task.

Forcing play across the field

Sometimes defenders will prefer to force the play across the field rather than down the touch-line. On these occasions it is necessary for the challenging player to adjust his position in order to deny the opportunity and the space for the attacking player to go down the touch-line. The great advantage in forcing play across the field is that it keeps the play in front of the defence and denies the attacking players progress towards goal.

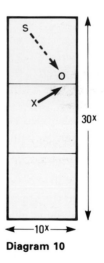

Diagram 10

ORGANISATION FOR PRACTICE

Practice takes place in a grid measuring 30 yards by 10 yards (Diagram 10). The server, S, passes the ball to O who is challenged by X. The task of X is to force O across the grid and prevent O from reaching the 30-yard line. All the techniques for producing an effective challenge should be employed by X. The practice should be repeated several times and then the players should rotate positions.

DEVELOPMENT OF THE PRACTICE

Practice is developed by introducing a covering player. Just as the challenging player needs to adjust his position in order to force play across the field, so too does the covering player. In Diagram 11, S serves the ball to O and X_1 moves into a position to challenge O and force him across the field. X_2 moves into a covering position so that he can challenge for the ball if X_1 is beaten. X_1 and X_2 must prevent O from crossing the 30-yard line. The task for X_1 and X_2 can be made more difficult by introducing a target player on the 30-yard line. In Diagram 12, O_1 is challenged by X_1 who is covered by X_2. O_1 must try to create an angle to pass the ball past X_1 and X_2 to reach O_2. X_1 and X_2 must try to block the pass.

The covering player's position is again determined by a consideration of the angle, distance, and communication between the covering player and the challenging player.

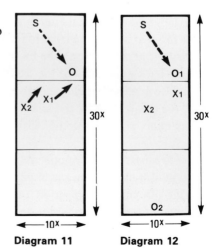

Diagram 11   **Diagram 12**

The angle. X_2 should be positioned just backward of square of an imaginary line drawn through X_1, parallel to the half-way line (Diagram 13).

The distance. The distance between the two players should never be more than 10 yards and, on the edge of the penalty area in the defending third of the field, it may be as little as two or three yards.

Communication. Again, the covering player should communicate with the challenging player, giving both information and encouragement. The information should concern the position of the challenger and where to force the opponent.

POINTS FOR THE COACH TO OBSERVE

1. When the challenging player is forcing his opponent down the touch-line, he should adopt a position that blocks the opponent's route inside. He should also employ all the techniques for making an effective challenge.

2. When the challenging player is forcing his opponent across the field, he should adopt a position that blocks the opponent's route down the touch-line. Again, he should employ all the techniques for making an effective challenge.

3. The covering player should position himself at the correct angle and the correct distance from the challenging player.

4. The covering player should communicate information and encouragement to the challenging player.

COMBINING THE SKILLS OF CHALLENGING AND COVERING IN A SMALL-SIDED GAME

The development from grid practices to small-sided games requires careful consideration. There is a danger that the game might be practised in too large an area, thereby making the physical task for the players too demanding. A relatively small space should be used initially, calculating on the most likely chance of success for the defending players.

Practice takes place in a grid measuring 30 yards by 20 yards, using full-sized portable goals. There are four players, including a goalkeeper, on each side. The players should be encouraged to shoot, if they have the space, as they can never be far from their opponent's goal. This will also emphasise to the challenging players that they must be close enough to block the shot. Emphasis should be placed on two special qualities:

■ Early decisions. The man nearest to the man with the ball should always move to challenge.

■ Clear communication. There should be clear communication between the players to establish who is to challenge the man with the ball. This should be followed up by the communication of information and encouragement from the covering player to the challenging player.

Sometimes there will be indecision as to which player is nearest to the man with the ball. In such circumstances there is a danger that either no player will challenge for the ball, or two players will challenge for the ball. Players will do well to remember that 'An early shout will sort it out'. Early calling, and talking to each other, is a most important part of defending. It greatly assists in making early and correct decisions and in combining the skills of the defending players.

DEVELOPMENT OF THE PRACTICE

Once the defending players feel comfortable in a small space, and are effective in combining their skills, the practice should be expanded. The next stage is to practise in a realistic space, in relation to numbers, but still in a small-sided game. It cannot be emphasised too strongly that a gradual expansion, in terms of space and numbers, produces the best results. The practice, therefore, is expanded to six against six, including two goalkeepers, in an area measuring 60 yards by 40 yards (Diagram 15). Full-sized goals are used.

The off-side law should be operative in the practice. If the off-side law is not

7 Forcing play across the field

A young defender in a good position and determined to force Keegan across the field. The covering player is also in a good position, both to cover his team-mate and mark Blissett.

8 Forcing play across the field – challenge and cover

Blissett being forced across the field. Both the challenging and covering players are in excellent positions.

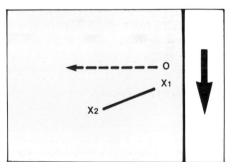

Diagram 13

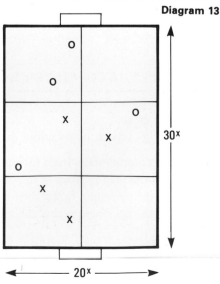

Diagram 14

used in a space of this size, it will lead to unrealistic defending as the defenders will be unrealistically stretched. Huge spaces will be created between defenders and effective covering will be difficult to achieve. Indeed, the practice will be self-defeating. This is one of the many occasions in coaching where if the coach blunders on the organisation, everything else will go wrong from that point onwards.

It may seem to be logical, once the players are efficient in the six-a-side game, to expand the practice into the eleven-a-side game. There are, however, a number of other important elements in defending which should be learned and combined with the skills of challenging and covering before embarking on practice in the full game.

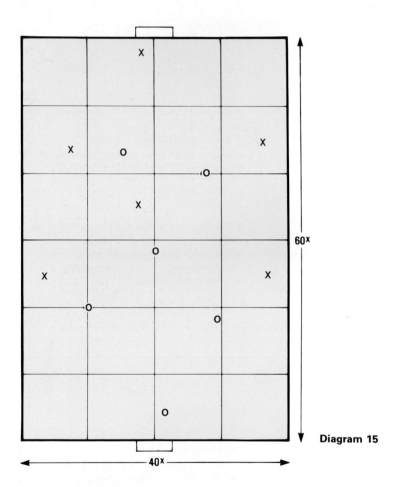

60ˣ

Diagram 15

40ˣ

POINTS FOR THE COACH TO OBSERVE

1. Observe that the organisation is correct and that the off-side law is obeyed in the six-a-side game.
2. Challenging players should adopt the correct techniques when:

  (i) Preventing opponents from turning with the ball.
 (ii) Keeping the play in front of the defence.
(iii) Forcing the opponent down the touch-line.
(iv) Forcing the opponent across the field.

3. Covering players should adopt the correct covering angle and distance and should communicate with the challenging player.
4. Players should be able to combine their understanding and their skills in making early and decisive decisions.

13
DEFENDING (2)
AS A TEAM

When a team loses the ball, or is subjected to skilful play by the opposition, it will often find itself outnumbered on the goal side of the ball. When a defending team finds itself in this situation, defenders who are on the goal side of the ball should retreat. At the same time, defenders on the wrong side of the ball should recover on to the goal side in order to redress the balance in their favour. Defenders, therefore, need to develop the skill of dealing with situations where they are outnumbered. They also need to develop the skill of recovery. When a defender is outnumbered, the temptation to challenge the man with the ball must be resisted. The exception to this rule is where the situation occurs in or around the penalty area and the attacker is closing in for a shot at goal.

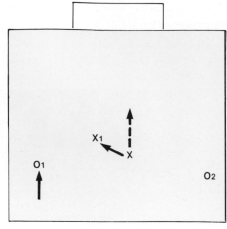

Diagram 1a

RETREATING FROM A POSITION ON THE GOAL SIDE OF THE BALL

There are two objectives in retreating:

- To allow time for other defending players to recover to a position on the goal side of the ball.
- To deny space to the back of the defence and thereby keep the opposition playing square or in front of the defence.

There are four considerations for a defender who is retreating:

The line of retreat. If the defender is in a central position, his line of retreat should be towards his goal. Although, in theory, his line of retreat should be direct, in practice it is more likely to be a zigzag along that line. In Diagram 1a, X is confronted with O_1 and O_2 in a central position. His ideal line of retreat is direct towards the goal but, because O_1 is running forward with the ball, X moves backwards and slightly to his right in order to defend the space which O_1 may attack. By defending the space to the back of the defence, X forces O_1 to pass square to O_2. X reacts by moving backwards and slightly to his left to position at X_2 (Diagram 1b). One can see that by adopting a zigzag line of retreat (although care must be taken not to get too far across the central line), X has achieved the two main retreating objectives.

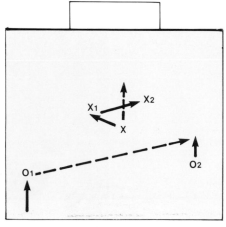

Diagram 1b

Keep the players in view. Defending in a situation where one is outnumbered by the attackers is difficult. If, however, the defender positions in such a way that either of the opponents, or the ball, goes out of view, the task becomes nearly impossible. The problem for the defender will occur each time he has to turn. The golden rule is: always turn into the play – never turn into a position where one has one's back to either the opponents or the ball.

In Diagram 2a, O_1 has passed the ball to O_2. X has turned away from O_1 and O_2 and the ball. For a period of time, X will be facing his own goal, thereby creating a blind-side situation for himself. O_1 is able to exploit the mistake by moving forward behind X and receiving a pass from O_2. In Diagram 2b, O_1 has passed the ball to O_2 but X has turned to face the play and can observe the movement forward of O_1. X is therefore able to retreat into the space which O_1 is trying to exploit. X thus keeps the play in front of him.

Maintain the space between the attackers and the defender. The retreat should be as slow as possible in order to allow time for other defending players to recover, but fast enough to maintain the space between the attackers and the defender. The more interpasses the attackers make, the more they serve the purpose of the defending player. The one pass the attackers must not be allowed to make is the one to the back of the defence. It should be remembered that the

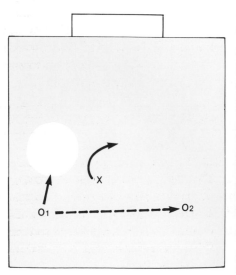

Diagram 2a

main objective of defence is to keep the opposition playing in front of you and deny them the opportunity to play behind you.

In Diagram 3a, X has failed to maintain the space between himself and the O players, with the result that O_1 has passed the ball past X into the space at the back of the defence for O_2 to run on to. In Diagram 3b, X has maintained the space between himself and the O players and is in the space which the O players are trying to exploit.

Drawing the shot. There comes a point in a defender's retreat, near to the edge of the penalty area, where the retreat must be halted. At this point the defender, clearly, cannot maintain the space between himself and the attackers. However, the attackers will have almost run out of exploitable space behind the defender – most of it will be covered by the goalkeeper.

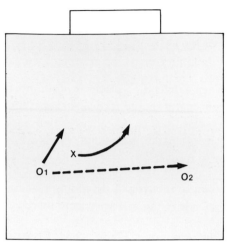

Diagram 2b

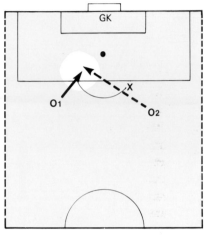

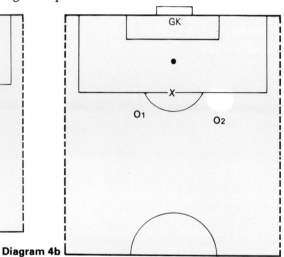

Diagram 4a   Diagram 4b

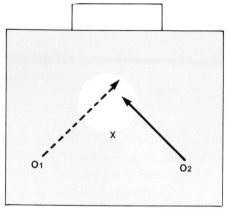

Diagram 3a

In Diagrams 4a and 4b, O_2 is in possession of the ball and X is faced with two defending options. He can either block O_2, thereby leaving a space which O_1 could exploit (Diagram 4a); or he can move off line and open up a space for O_2 to exploit by moving forward to shoot (Diagram 4b). Of the two possibilities, X should elect to draw the shot from O_2 in order to gain three advantages:

- The shot will be from a greater distance.
- The shot will be from a wider angle.
- X will still have a chance of making a challenge.

ORGANISATION FOR PRACTICE

The practice takes place in a grid measuring 30 yards by 10 yards, using a full-sized goal (Diagram 5). There are two attackers against one defender and a goalkeeper, and a server. S passes the ball to O_1 who can either go for goal himself or combine with O_2 to produce a shot at goal. X must try to delay O_1 and O_2 and, if possible, win the ball.

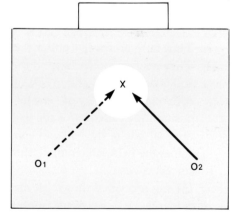

Diagram 3b

POINTS FOR THE COACH TO OBSERVE

1. The defender's line of retreat should block the attacker's route to goal and should invite the pass to be made in front of him.
2. The defender should keep both the attackers and the ball in view, and he should always turn towards the play.
3. The defender should maintain the space between himself and the attackers and he should adjust the speed of his retreat to achieve this objective.
4. When the retreat has to halt, the defender should draw the shot from the least vulnerable position.
5. By a combination of all these techniques, the defender should delay the attack.

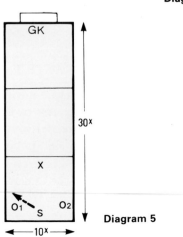

Diagram 5

RECOVERING FROM A POSITION ON THE WRONG SIDE OF THE BALL

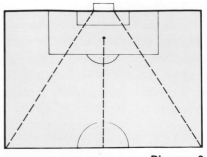

Diagram 6

When a defending player is outnumbered, it is important that one or more of his team-mates should recover to assist him as quickly as possible. Even in the best organised teams, defenders sometimes find themselves outnumbered by attackers. Players should understand, therefore, when to recover, how to recover, and how far to recover.

When to recover. A defending player should recover when the defenders on the goal side of the ball are outnumbered.

How to recover. Players should run as quickly as possible and take the shortest possible recovery route towards the danger area. Players on a flank should take a line back towards the near post and players in central positions should take a line back towards the penalty spot (Diagram 6).

How far to recover. Once a player reaches a position on the goal side of the ball, a reassessment of the situation should be made. This will lead to one of four possible decisions:

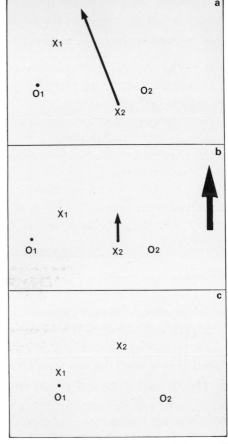

Diagram 7

■ Challenge the opponent with the ball.
■ Cover the defender challenging the opponent with the ball.
■ Mark an opponent who is not in possession of the ball.
■ Occupy important space on the goal side of the ball.

It may or may not be necessary, therefore, for a recovering player to continue his run once he is on the goal side of the ball.

There are three particular mistakes which players make in relation to recovery runs:

(i) They fail to recover – either the run is not made, or it is made too slowly.
(ii) They recover too far beyond the ball. In Diagram 7a, X_1 is outnumbered and is delaying O_1 and O_2. X_2 makes a recovery run but runs too far. Although the X players now have equal numbers, neither X_1 nor X_2 is in a position to challenge for the ball. In Diagram 7b, X_2 has recovered on to the goal side of the ball and encourages X_1 to challenge O_1 and force him across the field. Diagram 7c shows X_1 challenging O_1 with X_2 giving the correct cover.
(iii) Having recovered they relax mentally and fail to concentrate upon their defensive task. Recovery runs are a means to an end – the end is to be in a position on the goal side of the ball, performing a defensive duty.

ORGANISATION FOR PRACTICE

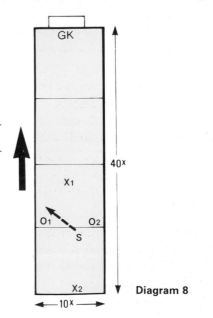

Diagram 8

The practice takes place in a grid measuring 40 yards by 10 yards, using a full-sized portable goal. There are two attackers against one defender and a goalkeeper, and an extra defender who should recover from a starting position 10 yards behind the play (Diagram 8). S passes the ball to either O_1 or O_2. X_1 tries to delay the attack while X_2 makes a recovery run. X_2 cannot start his recovery run until S has played the ball. The O players must try to attack the goal before X_2 recovers and the X players must try to win the ball, or at least prevent a shot at goal. X_1, by making an early call, should help to reposition the recovering player by instructing X_2 to either challenge for the ball or cover X_1.

DEVELOPMENT OF THE PRACTICE

The practice for retreating and recovering defenders should be combined and expanded to involve five defenders, a goalkeeper, and five attackers. The practice takes place in just over half the field and occupies its whole width. In Diagram 9, three defenders, X_3, X_4 and X_5 are outnumbered by five attackers. S passes the ball to any of the O players who must try to attack and score. When S passes the ball, X_1 and X_2 start their recovery runs. The X players must then try to delay the O players and then win the ball. The pressure on the defence can be increased by moving the practice nearer to the goal and by making the recovery runs for X_1 and X_2 longer.

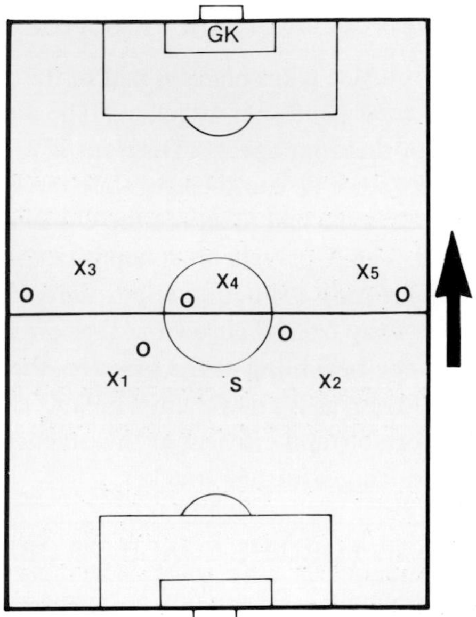

Diagram 9

POINTS FOR THE COACH TO OBSERVE

1. Defenders should adopt the correct lines of retreat.
2. Defenders should judge their lines of recovery so that they take the shortest line back to help the defence.
3. Defenders should judge the distance of their recovery run so that they do not recover too far beyond the ball.
4. Once defenders have recovered, they should concentrate on the performance of their defensive task.
5. The players, as a unit, should combine their skills to deny vital space to the attacking players and win the ball.
6. Players on the goal side of the ball should aid recovering players with verbal instructions.

KEEPING GOAL SIDE OF THE BALL

When players are on the goal side of the ball they should either mark players or space. It is appropriate to emphasise again that the aim of defence is to keep the opposition playing in front of the defence and to deny them the opportunity to play behind the defence. When a defending player is deciding where to position himself, he should be guided by the relative positions of the ball, the opponent, and the goal. In Diagram 10, X_1 and X_2 are marking O_1 and O_2 respectively. X_2 is positioned in accordance with the ball, his opponent and the goal. X_2 is in a position where the ball must be played across him, thus giving X_2 the possibility of an interception.

The nearer the defender and his immediate opponent are to the ball, the more important it is for the covering defenders to mark players. The farther the defender and his immediate opponent are away from the ball, the more important it is for them to mark space. Marking is not a matter of man-to-man marking or zonal marking – it is a matter of marking players *and* marking space. Good teamwork requires that these two objectives be achieved at the same time. In Diagram 11, O_1 is in possession of the ball and is marked tight by X_1. O_2, O_3 and O_4 are marked by X_2, X_3 and X_4 who increase their distance from their opponent the farther they are from the ball.

When adopting their positions, defenders should always remember the following considerations:

- If the ball is played into the space behind them, they should be able to beat their immediate opponent to the ball.
- If the ball is played to the feet of their immediate opponent, they should be able to make up the ground while the ball is travelling.
- They should keep their opponent and the ball in view.

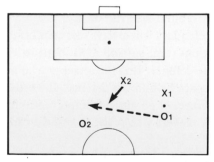

Diagram 10

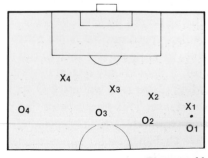

Diagram 11

ORGANISATION FOR PRACTICE

The practice takes place in half of the pitch. There are five defenders, a goalkeeper, and four attackers. The defenders should be positioned on the goal side of their opponents (Diagram 12). It is an advantage for the coach to act as a server, since he can then regulate the type of service.

S plays the ball to any of the O players, who must combine together and try to score. The X players must combine their defensive skills to prevent the O players from creating a shooting opportunity. The X players must also try to win the ball as far away from their own goal as possible.

At the beginning of the practice, the X team should have one more player than the O team as it gives them a greater chance of success. Once the X players are comfortable and efficient at the practice, their task can be made more difficult by introducing a further attacker.

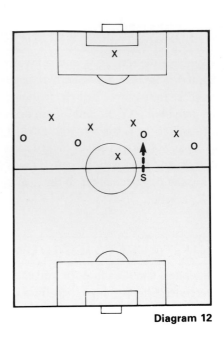

Diagram 12

POINTS FOR THE COACH TO OBSERVE

1. All the players should be in realistic positions and should be alert before the practice commences.
2. The defenders should position themselves according to the ball, the opponent, and the goal.
3. The defenders should deny the attackers the space behind them.
4. The defenders should force the passes to be played across them. Observe how many times defenders intercept passes.
5. The defenders should keep the ball and their opponent in view.

TRACKING AND MARKING PLAYERS

Even when defenders are on the goal side of the ball, and on the goal side of their immediate opponent, there is the possibility that an attacker will make a forward run and try to get behind one or more defenders. Defenders who watch the ball to the exclusion of their opponent are likely to fail to see an opponent making a forward run on their blind side, as has happened in Diagram 13, where O_2 has made a blind-side run on X_2.

Defenders will always feel comfortable against attackers who play in set positions (e.g. outside right, outside left, centre forward) and always play in front of the defence. It is the attacker who moves diagonally across the field or attacks the space behind the defence who causes defenders most problems. It is, therefore, of paramount importance that defenders should understand how to mark players who make cross-field runs with or without the ball.

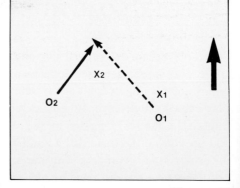

Diagram 13

Marking players who make cross-field runs with the ball

In Diagram 14a, O has dribbled the ball infield from a flank position and X has moved, correctly, with him, keeping on the goal side and preventing the ball from being played forward. In Diagram 14b, O has again dribbled the ball infield from a flank position, but X has retreated, incorrectly, towards his goal. O is therefore given space in which to run at the defence with the ball or pass the ball forward. X should only retreat towards goal if he can pass off O to another defending player who will track O across the field and keep him playing in front of the defence. This presupposes that the X team has got a free player in the position required. Generally speaking, if a challenging player can keep a close and effective challenge on his opponent and keep him playing in front of the defence, then the challenging player should track his opponent all the way.

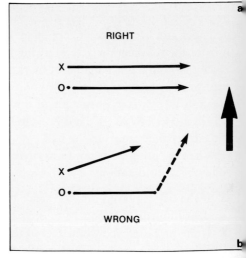

Diagram 1

Marking players who make cross-field runs without the ball

If attacking players make runs without the ball, they do so with one of two possible objectives in mind:

■ To attack a dangerous space.
■ To draw the defender out of a good defensive position.

It is of the utmost importance that defenders should determine quickly the objective of an attacker's movements.

In Diagram 15a, the central attackers O_1 and O_2 have made cross-over runs and X_1 and X_2 have followed on a man-for-man basis. It can be seen, in Diagram 15b, that there will be a moment when all four players cross in line end to end. At that moment the central defence becomes vulnerable, for space is opened up on either side. In Diagram 15c, O_1 and O_2 have again made cross-over runs, but on this occasion X_1 and X_2 have retreated a few yards to keep the movements of O_1 and O_2 in view. Although O_1 and O_2 have crossed over, X_1 and X_2 remain in their positions (Diagram 15d). At no point in the play were X_1 and X_2 vulnerable, and at no point did O_1 and O_2 create space.

Players who make runs without the ball to the back of the defence pose a very much more dangerous threat. The runs will take one of two forms: runs from a flank to central positions, runs from central positions to a flank.

Diagonal runs from a flank to central positions. These are the most dangerous runs and defenders dare not let attackers go on them unmarked. For defenders to track attackers effectively, they must keep on the goal side of the attacker and in order to do this they must keep their opponent and the ball in view. To be able to do this while running at speed does require practice.

In Diagram 16, O_2 is in possession of the ball and X_2 is moving across to challenge. O_1 makes a diagonal run from the flank to a central position and is tracked and marked by X_1. At positions 1 and 2, X_1 is on the goal side of O_1, having kept him to his left. At position 3, X_1 is still on the goal side of O_1 and has allowed O_1 to move to his right in order to achieve the correct marking position. X_1 has positioned, throughout, in accordance with the position of the ball, his opponent and the goal.

Diagonal runs from central positions to a flank. Usually these runs are designed to draw defenders away from central positions. Defenders must track players who make them, but they should know how far to go. In Diagram 17, O_2 is in possession of the ball and X_2 is moving across to challenge O_2. O_1 makes a diagonal run from a central position to the flank and is tracked by X_1. At position 1, X_1 is on the goal side of O_1, having kept him to his right. At position 2, where O_1 has just moved beyond the line between the ball and the near post, X_1 is still on the goal side of O_1 and has allowed O_1 to move to his left in order to achieve the correct covering position. At position 3, X_1 has correctly allowed O_1 to reach the touch-line without being closely marked. X_1 is still in a position to challenge O_1 if the ball is played to him, and he has also maintained a position on the goal side of O_1. It can be seen that considerable judgment is required by defenders when tracking attackers. That judgment is based on the position of the ball and the opponent, and their position in relation to the goal.

As defenders track opponents, spaces are bound to be created between defending players. These spaces should be filled in two ways:

■ By players on the goal side of the ball moving across to seal off central spaces.
■ By players recovering on to the goal side of the ball to occupy important spaces.

If all the spaces cannot be sealed off then the space to leave vacant is the space on the farthest flank from the ball.

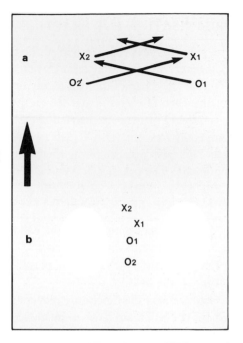

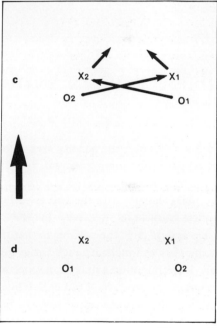

Diagram 15

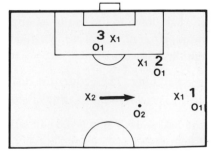

Diagram 16

ORGANISATION FOR PRACTICE

The practice takes place in half of the full pitch. There are five defenders, a goalkeeper, and five attackers. It is an advantage if the coach acts as the server. In Diagram 18, S passes the ball to any one of the O players. At the start of the practice each O player is marked on the goal side by an X player. Once play starts, the O players are instructed to make diagonal runs. They must also, of course, try to score. The X players practise tracking players with and without the ball. They also practise filling the spaces vacated by defenders who track opponents. The practice is eventually developed into an eleven-a-side situation.

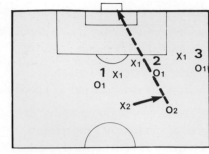

Diagram 17

POINTS FOR THE COACH TO OBSERVE

1. The defenders should keep the ball and their opponent in view and should constantly adjust to their movements.
2. Observe how the challenging player marks his opponent who runs with the ball across the field.
3. Observe how the defending players mark opponents who run across the field without the ball from flank to infield, and vice versa.
4. The defenders should keep on the goal side of their opponents while tracking their runs.

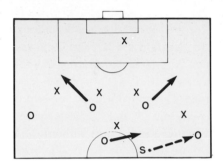

Diagram 18

DEFENDING IN AND AROUND THE PENALTY AREA

For the defender, the penalty area is the one area, above all others, where there are no prizes for coming second. It is essential, therefore, that defenders are first to the ball and are prepared to attack it. Defenders should move to meet the ball and make contact with the ball as early as possible, which usually means at the highest point in its trajectory that they can reach.

Defenders have the advantage that the ball will usually be coming towards them. This will make it much easier to move into the line of flight and attack the ball. Determination and courage, particularly when heading is involved, are important qualities required of defenders in this situation. Having reached the ball first, the defender must play the ball clear of the attacking players, preferably to a team-mate. If no team-mate is available, defenders should play the ball high, long, and wide.

Play the ball high. Height means time and in the penalty area time favours the defence. It is better to play the ball straight up in the air in the six-yard area than play the ball down to the feet of an opponent on the edge of the penalty area. The technique required, therefore, whether from foot or head, is to strike the ball through the bottom half.

Play the ball long. The greater the distance achieved from the clearance, the greater the certainty that the immediate danger is cleared.

Play the ball wide. Playing the ball wide usually means that the ball is played a safe distance, and at a safe angle, from goal. If the ball is crossed from the opponent's right flank, for instance, defenders should try to clear the ball in the direction of the opponent's left flank, for one can expect this area to be least heavily populated with opponents. Having cleared the ball, the defenders should move out from goal in order to support the attack, to play opposing players off-side, and to take the pressure off the goalkeeper.

1 Attacking the ball – being first to the ball

1a In position to receive a cross from the left flank.

1b Moving to attack the ball in the area of the near post.

1c First to the ball and playing the ball safely away from goal.

2 Playing the ball high, long and wide

2a Moving to attack the ball.

2b Heading the ball through the bottom half and going for height, distance and width.

ORGANISATION FOR PRACTICE

The practice takes place in the defending third of the field on a full-sized pitch. In Diagram 19, S passes the ball to O_1, who crosses the ball into the penalty area. O_1 should be encouraged to cross the ball from a variety of positions on the flank and at varying heights. X_1 and X_2, opposed by O_3, challenge for the ball and try to play it to X_3 or X_4. Failing that, they must clear the ball high, wide, and clear of the penalty area.

The practice is repeated by O_2 from the opposite flank. It is important that defenders should have practice clearing balls from each flank as most defenders are strong from one side and weaker from the other.

Diagram 19

DEVELOPMENT OF THE PRACTICE

The practice may be developed in several ways:
1. By introducing a goalkeeper into the practice. This helps the defenders to appreciate which balls they must go for and which are more efficiently dealt with by the goalkeeper. This development also enables the necessary element of calling to be coached in the practice.
2. By introducing a second attacker into the practice so that there are two against two, plus a goalkeeper, in the penalty area.
3. By introducing two O players on the edge of the penalty area. These players can either wait on the edge of the penalty area for a poor clearance or mark X_3 and X_4. They should be encouraged to vary what they do.

POINTS FOR THE COACH TO OBSERVE

1. The players should be in realistic positions to start the practice.
2. The defending players should move to be first to the ball and should attack the ball by taking it at the highest possible point in its trajectory.
3. The defenders should play the ball clear of the attacking players, ideally to a team-mate. Failing that, they should play the ball high, long, and wide.
4. The defenders should move out from goal after clearing the ball.

MENTAL CONCENTRATION

Frequent reference has been made to the fact that players require a high level of mental concentration. Knowledge and understanding are of little value if they are not accompanied by the concentration necessary for the successful application of that knowledge. Soccer is a game of judgments and decisions in rapidly changing circumstances. Concentration, therefore, is fundamental to successful performance and requires to be coached just as any other facet of the game. Concentration is likely to break in three circumstances: when the play is stopped for a goal-kick, corner, throw-in etc; when the ball changes hands; when a player becomes fatigued. A break in concentration by an attacker may simply mean a lost chance. A break in concentration by a defender, however, could mean a lost match.

The application of all the defensive techniques are brought together by coaching in the small-sided game, followed by the eleven-a-side game. The practice takes place in a grid measuring 60 yards by 40 yards, using full-sized portable goals (Diagram 20). The situation is six against six, including two goalkeepers. Balls are placed at 10-yard intervals round the touch-lines so that when the ball goes out of play, the attacking team can play a ball in very quickly. This requires maximum concentration from the players who must adjust their thinking with equal speed. The coach should also give a number of free kicks which, again, will make it necessary for the players to adjust their thinking quickly.

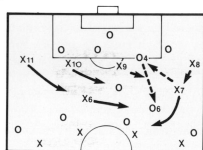

Diagram 21

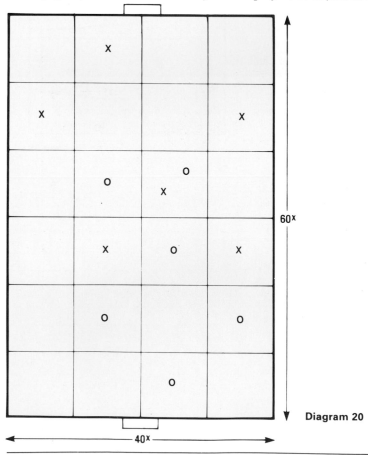

60ˣ

Diagram 20

40ˣ

POINTS FOR THE COACH TO OBSERVE

1. Players should concentrate when the ball changes hands.
2. Players should concentrate when the game is stopped.
3. Players should concentrate on the game and not over-react to receiving a knock, gamesmanship, or what they consider to be bad refereeing decisions or bad luck.

COMBINING THE SKILLS OF DEFENDING IN THE ELEVEN-A-SIDE GAME

Good teamwork is not achieved by accident. It is achieved by combining the understanding, the techniques, and the skills of eleven players. To achieve the best results, teamwork should be coached carefully and patiently in an eleven-a-side situation. The task of the coach is to weld together the individual defensive skills of the team and ensure that the sum of the whole exceeds the sum of all the separate parts.

Reference has been made to the fact that defending will be made more difficult if a team allows itself to become stretched. A major factor in coaching defensive skills, therefore, is to achieve team compactness as a necessary prerequisite and framework for the performance of individual skills. There are three ways in which team compactness can be achieved:

By forward players working hard to recover and challenge the opponent with the ball, the moment the ball is lost. In Diagram 21, X_7 has played an inaccurate pass which has been intercepted by O_4 who plays the ball first time to O_6. The six forward X players immediately make recovery runs to achieve compactness by:

- Getting goal side of their opponents.
- Challenging the player with the ball.
- Decreasing the space between the back defender (excluding the goalkeeper) and the most forward defender.

By defending players moving across the field when the opposition has possession of the ball on a flank, in order to lock the ball in that quarter of the field. In Diagram 22, the ball has been played by O_2 to O_3 in a flank position. The six forward X players make recovery runs back and across the field in order to lock the ball in the shaded quarter of the field, so establishing numerical superiority. The X players have succeeded in achieving compactness in that area of the field.

By the rear and midfield players moving forward when they have possession of the ball and the ball is played forward. In Diagram 23, the goalkeeper, X_1, has rolled the ball to X_2 who, in turn, has played the ball forward to X_3. Having played the ball forward, all the rear and midfield X players, including X_2, make their movements forward. The X team has established a numerical superiority of ten against seven in the shaded area and has also achieved compactness. Such compactness is important for support in attack and guarantees that if the ball is lost, the opposition will have the minimum of space and time in which to launch their attack.

ORGANISATION FOR PRACTICE

The practice takes place in the attacking third of the field with 22 players on the field. In Diagram 24, S plays the ball to the O goalkeeper from a position just inside the X team's attacking third of the field. The O players then spread out.

The development of the practice goes through several stages:

1. The O goalkeeper plays the ball to his left flank. The X players must recover and move across the field and try to win the ball on that flank. The O players must try to make progress down the field or change the direction of play to their right flank.
2. The same practice is repeated with the O goalkeeper playing the ball out to his right flank.

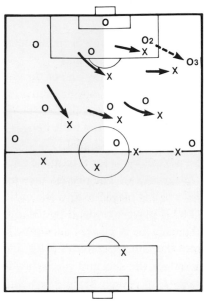

Diagram 22

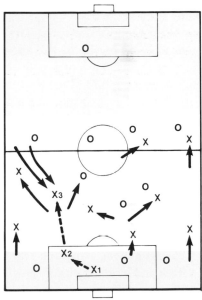

Diagram 23

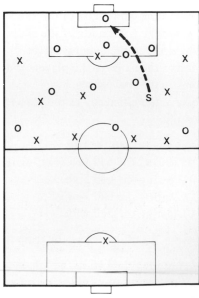

Diagram 24

3. The same practice is repeated with the O goalkeeper free to play the ball out to either flank.

4. S plays the ball to any of the O defenders. The O players then spread out and the above practice is repeated.

5. S plays the ball to any one of the X players. The X players try to score and when they lose possession they must immediately try to win back the ball. The purpose of this practice is to give the X players practice in concentrating on their defending skills when the ball changes hands. Having won the ball, the X players must again attack the O goal.

6. The next phase is for S to move back to a position just inside the X half of the field (Diagram 25). The players take up positions relative to the position of the ball. The ball is played to any one of the O players and the O players attack the X goal. The X players respond by defending in the middle third of the field. Having won the ball, the X players must attack the O goal.

7. From the same position, S plays the ball to any of the X players. The X players attack the goal and when they lose possession of the ball they must concentrate upon their defensive skills in winning back the ball. Having won back the ball, the X team must again attack the O goal.

8. The third phase is for S to move into a position just outside the X team's defending third of the field (Diagram 26). From that position the ball is played to any one of the O forward players. The O players must attack the X goal and the X players must try to win the ball and then attack the O goal.

9. The final phase is for S to play the ball from the same position, just outside the X team's defending third of the field, to any one of the X players. The X team must attack the O goal. If they lose possession, however, they must immediately concentrate upon defending.

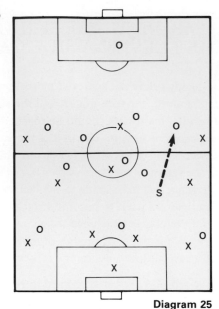

Diagram 25

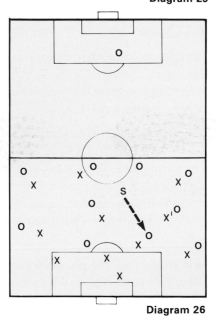

Diagram 26

POINTS FOR THE COACH TO OBSERVE

1. Observe that the players are always in realistic positions and alert before each practice commences.

2. Observe the compactness of the team in relation to:

   (i) Forward players recovering when the ball is lost.

   (ii) Players moving across the field to lock the ball on the flank.

   (iii) Back and midfield players moving forward when the ball is played forward.

3. Observe the mental concentration of the players when the ball changes hands.

4. Observe the combining of the skills of the players in retreating and recovering.

5. Observe the combining of the skills of the players in challenging for the ball and covering the challenging player.

6. Observe the skills of the players in tracking opponents and adjusting their positions to fill vital spaces.

7. Observe the efficiency of the players in attacking the ball near to their goal in relation to:

   (i) Being first to the ball.

   (ii) Clearing the ball to a team-mate.

   (iii) Clearing the ball high.

   (iv) Clearing the ball long.

   (v) Clearing the ball wide.

8. Observe the efficiency of the team in:

   (i) Winning the ball in the opponent's half of the field.

   (ii) Preventing shots at their own goal.

14
SET PLAYS (1)
DEFENDING

It is a fact that over 40 per cent of all goals are scored from set plays (free kicks, corners and throws). The more important the game, and the more evenly matched the teams are, the more likely it is that the winning goal will be scored from a set play. Why do teams find it so difficult to defend at set plays? There are two particular reasons:

■ The attacking team can place a large number of players in pre-planned attacking positions.
■ It is impossible to exert a high degree of pressure on the service as, with the exception of a throw-in, the defending players always have to be ten yards away from the ball.

There are two further reasons, self-inflicted as it were, which have some bearing on the problem:

■ There is a general lack of detailed defensive organisation at set plays.
■ It is a fact that many players lose their concentration when the game stops.

The salvation for players with a concentration problem is to have something to concentrate upon. Lack of detailed planning accentuates the problem for players whose concentration is inclined to falter. There are, therefore, three prerequisites to successful defending at set plays:

Individual and team discipline. Discipline is important as the efficiency of the team as a whole ultimately depends on each individual performing thoroughly the task to which he is assigned.

Detailed planning and organisation. Planning is important as it is the best guarantee of making the task of one's opponents as difficult as possible. It is also the best guarantee of getting the best out of the players as individuals and as a team.

Concentration. In order to perform well, a player must be alert and watchful of what is happening. It is not sufficient for a player to know the detail of what to do. He must concentrate on giving an overall performance.

In tactical terms, the basic problem in all set plays is twofold:

■ Marking players.
■ Marking space.

We shall consider the above factors in relation to free kicks, corners, throws and goal-kicks.

FREE KICKS

Free kicks in the attacking and middle thirds of the field

When a team is awarded a free kick, especially in the middle third of the field, the players' reaction will usually be to try to take the kick quickly. This will be for two main reasons:

■ To take advantage of the space which is awarded to them with the free kick as the opponents must be at least ten yards away from the ball.
■ To take advantage of any breakdown in concentration by the defending players.

To combat this, whenever and wherever a free kick is conceded, a defending player should move quickly into position, ten yards from the ball, in line between the ball and his own goal. By doing this, the player immediately blocks the direct forward ground route.

The effect of achieving that objective will be to delay the attack in one of two possible ways:

■ By making the opponents pass the ball along a less penetrative route.
■ By making the opponents use more difficult techniques, such as playing the ball over the head of the challenging player, thus giving the receiving player a more difficult pass to control or a more difficult ball to pass first time.

The time which is gained by challenging the kick should be used to ensure that all opponents in advance of the ball are marked, and all important spaces are sealed off.

The point should be made at this juncture that players who dispute free kicks, and argue with the referee, not only offend the laws and the spirit of the game, but also render a tactical disservice to their team. Indeed, players who argue with referees only succeed in displaying their indiscipline and lack of concentration. They never succeed in causing referees to change their minds.

Direct free kicks near to the penalty area – setting a wall

When a free kick is conceded near to the penalty area, it is wise for the defending team to set up a wall to defend part of the goal. Unless a team is well organised, practised, and disciplined when under pressure, confusion will reign supreme in the matter of setting a defensive wall. There are four fundamental questions which must be decided:

Who positions the wall? The job of setting the wall in position should be done by an outplayer, not the goalkeeper. The reason for this is that if the goalkeeper sets the wall, he must position himself in line with a post and the ball while he satisfies himself that the wall is in position (Diagram 1). For a period of time, therefore, if only for a few seconds, the whole of the goal is exposed.

The task of the goalkeeper is to position immediately to stop the major threat to his goal. That threat is the quick direct shot. The position of the goalkeeper must be:

■ Where he can see the ball, not behind the defensive wall.
■ Near to the centre of the goal.

The outplayer nominated to set the wall should position himself ten yards from the wall, behind the ball and in line with the post on which the wall is to be set (Diagram 2). Which post is chosen must be predetermined. If the kick is at a wide angle, then the wall should be set on the near post, thus greatly reducing the danger of the driven shot. If the kick is in a central position, the choice should rest with the goalkeeper but should still be predetermined.

The player lining up the wall, X_9 in Diagram 2, should only position one

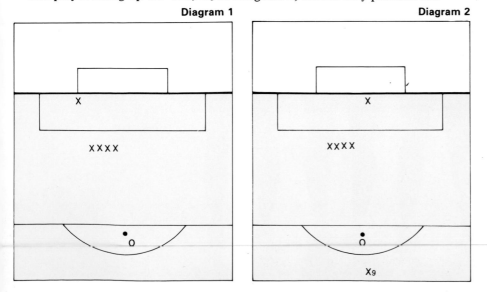

Diagram 1   **Diagram 2**

player. That player should be in a direct line between the ball and the post. He must also be ten yards from the ball. Once that player is lined up, it is vital that he does not move his position until after the kick is taken. While other players move to complete the wall, the player who has lined up the wall can assume other defensive duties.

How many players in the wall? The answer to this question very largely depends on the position of the ball. However, it is a mistake to place too many players in the wall as opponents in dangerous positions must be marked.

If, for example, six players were placed in the wall to defend against a central free kick in the 'D' there would be two disadvantages: the potential numerical situation outside the wall would be eight attackers against four defenders; the goalkeeper would have to move well across his goal, away from a central position, in order to see the ball. The answer to the question, therefore, lies in the following guide (Diagram 3):

- ■ If the kick is in a central position, in the 'D', the wall should contain four or five players.
- ■ If the kick is between the 'D' and the corner of the penalty area, the wall should contain three or four players.
- ■ If the kick is down the side of the penalty area, the wall should contain two or three players.

As the position of the kick goes out towards the touch-lines, or out towards the edge of the defending third of the field, so the number of players in the wall should be reduced until finally just one player threatens the kick.

Teams should be organised in such a manner that they know exactly how many players are required in a wall in any given situation. The goalkeeper, however, can eliminate and possible confusion by shouting the number required.

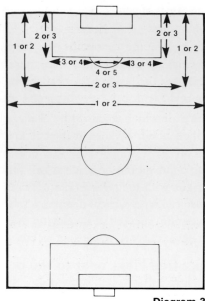

Diagram 3

1 The wall – preventing swerve, sizing and protection

This photograph is taken from the position of the kick and shows clearly the kicker's view of the player on the end of the wall preventing a bent shot round the outside of the wall. Note that the players are correctly sized, with the tallest on the outside and the shortest on the inside. Also shown is the correct protection by the players.

How do the players in the wall line up? If it has not been predetermined which players go into the wall, then confusion is likely to ensue and it becomes a matter of chance whether the number of players required arrive in time.

Players should know exactly who goes into which wall, which two players on the right-hand side, which five in the central position, which three on the left and so on. It is also worth stressing that it is a mistake to lock up the best defending players in the wall. Equally, of course, faint-hearted players can be a liability in a wall. Selecting players to go into the wall is just another extension of management, the criteria of which is to get the best out of the players as individuals and as a team. Once the players know which of them is going into the wall, and which one of them will be lined up between ball and post, there are three factors to consider:

■ If there are three or more players in the wall, one of them should always be outside the player who is lined up; that is, outside the line between ball and post. The reason for this is to prevent the ball from being swerved round the outside of the wall and into the goal.

■ The players should position according to size so that the tallest is on the outside and the shortest is on the inside. The reason for this is that the tall players will block a greater part of the goal which is least accessible to the goalkeeper.

■ The players must position close together and their feet should also be close enough to prevent the ball from going between their legs.

It is also important that players in a wall should give themselves the maximum possible protection. This they can achieve by crossing their hands in front of their lower abdomen and slightly bowing their heads so that the ball does not hit them directly in the face.

When does the wall break? It is a greater sin for the wall to break early than it is for the wall to break late. The wall should break once the kick is taken as it is unlikely that the wall will remain at the correct angle. Breaking, however, does not mean all the players moving off in different directions. On most occasions the best advice is for the wall to move, en bloc, towards the ball. Thus, as the attackers play the ball to the side to widen the angle for a shot at goal, so the defensive wall moves closer to the ball to narrow the angle. Obviously the quicker this is done, the more likely the defenders are to block the shot.

Sometimes players in the wall link arms or hold each other round the waist. Neither of these methods is satisfactory for two reasons:

■ The personal protection is minimal.
■ The movement, after the kick is taken, is restricted.

It would be easy, but wrong, to pretend that cheating is not attempted in the matter of setting up a defensive wall. The major form of cheating is to place the wall very much less than ten yards from the ball. Some take the view that it is the job of the referee to decide how far back the wall should be. This is not the case. The decision on how far back the wall should be was decided some time ago by those who wrote the laws. It is the task of teachers and coaches to ensure that the players are aware of the law.

They should also be aware of another fact. Defensive walls are always erected in parts of the field where the markings assist in determining where any ten-yard point is. Defenders, therefore, who position five or six yards from the ball are asking for trouble. They deserve to be cautioned.

It is vital that the wall is placed ten yards away from the ball, not only because that is the law, but also because there are considerable dangers if the wall is set five yards away from the ball and then moved back by the referee.

In Diagram 4, it is clear that four players will seal off more of the goal at point

A than at point B. At point B, a team would be extremely vulnerable to a direct shot. Furthermore, by placing the wall at point A, the goalkeeper will have to move farther across his goal in order to see the ball. This position makes him rather vulnerable to a ball chipped over the wall.

Organising a defensive wall is a simple, but detailed, piece of organisation. It is not so simple, however, to obviate the need for practice. Having organised the defensive wall, there is still the fundamental defensive job to be done. The task is twofold: marking players and marking space.

Direct free kicks near to the penalty area – sealing off vital space

The points have already been made that it is a mistake to lock up too many players in the wall and use one's best defenders. It is also wise, in defending against free kicks around the penalty area, to withdraw all eleven players into defensive positions.

How the players outside the wall are deployed is of immense importance. The precise positioning of the players depends mainly on the positioning of the ball. There are three basic positions for the ball:

Free kicks in the 'D'. The vital area to seal off when defending against free kicks in the 'D' is the area between the six-yard area and the penalty area, measuring roughly 20 yards by 12 yards (the white area, Diagram 5).

In Diagram 5, X_5 should place himself in a line between the ball and a position just inside the post. He should be able to stop a direct shot just inside the goalkeeper's left post.

The positions of X_2 and X_3 should not be wider than the width of the six-yard area, but it may be necessary for them to make a slight adjustment to their position in order to mark opponents. They should place themselves in a half-turned position so that they can move quickly into the six-yard area to clear the danger from possible rebounds off the goal structure or the goalkeeper.

The positions of X_9 and X_{10} are essentially to threaten the kick as there is a strong possibility that the angle of the shot will be changed by a short pass, to one side or the other, for a second player to shoot.

Free kicks between the 'D' and the corner of the penalty area. As the position of the kick moves to the side of the 'D', so the direct threat on goal decreases and the vital space to seal off increases. That space is about 32 yards by 12 yards (the white area, Diagram 6).

Diagram 6 shows that there are only three players in the wall since the kick is near to the corner of the penalty area. The kick is threatened by one player, X_9, from the inside. This is important because if the angle of the kick is changed, it is more dangerous on the inside than the outside.

X_3 is positioned to meet the threat to the outside of the wall. As it is the left full-back's normal defensive position, he should be the best player in the team to defend that space. X_4 is positioned in line between the ball and a point just inside the far post.

X_5 is positioned outside the far post to deal with high crosses. It is important that this player is a good header of the ball. The position is usually best occupied by the centre-half.

Free kicks down the side of the penalty area. As the position of the ball is moved down the side of the penalty area, still more space has to be sealed off. In Diagram 7, X_3 still defends the space on the outside of the wall and X_9 threatens the kick from a position square on the inside. The most critical position of all, however, is that of X_4 who is defending the space in the area of the near post. The threat to the near post, particularly from an inswing kick, is great from all flank free kicks in positions just outside the penalty area. The threat remains from those taken even farther out.

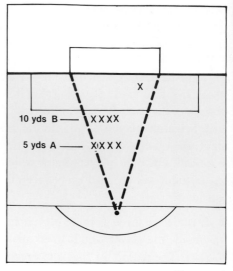

Diagram 4

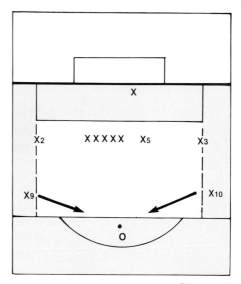

Diagram 5

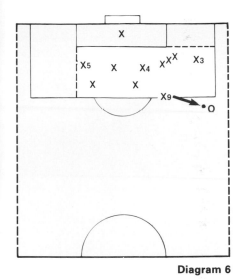

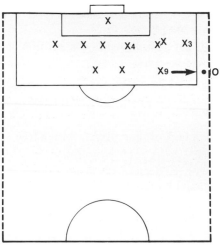

Diagram 6   **Diagram 7**

Other players will almost certainly have to adjust their positions slightly in accordance with the positions adopted by opponents. The player defending the near post, however, must not compromise his position.

Indirect free kicks inside the penalty area

Indirect free kicks inside the penalty area are not a frequent occurrence. This is not a reason, however, for any lack of preparation and organisation.

It is important to appreciate that the direct shot is unlikely, unless the kicker blasts the ball hoping for a ricochet into the goal. It is most likely that the angle of the ball will be changed and that the shot will come on the second touch – interpassing movements will certainly not be in the minds of the attacking players.

If the ball is in a good shooting position, which will be the case on most occasions, the defence should do two things:

- Cover as much of the goal as possible with a defensive wall. It could be, because of the ten-yard law, that the wall will have to position on the goal-line, with all eleven players between the posts. If this is the case, the goalkeeper should position in the centre of the wall.
- Once the kick is taken, and before the second touch is made, the wall should converge on the ball. This gives the best chance of smothering the shot and also gives an outside chance of catching opposing players off-side.

ORGANISATION FOR PRACTICE

Practising set plays is time consuming and involves little physical movement. Because of this, the players will get cold more easily than in a normal coaching session and may, if special care is not taken, become bored. It is essential that neither of these two things should happen as the players must apply maximum concentration to their task.

Coaches should refrain from practising set plays in bad weather: to do so is counter-productive. Even on a mild day it is important that players should be comfortable and, if necessary, they should wear track suits and sweaters. One must be cautious, however, of taking the line of least resistance by working everything out with the players using a blackboard. It cannot be done. There is no substitute for practice.

Practice in defending against free kicks around the penalty area takes place in six phases.

1a. Organisation of the whole defence against free kicks inside the 'D' without opposition.

1b. Defending against free kicks in the 'D' with a full attack of nine players being given a free choice in selecting their positions.

1c. After the necessary points and adjustments have been made a competition of five to ten free kicks, from inside the 'D', should be taken.

2a. Organisation of the whole defence against free kicks in the area from the edge of the 'D' to the corner of the penalty area, on the right-hand side, without opposition.

2b. Defending in the above area against a full attack of nine players with a free choice of selecting their positions.

2c. After the necessary points and adjustments have been made a competition of five or ten free kicks, inside the above area, should be taken.

3. As in Phase 2 but on the left-hand side.

4a. Organisation of the whole defence against free kicks in the area to the side of the penalty area, on the right-hand side, without opposition.

4b. Defending in the above area against a full attack of nine players with a free choice of selecting their positions.

4c. After the necessary points and adjustments have been made a competition of five or ten free kicks, inside the above area, should be taken.

5. As in Phase 4 but on the left-hand side.

6. A game is played in one half of the field. The coach blows his whistle at frequent intervals and places a ball in the position from which a free kick must be taken. Inside a short space of time, the coach should ensure that a large number of free kicks are taken from a wide variety of positions, including positions inside the penalty area for indirect free kicks.

POINTS FOR THE COACH TO OBSERVE

1. Observe that an outplayer always sets the wall in position.
2. Observe that the correct number of players are placed in the wall and that they:
   (i) Prevent the bent shot round the outside of the wall.
   (ii) Are sized correctly – tallest on the outside, shortest on the inside.
   (iii) Protect themselves correctly.
3. Observe the position of the goalkeeper in relation to the wall.
4. Observe that the kick is always threatened from the inside position.
5. Observe that the players seal off the vital spaces.
6. Observe that the players outside the wall know when to adjust their position to mark opponents and when to retain their position in space.
7. Observe that the players know how to defend against indirect free kicks in the penalty area.

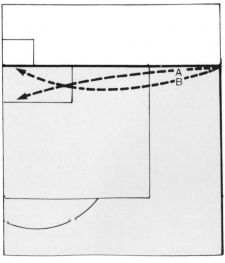

CORNER KICKS

Defending at corner kicks involves exactly the same principles which apply at free kicks.

It is advisable to detail a player to threaten the kick from a distance of 10 yards. There are two reasons for this:

To disturb the kicker. The position which the defending player adopts will depend on whether the attacking player takes an inswing or an outswing kick. If the kick is an outswinger, then he will position near to the goal-line in position A, Diagram 8. If the kick is an inswinger, he will position further out from the goal-line in position B.

Diagram 8

The technique of threatening the kick is to position a yard inside the anticipated line of flight and move into the line as the kicker is approaching the ball. The late movement of the defending player may cause the kicker to look at the defender instead of the ball, or change his mind about the line of the kick. If the kicker does either of the above, it will adversely affect his technique.

The opponents may decide to play the ball short. Should this happen, the defending player is in a position to try to prevent the opposition moving nearer to the goal. He is also in a position to delay the cross into the goal-mouth. It should, however, be understood that if the opposition does take a short corner, a two-v-one situation in the attackers' favour is not satisfactory from the defensive point of view.

The position of the goalkeeper

The position of the goalkeeper is critical. The major threat to the goal from corners is caused by the inswing kick directed towards the front half of the goal. Attacking teams will not only use the inswing technique frequently, but they will also support that play by placing several players in the area of the near post, one or more of whom are likely to be on the goal-line.

Should the goalkeeper position himself at the far post, he places himself at a severe disadvantage in dealing with the inswing kick to the near post. Indeed, his route across goal may be blocked by a mass of defenders and attackers. The best position for the goalkeeper, therefore, to deal with the major threat to his goal is half way across the goal.

The position of the goalkeeper's feet is also important. He should be in a sideways position so that he has the best view of all the movement in the penalty area at the same time as being able to observe the kicker. This means that the goalkeeper's feet will be along the goal-line, rather than across the goal-line.

2 Threatening the outswing corner kick
2a No 10 moves into the line just before the kick is taken.

2b Into line – a yard or so from the goal-line as the ball leaves the kicker.

3 Threatening the inswing corner kick

3a No 10 is in line as the kick is taken some two or three yards from the goal-line.

3b The kicker has pulled the ball (top of the picture) inside the challenging player.

3c Both players watch the ball go harmlessly behind the goal.

The position of the players on the posts

The near post. The player on the near post (the post nearest to the kicker) should be a yard off the goal-line and at least one yard in front of the post (Diagram 9). He should be more concerned about the space in front of him than the space behind. Indeed, if he goes back into the goal he is likely to add to the difficulties of the goalkeeper. He must be prepared to seal off the space near to the goal-line and in front of the near post.

Should the goalkeeper come out from goal to take a high cross, then he should tuck in, on the goal-line, inside the post to defend the goal. He will certainly have time to achieve that objective.

The far post. Most goalkeepers feel more comfortable, if they position half way across their goal, if the player defending the far post is in a position along the goal-line, inside the far post (Diagram 10). This is perfectly satisfactory as it

4 The foot position of the goalkeeper along the goal-line

The foot position of the goalkeeper is along the goal-line, not across it. The goalkeeper therefore has a good field of vision for the whole penalty area. Note also the position of the full-back inside the far post.

Diagram 9

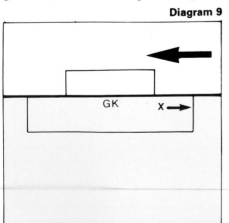

Diagram 10

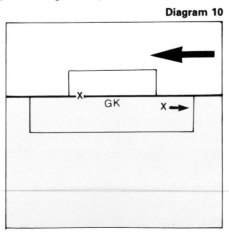

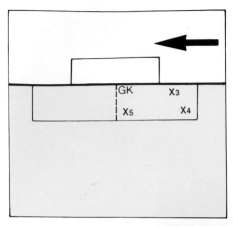

Diagram 11

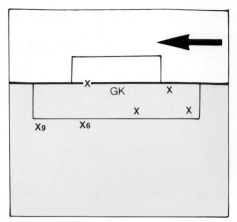

Diagram 12

should be remembered that it is unwise to force something upon the goalkeeper which makes him feel less comfortable. The player at the far post should position along the goal-line, not across the goal-line, in order to achieve the best position of observation.

Defending the near-post area

The player on the near post cannot defend the near-post area alone. The area must be reinforced by two further players who possess two particular qualities: the ability and determination to attack the ball and be first to the ball; and the ability to head the ball well.

Diagram 11 shows the positions of the two players in question, X_5 and X_4. X_4 should position a couple of yards inside the six-yard area. His concern must be with the space in front of him and the space between himself and X_3. The foot position of X_4 is very important and should be that of a standing sprint start. This will enable him to move quickly into the space in front of him. X_5 will be a yard inside the six-yard area and in the front half of the goal. His foot position must also enable him to move quickly to attack the ball in front of him.

Defending the far-post area

Whilst the near-post area is the most vulnerable, it must not be assumed that goals cannot, or will not, be scored in the area of the far post.

In Diagram 12, X_6 is positioned in the back half of the goal and a yard outside the six-yard area. Likewise, X_9 is positioned at the back of the six-yard area and a yard outside the area. Both X_6 and X_9 are in positions to make aerial challenges for the ball in the far-post area. Both of them must position in a manner which gives then the chance to observe movements in the back half of the penalty area.

Defending the area between the six-yard and the eighteen-yard lines

As the ball goes out from the goal area, so the danger becomes less. There is the possibility, however, that the ball may be played directly into the area between the six-yard line and the eighteen-yard line, or that the ball may be partially cleared into that area. The final three players should, therefore, be deployed in that area (Diagram 13).

X_7, X_8, and X_{10} are positioned in line with the penalty spot. These are rough guidelines as the positions of opponents may cause one or more of them to adjust their positions. Their main task is to prevent a strike at goal from the edge of the penalty area.

X_{10}, however, has an additional task: he must watch the situation in the area of the kicker. If the opposition introduces a second attacker into that area, thereby creating a two-v-one situation for a short corner, then X_{10} must move out to the

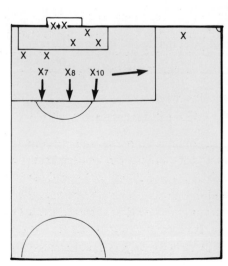

Diagram 13

corner to equalise the numbers. Should that happen, then X_7 and X_8 must adjust their positions.

Once the ball has been cleared by the defence, the whole defence should move up and out of the penalty area as quickly as possible in order to support the ball and play as many opponents as possible off-side.

ORGANISATION FOR PRACTICE

Practice in defending at corners takes place in three phases:

1. All the players should be placed in position, and the detail of their task explained and practised, without opposition. This should be done for both right- and left-hand corner kicks. Once the players feel comfortable in performing their tasks as a team, opposition can be brought in.
2. Practice should take place from the right-hand side. Nine attacking players should be introduced into the practice and given freedom to position where they wish. The kicker, however, should be instructed to serve a particular type of ball (inswing, outswing, drive, near post, far post). Later, the kicker should be encouraged to vary the service as much as possible. The phase should end with a competition of five or ten corner kicks.
3. As in Phase 2, but from the left-hand side.

POINTS FOR THE COACH TO OBSERVE

1. Observe the technique of the player threatening the kick.
2. Observe the position of the goalkeeper.
3. Observe the position of the players in the near-post area, and how they attack the ball.
4. Observe the position of the players in the far-post area, and how they deal with balls played into their area.
5. Observe the position of the players between the six-yard line and the eighteen-yard line, and how they deal with balls played directly into that area and balls partially cleared into that area.
6. Observe the reaction and adjustments of the players to a short corner.
7. Observe how quickly the players move out of the penalty area once the ball is cleared.

THROWS

Defensive problems are always likely to accrue if attacking players are left unmarked. In this respect, the situation at a throw-in is no different from any other defensive situation. Why then should there be such defensive problems at throws? There are two basic reasons:

- Players do not seem to be aware of how many goals are scored from throws.
- Players frequently lose their concentration at throws.

The throw-in occurs more frequently than any other type of set play. For the most part, efficient defending at throws involves only the implementation of the principles of defending. Special tactical arrangements, as in the case with corners and free kicks near to the penalty area, are neither necessary nor possible. The exception is the long throw in the attacking third of the field. Even the fact that players cannot be off-side from a throw-in is not a source of major problems.

Defending players should concentrate on three things:

- Move into marking positions while the ball is being retrieved.

■ Mark tight in the area of the ball, including the thrower.
■ Place the player receiving the ball under severe pressure, thus making either control or one-touch play difficult.

Defending from throws should be considerably easier than defending in normal fluid play as defenders are afforded much more time in which to make their decisions. Provided defenders concentrate, that time is invaluable.

Long throws in the attacking third of the field

This is one type of throw which does merit special tactical consideration. Many teams now have at least one player who is technically capable of throwing a ball from a position on the touch-line level with the penalty area to pitch well into the six-yard area. The one thing long throwers do not have on their side is the element of surprise – everyone can see when a long throw is coming.

The defensive arrangement should involve four considerations:

■ Marking from behind the player receiving the throw.
■ Marking the space in front of the player receiving the throw.
■ The goalkeeper positioning in the front half of the goal.
■ Sealing off as much space as possible inside the penalty area.

In Diagram 14, the possible arrangement of the defending players is shown.

ORGANISATION FOR PRACTICE

The short throw. Practice for all throws, except the long throw in the attacking third of the field, should take place in both small-sided games and eleven-a-side games. Players should be encouraged to be alert, to concentrate, and to perform quickly their defensive duties once a throw-in has been conceded.

The organisation of the practice should make it possible for throws to be taken quickly. Balls should be placed a couple of yards from the touch-lines at five- or ten-yard intervals. The attacking players should pick up the nearest ball to the point where the ball went out of play, and be allowed to take the throw from that point.

Within that organisation, the game should proceed normally, with no attempt to produce a glut of throws. The coach may rest assured there will be enough throws, in the normal course of play, to provide adequate practice.

Diagram 14

Diagram 15

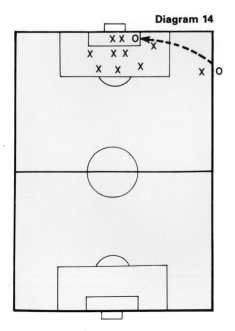
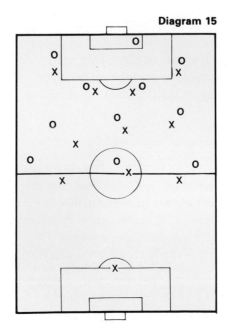

The long throw. The long throw in the attacking third of the field should be organised in much the same way as corners:

1. Players should be positioned to deal with the long throw from the right-hand side without opposition. Once the necessary points and adjustments have been made, opponents should be brought into the practice.

2. Eight attacking players should be brought into the practice and given freedom to position where they wish. The phase should end with a competition of five or ten throws. The thrower should now be allowed to vary the service if he wishes.

3. As in Phase 2, but from the left-hand side.

POINTS FOR THE COACH TO OBSERVE

1. Observe that the organisation for practice is correct, and that there is a sufficient number of balls down each touch-line.

2. Observe that the defending players move into marking positions while the ball is being retrieved and retain their concentration.

3. Observe that the marking is tight in the area of the ball, including that of the thrower.

4. Observe that the player receiving the ball is put under severe pressure.

5. Observe when a long throw is taken:
   (i) The player receiving the ball is marked from behind, and that a defending player also occupies the space in front of the receiving player.
   (ii) The goalkeeper positions in the front half of the goal.
   (iii) As much space as possible, inside the penalty area, is sealed off.

GOAL-KICKS

Defending from a goal-kick is the one situation in which the defending team should be able to guarantee that all eleven defending players are on the goal side of the ball. It should also be possible to guarantee that every opposing player is correctly marked. As the ball must travel at least 12 yards before a second player can play the ball, a challenging player can be present wherever the ball is played. These factors should add up to a strong possibility of winning back the ball in the opponent's half of the field.

Many goalkeepers happily assist the defender to win back the ball by aimlessly kicking the ball long to the half-way line. This only serves to make the task of the defending players a good deal easier than it should be. Some teams even have an outplayer taking goal-kicks. This should assist the opposition even further as the kicker, having played the ball, is effectively out of the game until he can move outside the penalty area to take up a position of advantage.

In Diagram 15, the O goalkeeper is taking a goal-kick. The X team has ensured that every O player is marked as none is in a position to receive the ball without being challenged. Some coaches will not like the arrangement of the X players in Diagram 15 because the X team does not have an extra player at the back; but that really would be ultra cautious and negative thinking.

Efficient defending from goal-kicks is not unlike defending from throws. It requires the implementation of three elements:

■ Players should position while the ball is being retrieved.
■ Players should concentrate hard while waiting for the kick to be taken. The delay is likely to be longer in the taking of goal-kicks than it is in the case with throws, so beware of positioning correctly and then losing concentration.
■ Ensure that the player receiving the ball is put under maximum pressure.

ORGANISATION FOR PRACTICE

It is best for the practice to take place in a full eleven-a-side game. If concentrated practice is required, the coach should stipulate that the team winning the ball from the goal-kick should make three consecutive passes and then return the ball for a further goal-kick. It should be appreciated, however, that the fundamental problem is lack of concentration. Improvement in this quality is best achieved in the normal ebb and flow of a practice game.

POINTS FOR THE COACH TO REMEMBER IN ALL SET PLAYS

Efficient defending requires:

1. Detailed planning and organisation.
2. Rehearsal to co-ordinate and integrate the performance of the individual with that of the team.
3. Mental concentration.
4. Discipline.
5. Application.

SET PLAYS (2)
ATTACKING

Between 40 and 50 per cent of goals are scored from set plays; more important, vital matches are often decided by a goal from a free kick, a corner or a throw-in. The reasons for this are perfectly understandable and are basically threefold:

■ In vital matches the marking is usually tighter than normal and less time and space is therefore available for attacking players to play the ball.

■ When there is less time and space it is also more difficult to get players forward into advanced attacking positions.

■ In matches with tight marking there are usually more fouls, and therefore more free kicks.

There are five basic advantages in attacking at set plays as opposed to attacking in the normal course of fluid play

■ The kick, or throw, is always made with a ball which is dead still. Control problems are therefore eliminated.

■ The opponents should be ten yards away from the ball, except at a throw-in. There is therefore no pressure on the kicker.

■ Large numbers of attackers, eight or nine is not uncommon, can move forward into advanced attacking positions without incurring risk.

■ Players can be placed in pre-planned attacking positions to maximise the use of individual abilities.

■ Rehearsal can produce high levels of timing and co-ordinated movement.

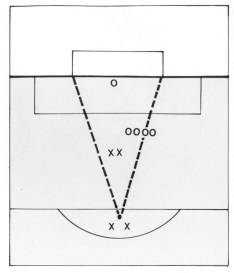

Diagram 1

These five factors conspire to make defending at set plays extremely difficult. Defending at set plays, however, can be made even more difficult if attackers concentrate on playing the percentages. They should aim to provide the service, and the arrangement of players, which will produce the best results on most occasions.

The point should be made strongly that some coaches are obsessed with variety at set plays. Variety for its own sake has nothing to commend it. For the most part, these men succeed only in varying the play from something which succeeds to something which fails. The best variety is variety on a theme which is known to pay high dividends and which will keep the opposition guessing.

The one precept of attacking at set plays which should be lodged in the minds of coaches and players is this: *The more direct and simple the play, the more likely it is to succeed*.

DIRECT FREE KICKS

Direct free kicks around the penalty area divide into two categories: when there is a good chance of scoring with a direct shot; and when there is a poor chance of scoring with a direct shot. If there is a good chance of scoring with a direct shot, then all other considerations should be eliminated. The best chances arise from free kicks inside the 'D'.

Free kicks in the 'D'

If a free kick is awarded in the 'D', it is a certainty that the defending team will erect a wall to block part of the goal. The purpose of the wall is to protect part of the goal from a driven shot.

The goalkeeper will usually position slightly off centre of his goal so that he can see the ball and protect his goal from a chip over the defensive wall, or a driven shot into the part of the goal not protected by the defensive wall. Attacking tactics, therefore, should be based on obscuring the goalkeeper's view of the ball in order to slow down his reactions to any shot – driven or chipped.

2 Approaching the ball at different angles

2a Moving towards the ball at different angles.

2b The first player crossing in front of the ball, and the second player in close behind to use the first player as a screen.

2c The shot is a chip over the attacker's wall.

Obscuring the goalkeeper's view. This tactic is easily achieved by using two attackers to complete the defensive wall, thereby blocking the whole of the goal. In Diagram 1, the two X players are used to complete the defensive wall. It is important to note that they are positioned less than ten yards from the ball. This is for two reasons:

- If they were ten yards away from the ball and level with the defensive players they would be off-side.
- By moving to a position six or seven yards from the ball, they block more of the goal than they would at nine yards.

They could, of course, position one or two yards from the ball. This would have advantages in terms of blocking the goal and the goalkeeper's view. However, the players would be too far away from the goal to have a reasonable chance of attacking the goal, after the shot, to score from rebounds from the goal structure or the goalkeeper.

Six or seven yards distant from the ball, therefore, achieves the dual objectives of:

- Blocking the goalkeeper's view.
- Attacking the goal for rebounds.

It is important that the two attackers should function in the following manner:

- They should stand close together with their feet also close together. If this position is not adopted the goalkeeper will gain a sight of the ball.
- They should break after the ball has been kicked. It is essential to keep watching the ball until the ball has been kicked. If they break early then the goalkeeper will gain a sight of the ball.
- When they break, the outside player should spin to his right and the inside player should spin to his left. Both players should converge on the goal and attack the ball if there is a rebound.

Taking the kick. Two players should position to take the kick. There are four basic reasons for this:

- The opposition will be in doubt as to which player is going to strike the ball.
- The two players approach the ball at speed from different angles, so making different types of kick possible. It is even better if one of the players is right footed and the other left footed.
- By approaching the ball at different angles it makes decoy play very much easier.
- The player not striking the ball can act as a screen.

The two players will have decided from their assessment of the situation which type of kick has the best chance of scoring, and which one of them is best equipped to take the kick. The decision may be made that one player will make his run, slightly earlier than the other, to act as a decoy for the second player to strike the ball. If this is the case, then the player running as a decoy should run slightly in front of the ball, rather than over the ball, in order to act as a screen for the player striking the ball.

1 Obscuring the goalkeeper's view of the ball

The two attacking players in the dark shirts are six or seven yards from the ball and are obscuring the goalkeeper's view of the ball.

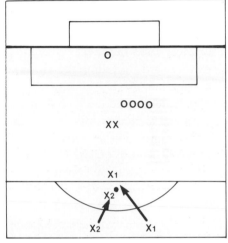

Diagram 2a

Diagram 2b

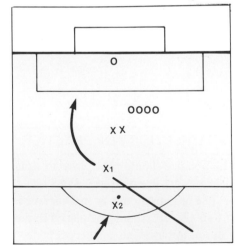

In Diagram 2a, X_1 is positioned between the ball and the goal as X_2 enters his kicking stride. As the ball is propelled forward, X_1 should be outside the line of the goal but bending his run to attack the goal for possible rebounds (Diagram 2b).

X_1 and X_2 should practise synchronising their runs. It is also important that a clear understanding between the two players involved in the kick and the two players completing the wall is established. This understanding should be based on the following:

(i) The attacking players in the wall will stand firm for the player making the first run in order to block the goalkeeper's view of the kick. This does not necessarily mean that the player making the first run will not play the ball. It does mean that he will not attempt to drive the ball through his own wall.

(ii) The attacking players in the wall will always break for the second player taking the kick, but will continue to watch the ball as they turn to attack the goal for rebounds.

It is probable that defending teams will withdraw all eleven players to defend against free kicks in the 'D'. Attacking teams can afford, therefore, to send nine players forward, including the kicker. Attacking players should position close to each defending player who is marking space to the side of the wall. Defenders do not like being treated in this way and they usually defend less well under such physical and mental pressure.

In Diagram 3, all the O players to the side of the wall, are marked by the attacking X players. O_7 and O_8 are not marked as they are positioned to threaten the kick. X_4 is positioned behind the two X players involved in the kick and will move forward into the 'D', as the kick is taken, to deal with any ball which is cleared to the edge of the penalty area. All the other X players, including the kicker, should concentrate on attacking the six-yard area after the kick is taken.

3 Attacking the six-yard area after the kick is taken

3a Approach to take the kick.

3b The kick is taken by the second player to the ball and the ball is driven through the attacker's wall.

3c Several attackers have converged on the goal, hoping for a rebound.

3a

3b

3c

ORGANISATION FOR PRACTICE

The practice should take place on a pitch using a penalty area. The precise markings are essential to the practice. There are three phases to the practice:

1. The organisation is as in Diagram 1. The goalkeeper, plus the defensive wall of four players, should be placed in position. Two attacking players should position to block the goalkeeper's view of the ball and two further attacking players should position to take the kick.

The players should practise four basic shots:

- Chip shot over the defensive wall.
- Chip shot over the attackers' wall.
- Swerve shot round the outside of the attackers' wall.
- Drive through the attackers' wall.

Once the attacking players have synchronised their movements and combined their understanding, the practice should be expanded.

2. The organisation is as in Diagram 3. The remainder of the defence is brought

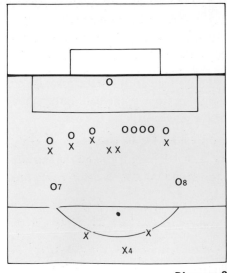

Diagram 3

into the practice and the players are allowed to position where they please. Five further attackers are introduced. Four are deployed in occupying defenders to the side of the wall and one is positioned just outside the 'D'. Practice at each of the four types of shot taken in the previous phase then takes place.

3. Once the attacking players are comfortable in their performance, a competition of five or ten shots should be held from varying positions inside the 'D'.

4 Swerving the ball round the attacker's wall

4a Into the kicking stride – the ball is kicked with the outside of the right foot.

4b The ball is swerved round the outside of the attacker's wall.

4c The goalkeeper is well beaten.

POINTS FOR THE COACH TO OBSERVE

1. The two attacking players completing the defensive wall should do the following:
    (i) Position less than ten yards from the ball.
    (ii) Block the goalkeeper's view of the ball.
    (iii) Attack the goal for rebounds after the kick has been taken.
2. The two players involved in the kick should do the following:
    (i) Approach the ball from different angles.
    (ii) Produce effective decoy movements.
    (iii) Produce an effective screen if the second player is striking the ball.
    (iv) Make a direct shot at goal.
3. The two attacking players in the wall should co-ordinate with the two players involved with the taking of the kick.
4. The attacking players should mark the defending players marking space to the side of the wall. They should attack the six-yard area once the kick is taken.
5. One attacking player should remain in the 'D' to deal with a ball which is partially cleared.
6. Observe the percentage success of the various types of shots.

Free kicks from the side of the penalty area

The wider the angle around the penalty area from which a free kick is taken, the more important it is to observe two fundamental principles:

■ Play the ball to the back of the defence.
■ Challenge the free defending players.

On most occasions, the area to aim for will be the area of the near post. The chances of success will be increased if the ball is hit with inswerve, i.e. with the ball spinning and swerving in the direction of the goal.

The difficulty for defending players who are trying to clear a ball which is played behind them, and is swerving and spinning away from them, is immense. The task for attacking players is made easier by the fact that if they strike with the spin the ball is likely to go downwards.

Analysis reveals that the chance of success at the near post from such a kick is 90 per cent better than attacking the far post. The evidence is irrefutable.

In Diagram 4, X is positioned for a free kick just outside the corner of the penalty area. From such a position, a defending team would normally erect a wall with two, or possibly three, players in it and the goalkeeper would position in the back half of the goal. The positions of O_3 to O_{10} are realistic.

The most vulnerable space in these circumstances is in the area of the near post. There is nothing the defence can do to stop the ball being played into that area. Should the defence position a player in line with the ball and the front half of the goal, the ball can still be played round or over the player. Given an accurate kick, therefore, the situation is dangerous. The kick from the right is best taken by a left-footed player, and the kick from the left by a right-footed player.

If the attackers challenge the defending players level with the wall (O_4, O_5, O_6, and O_7 in Diagram 4), and try to create a numerical advantage on the inside of the wall (Diagram 5), then the situation becomes even more dangerous. Given the accuracy of the kick, and the determination of the X players to be first to the ball, the situation for the O players becomes perilous. The X players have all to gain and the O players have all to lose.

Sometimes defenders do not defend the space on the outside of the wall, the space occupied by O_3 in Diagram 5. It is for that possible eventuality that two players should position to take the kick. If the space outside the wall is not defended, then one of the X players should attack the space and receive the ball at the back of the defence, as has happened in Diagram 6. X_2's main concern now, before he delivers the ball, is to check on the position of the goalkeeper; only disaster should now await the O team.

The attacking team must not make the mistake of sending too many players in to attack the back of the defence. Two attacking players should be positioned on the edge of the penalty area (Diagram 7) to deal with partial clearances. They will also be in a good position to counter any possible threat of a quick breakaway.

It can be seen that there are four key factors which contribute to successful free kicks from wide angles around the penalty area:

- Understanding in percentage terms what will pay the highest dividends.
- Simplicity and directness of concept.
- Accuracy of the kick.
- Determination by the attacking players to challenge opponents in the area inside the wall and to be first to the ball.

One further point is well worth making. A scatter-graph of free kicks awarded in the attacking third of the field reveals that a very high percentage are awarded in flank positions – the shaded areas in Diagram 8. It is sensible, therefore, to devote a proportionate amount of practice time to the types of free kick which one knows, in percentage terms, will occur.

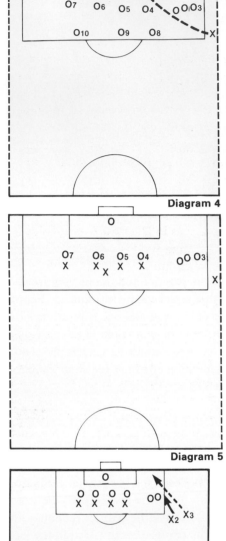

Diagram 4

Diagram 5

Diagram 6

5 A left-footed free kick from the right-hand side of the penalty area

5a The first player makes his movement to run past the ball and attack the space on the outside of the defender's wall.

5b No 11 uses the player as a screen.

5c A left-footed kick, hit with spin and swerve to the area of the near post.

5a

5b

5c

ORGANISATION FOR PRACTICE

The practice must take place on a pitch in the attacking third of the field. There are six phases to the practice:

1. The defenders position as in Diagram 4 and X practises hitting the target area in the front half of the goal. The assumption is that X will only need a few kicks to establish his accuracy and move on to the next phase. If this is not so, then X should practise on his own.

2. Five attacking players are brought in to challenge the defending players on the inside of the wall and a second X player is positioned in the area of the ball, as in Diagram 5. The position of O_3 must be varied to provide practice in attacking the space outside the wall in addition to attacking the space in the front half of the goal.

3. Once the players are comfortable, and are achieving success in the previous phase, the practice should be expanded to include the remainder of the O and X players, as in Diagram 7. A competition should take place, involving five or ten kicks, from various positions on the corner of the penalty area and out towards the touch-line.

4, 5, 6. The three previous phases are repeated, but from the left-hand side of the penalty area.

POINTS FOR THE COACH TO OBSERVE

1. Observe the accuracy of the kick into the front half of the goal.
2. Observe the ability of the two attackers on the ball to exploit space to the outside of the wall.
3. Observe the ability of the attackers to challenge defenders inside the wall, get close to their opponents, and then check away to be first to the ball.
4. Observe the ability and determination of the attacking players to attack the ball.
5. Observe the percentage success of the attacking players.

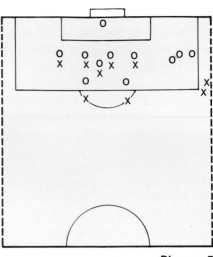

Diagram 7

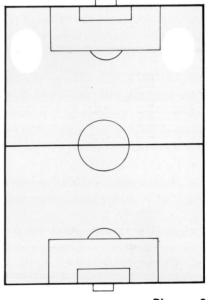

Diagram 8

INDIRECT FREE KICKS

There are two areas of the field in which special consideration needs to be given to indirect free kicks. These areas are in the 'D' and inside the penalty area. Consideration should also be given to free kicks taken outside the attacking third of the field.

Free kicks inside the 'D'

All the principles discussed earlier in this chapter apply, the one difference being that the direct shot must be made on the second touch by a second player. A slight adjustment in the positioning of the attacking wall is the main requirement.

6 Challenging the free defending players on the inside of the wall

Maximum pressure is exerted by the dark-shirted players. There is certainly no free defending player in the six-yard area.

7 Taking indirect free kicks

7a Shaun Brooks, on the ball, prepares to take the kick.

7b Brooks plays the ball with his toe end, opening up an angle for Steve MacKenzie, No 7, to shoot for goal.

In Diagram 9, X_1 will make a short pass for X_2 to shoot. X_3 and X_4, a couple of yards away from the ball, are blocking the goalkeeper's view. They must break as late as possible, leaving the goalkeeper as little time as possible to see the ball.

Whether the ball is played slightly to the right, or to the left, on the first touch will depend very much on how X_1 and X_2 see the situation and which angle to goal they wish to widen. For example, if X_2 plays the ball a yard to the left, it will open up an angle to attack the area of goal to the goalkeeper's left. That could be particularly dangerous if X_1 swerved the ball away from the goalkeeper with his left foot.

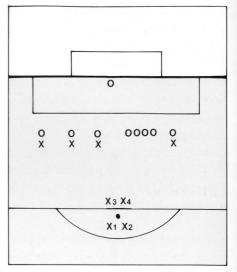

Diagram 9

Free kicks inside the penalty area

These do not occur with any great regularity but a team should be prepared for the situation when it does occur. One can expect all eleven defending players to be withdrawn into the penalty area. If the kick is within ten yards of goal, then the probability is that all eleven will be on the goal-line between the posts. In such circumstances it is also probable that the whole team will advance towards the ball in a block once the ball is in play and before the shot is taken.

There are four important factors to consider:

- If the kick is at a narrow angle then the first touch should widen the angle. In Diagram 10, X_1 has widened the angle for X_2 to shoot through.
- If the ball is less than ten yards from the goal, as is the case in Diagram 10, then the ball should be played backwards on the first touch to give the second player more time and more space for the shot.
- It is important to observe the position of the goalkeeper and direct the shot over the heads of defenders in the area where the goalkeeper is not positioned.
- The players taking the kick should try hard to remain calm in a situation which often lends itself to utter confusion.

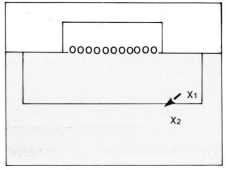

Diagram 10

ORGANISATION FOR PRACTICE

The practice should take place in the penalty area on a pitch and should, ideally, form part of a concentrated session on direct and indirect free kicks.

POINTS FOR THE COACH TO OBSERVE

1. The two players in the attackers' wall should adjust their position so that they are a couple of yards from the ball. They should break as late as possible.
2. The players taking the kick should assess the situation and attack the most vulnerable area of the goal, widening the angle of the kick if necessary.
3. If the kick is less than ten yards from the goal, they should give themselves more time and space by playing the ball backwards for the shot.
4. Observe the accuracy of the execution.
5. The players involved in the kick should remain calm.

Free kicks outside the attacking third of the field

When free kicks are awarded in positions outside the attacking third of the field, and more especially in the middle third of the field, a premium should be set on taking the kicks quickly. The principal reason for this is to take advantage of any breakdown in concentration by the defending players. Attackers should be mindful of two things:

- Two players should move to the ball quickly in order to bring about a quick free kick and a change in the direction of play.
- Players in advance of the ball should get into position either behind, or on the goal side, of their immediate opponent.

There is no need for moves to be worked out like a game of chess. A clear understanding of the percentages, the importance of capitalising on opponents who lose their concentration, and simplicity and directness of concept are the stuff of which success is made.

ORGANISATION FOR PRACTICE

The practice should take place in an eleven-a-side game in the middle or the defending thirds of the field. The coach should control the practice by whistle, stopping the game frequently to award free kicks. He should also indicate verbally which team has been awarded the kick. It is not wise, however, to keep such a practice going for too long. Ten to fifteen minutes is quite sufficient for one session.

POINTS FOR THE COACH TO OBSERVE

1. The players near to the ball should move quickly to make possible a quick short free kick. Observe that the angle of the ball is changed.
2. Players in advance of the ball should try to get behind their opponents and goal-side of their opponents.
3. The whole play should be characterised by simplicity, forward thinking, forward movement and forward passing.

CORNER KICKS

Corner kicks are, without question, a major source of goals. The type of kick which produces most of these goals is the inswing aimed at the front half of the goal.

Inswing corner kicks

It is important that attacking players should be selected carefully for the various roles which are required. Chief amongst these is the kicker himself. The kicker must be able to guarantee 80 per cent accuracy in his service. His task is to send the ball into the six-yard area between head and bar height, ideally swinging the ball into the front half of the goal. In Diagram 11, he will be aiming for area A from the left-hand side of the field and area B from the right. Most players could achieve that objective in two or three kicks out of ten. The difference between that, and eight out of ten, is practice.

The team should be organised to support the kick. The first phase of that organisation must be in the six-yard area. Four players are needed to provide for all eventualities and their precise positions and functions are important.

In Diagram 12, X_1 is positioned at the near post. His task is to move out towards the ball and to flick it on across the goal if it is low in flight. He also has an important function in medium and short corners which will be discussed later in this chapter.

X_2 is positioned near to the goal-line inside the near post. As the kick is taken he should move out towards the edge of the six-yard area. From that position he can attack any ball below bar height entering the area. The movement, therefore, of X_2 is out towards the six-yard line, and then possibly back in again to attack the ball. Some may wonder why he should not position on the edge of the six-yard area in the first place. There are two basic reasons:

- The goalkeeper's view is obstructed both by X_2 and the player who will be marking him.
- X_2 is more likely to achieve space by moving out and then in towards goal.

Diagram 11

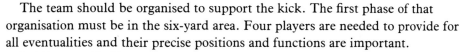

Diagram 12

8 The inswinging corner kick

8a Note the placement of the ball and also the fact that a corner flag is in position. This is a detail of practice which is often ignored. A different technique becomes possible if the corner flag is not in position.

8b A left-footed inswing kick to the area of the near post.

227

X_2 must, of course, be tall and a good header of the ball. It will not always be advantageous for him to head the ball for goal. Sometimes his best ploy will be to head across goal to X_3 or X_4.

The task of X_3 is similar to that of X_2 but his starting position is in the back half of the goal. His movement out from goal towards the edge of the six-yard area must allow him to watch the ball all the time. If the ball is flicked on, or deflected in any way, it is likely that X_3 or X_4 will be fully employed.

The task of X_4 is to position at the far post and move out backwards, watching the ball from that position. His function is to seize any chance in the area of the far post. He is sure to be kept busy. X_3 and X_4 need not be tall but they must be quick.

All four X players in the six-yard area, especially X_3 and X_4, should be vigilant and ensure that they are not caught off-side when the service is outside the six-yard area or the kick is partially cleared.

The second phase of the organisation to support the kick involves three players.

In Diagram 13, X_5 is positioned to the far side of the penalty area. From that position he will attack the far post from a position just outside the six-yard area. X_6 is positioned near to the edge of the penalty area. From that position he will attack the mid-goal area from a position just outside the six-yard area. X_7 will retain a position on the edge of the penalty area to deal with any ball which rebounds or is partially cleared.

9 The four attacking players inside the six-yard area can be seen performing their functions.
10 Their starting positions.

11 Taking a medium corner kick

11a The ball is played to the attacking player, coming along the goal-line towards the edge of the penalty area.

11b The kicker, No 3, moves to a wide angle to receive the return pass.

11c No 3 now prepares to cross the ball into the six-yard area.

Medium corner kicks

If it is decided to take a medium corner kick, X_1 should move out towards the kicker to receive the ball just inside the penalty area, as shown in Diagram 14. From that position, X_1 can do one of two things:

■ If he is unmarked he can turn and play the ball across goal.
■ If he is marked he can play the ball for X_8 to cross from a wider angle.

When a medium corner is being taken it is important that the players in the six-yard area, and on the edge of the penalty area, delay their movements. The time to make the movement is when the player is actually crossing the ball.

Short corner kicks

The purpose of short corner kicks, like medium corner kicks, is to achieve a more advantageous position for crossing the ball. By taking the short corner, it is possible for the cross to be made from a position nearer to goal and at a wider angle.

Advantage can be taken of the law concerning the position of opponents (ten yards from the ball). This is particularly the case if the attackers have a numerical advantage in the area of the kick. In Diagram 15, X_1 has moved out along the line and is within a yard of the kicker, X_8. O is the defender and is ten yards away. Normally, there is no special advantage to be gained from a short corner unless the attackers have more players in the area of the ball than the defenders.

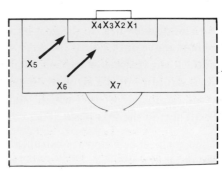

Diagram 13

Experience and analysis have proved that corner kicks to the near post will produce more goals than corner kicks to the far post. Inswing corner kicks will produce more goals than outswing corners. Variety on a theme is far better than variety based on the sole criteria of doing something different. The time to play to the far post, for example, is when defenders have been drawn to the near post, which may be the case from a medium or short corner. This is the logical and commonsense approach to soccer.

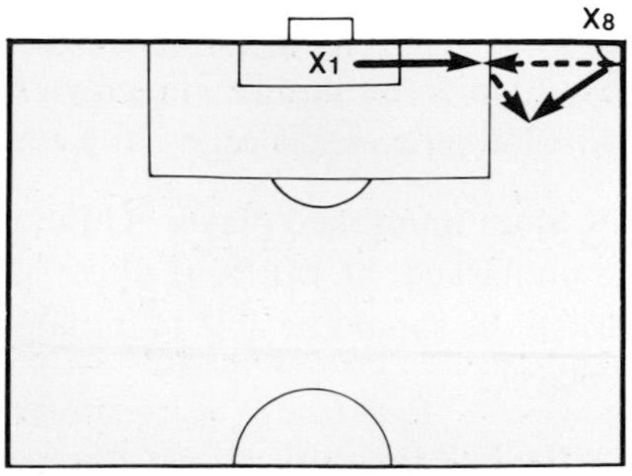

Diagram 14

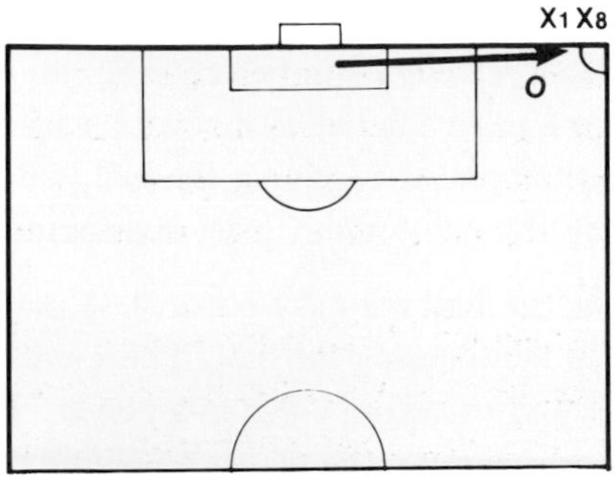

Diagram 15

ORGANISATION FOR PRACTICE

The practice must, of course, take place on a pitch. There are six phases to the practice:

1. Practise the kick with the four attacking players in the six-yard area, as shown in Diagram 12.

2. Expand the practice to include the three players positioned on the edge of the penalty area, as shown in Diagram 13. The players should practise all three types of corner kick and concentration should be upon timing movements in relation to the release of the ball.

3. Once the attacking players feel comfortable the whole defence should be brought into the practice. The defenders should be allowed to position where they please. Each of the three basic plays should be practised with opposition. If necessary, defenders should be conditioned to allow medium and short corners to be practised.

At the end of this phase, a competition of five or ten kicks should be taken.

4, 5, 6. The three previous phases are repeated, but from the left-hand side of the field.

POINTS FOR THE COACH TO OBSERVE

1. Observe the technique and accuracy of the kick.
2. Observe the movements of each of the four attackers in the six-yard area.
3. Observe the timing of the movements of the two players from the edge of the penalty area.
4. Observe the performance of the attacker on the edge of the penalty area.
5. Observe the play from the medium corner kick, especially the situation prior to delivery of the ball into goal. Have the defenders been drawn towards the near post? Where is the most vulnerable area?
6. Observe, similarly, the play from the short corner. Was the decision to take a short corner correct?
7. Observe the percentage success from the various plays.

THROWS

In any game, at any level, one can expect to receive more attacking throws than any other type of set play. That in itself is good enough reason for giving the matter some thought. Players appear to relax their concentration more at throws than in any other situation. The probable reason for this is that throws look deceptively innocuous. Thus, the potential danger from a throw-in is greatly underestimated.

There are six key factors to consider in attacking from a throw-in:

Take the throw quickly. Defending players who lose their concentration are vulnerable and they should be exposed as quickly as possible. The sooner the

12 The six-yard area is heavily populated with both attackers and defenders – the dark shirted players are attacking.

13 A moment of pleasure for the attacking players as practice is rewarded.

throw-in is taken, therefore, the better. This means that the nearest man to the ball should take the throw. The only exception to this is when the team's specialist long thrower is called into action in the attacking third of the field.

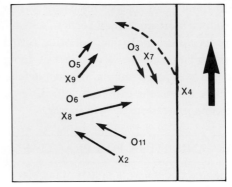

Diagram 16

Throw to an unmarked player. On most occasions, if there is an attacking player who is unmarked, he will be the best player to receive the ball. Since he is unmarked, he should be able to initiate forward movement quicker than any other player.

Throw the ball forward. Soccer is a forward-thinking game and on no occasion should this be better exemplified than at a throw-in. Balls thrown forward past opponents leave defenders on the wrong side of the ball and with the problem of making a recovery run before they can defend effectively. The exception to this, of course, is if the ball is thrown backwards to an unmarked player. However, an unmarked player receiving the ball will think, first and foremost, in terms of playing the ball forward past opponents.

Throw the ball for easy control. A player taking a throw should appreciate that he is in fact passing the ball. There is a difference between throwing a ball *at* a player and throwing a ball *to* a player. The ball should be thrown at a pace and an angle which gives the player receiving the ball as few control problems as possible. The service should also make a defender's task of challenging for the ball as difficult as possible.

If the thrower intends the player to head the ball back to him, the ball should be aimed at chest height. This will enable the player to move easily towards the ball and head the ball through the top half, thus ensuring that the ball is returned to the thrower's feet.

Create sufficient space to make the throw effective. One of the most frequent mistakes which inexperienced players make is to position too close to the thrower. Players should spread out at a throw-in for two basic reasons:

■ To make it difficult for defenders to mark opponents and cover each other.
■ To establish the space for movement and exploitation of space.

In Diagram 16, X_4 is taking the throw. X_7, X_9, X_8, and X_2 have spread out. As X_4 prepares to throw the ball, X_7, marked by O_3, and X_8, marked by O_6, move towards the thrower. The resulting space created by X_7 can be exploited by X_9 and the space created by X_8 can be exploited by X_2.

Try to get the thrower back in the game. The thrower should not consider that his task is finished once he has thrown the ball. He should think in terms of supporting the player in possession of the ball and moving to create a numerical advantage in the area of the ball.

ORGANISATION FOR PRACTICE

The practice should take place initially in a six-a-side game, including two goalkeepers, in an area measuring 60 yards by 40 yards (Diagram 17). Balls should be placed a couple of yards from each touch-line and five or ten yards apart. A normal small-sided game should be played, the only condition being that the player taking the throw should pick up the nearest ball to the point where the ball went out of play.

DEVELOPMENT OF THE PRACTICE

The practice should be developed into a full eleven-a-side game. As in the small-sided game, balls should be placed a couple of yards from each touch-line and the same condition for taking the throw should be adopted.

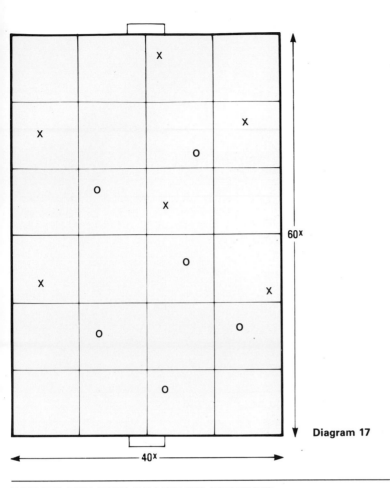

60^x

40^x

Diagram 17

POINTS FOR THE COACH TO OBSERVE

1. The nearest player to the ball should pick up the ball and take the throw as quickly as possible.

2. If there is an unmarked attacking player in the area of the ball, the ball should be thrown to him.

3. The ball should be thrown forward unless there is an unmarked player behind the line of play.

4. The throw should make control and one-touch play easy.

5. The attacking players should position far enough away from the thrower to make it difficult for the defending players to mark opponents and cover each other.

6. Observe the movement of the attacking players at the throw and the exploitation of the space thereby created.

7. The player taking the throw should get back into the game by either supporting the player in possession of the ball, or moving to create a numerical advantage in the area of the ball.

The long throw-in in the attacking third of the field

The long throw is especially dangerous when it is aimed at the area of the near post. In addition to a long, fast, accurate throw of low trajectory from the thrower, there should be a tall player who is a good header of the ball positioned to receive the ball in the area of the near post, and well-organised team support to attack the spaces into which the ball may be played.

In Diagram 18, X_4 throws the ball to X_5 in the near-post area. The starting position of X_5 should be at the near post and he should move from that position as late as possible to meet the ball. X_9 is positioned to attack the space behind X_5 in case the ball is flicked on. All the other X players are positioned to attack spaces inside the penalty area, covering the 180 degrees into which the ball may

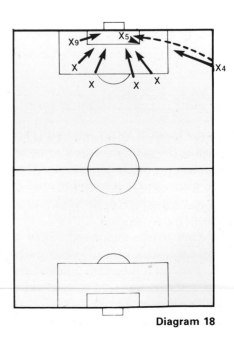

Diagram 18

be played. The timing of their movements is important and they should move as late as possible to attack the space.

It should be understood that without the organised support of the team the long throw is of no advantage. It is the combination of the long throw with the skills of the supporting players which maximises team performance and gives the best chance of success.

ORGANISATION FOR PRACTICE

The practice should take place in the attacking third of the field. It is important to use a pitch so that the distances, angles and spaces are correct. The basic organisation is as shown in Diagram 18. There are four phases in the practice:

1. Seven attackers rehearse the play from a long throw from the right-hand side without opposition. When the necessary adjustments have been made, opponents are brought into the practice.

2. Nine opponents, including the goalkeeper, are allowed to position where they wish in defence of the throw. The thrower should now be allowed to vary his service and occasionally make a short throw. The practice should conclude with a competition of five or ten throws.

3, 4. The two previous phases are repeated from the left-hand side of the field.

POINTS FOR THE COACH TO OBSERVE

1. Observe the quality of the throw. It should not only be accurate but should be fast and of a low trajectory. A throw of high trajectory makes the receiver's task difficult in terms of timing the run to meet the ball and deflecting the ball to his team-mates.

2. Observe that the thrower follows in towards goal after making the throw.

3. Observe the play of the receiver at the near post in respect of:
    (i) Starting position.
    (ii) Movement to meet the ball.
    (iii) Heading the ball down for his team-mates.

4. Observe the play of the support players in respect of:
    (i) Positioning to be able to attack through 180 degrees.
    (ii) Positioning to create space to move into in order to attack the ball.
    (iii) Timing movements to synchronise with the throw, the movement of the players in the near-post area, and the ball headed down in front of goal.

GOAL-KICKS

At many levels of soccer, goal-kicks seem to be regarded as simply a means of restarting the game. In a great many instances, this amounts to giving the opposition the ball in the region of the half-way line. It is ironic that, whilst most teams would accept the need to work hard to create space once possession of the ball has been achieved, they fail to apply that thinking in the easiest situation of all.

It is not an uncommon sight, even at the highest level, to see a goalkeeper taking a goal-kick with all twenty outplayers packed into the middle third of the field. The ball is propelled into that area over a distance, usually in excess of 50 yards, and nothing could be more calculated to make the task easier for the defending players.

The fundamental reason why players do not spread out at goal-kicks is that they are afraid of losing the ball near to their own goal. In effect, they are saying that they do not trust their passing or their ball control.

It is often the case that the goalkeeper is the worst kicker of the ball in the team. Indeed, outplayers are sometimes called upon to take goal-kicks. They usually get the job on the credentials of being able to kick the ball further upfield than the goalkeeper.

There are three basic factors in taking goal-kicks:

Spreading out side-to-side and end-to-end to create space for the ball to be played into. In Diagram 19, the X players are positioned correctly for a goal-kick from the right flank. They have spread out over half the field. There are also four players at various points round the penalty area. Any one of these four could be used for a short goal-kick. This is important because taking short goal-kicks, or even threatening to do so, has the effect of drawing opponents towards the penalty area. This in turn, creates space behind opponents.

In Diagram 20, each one of the X players is marked. This, in itself, is unusual as the O team would normally like to have a spare player at the back. However, there are four passes which are possible:

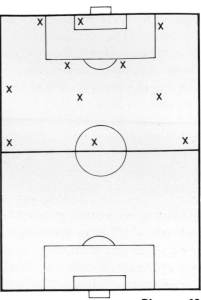

Diagram 19

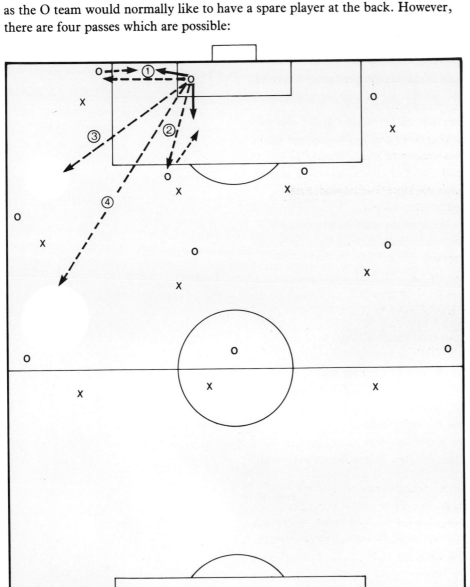

Diagram 20

Pass One is short, approximately 12 yards to the right flank player positioned near to the goal-line.

Pass Two is short, approximately 12 yards to the right central player positioned near to the edge of the penalty area.

Pass Three is of a distance of 30 to 35 yards to a player on the right flank wide on the touch-line.

Pass Four is of a distance of 40 to 50 yards to a player wide on the right flank near to the half-way line.

In each of the four passes, the X player is likely to be challenged. The challenging player, however, is unlikely to be covered because the spaces between the defending players are too great.

The quality of the pass. A goal-kick is a pass and the qualities of good passing should be evident. The pace and angle of the pass are of particular importance.

In each of the four examples given in Diagram 20, the pass should be directed to the receiving player's left foot, the foot furthest from the opponent. This makes receiving the ball easier and challenging for the ball more difficult. Furthermore, in the first two passes the ball should be played firmly. In the last two passes the pace of the pass should bring the receiving player towards the ball and away from his immediate opponent.

There will always be several passing options if players are prepared to spread out. If a good quality pass is made, controlled possession should be established.

Movement of attacking players. Even before the ball is brought under control by the receiving player, attacking players should be moving either to support the player with the ball or to create more space in important areas. Having established controlled possession, it is the movement of players to create more space which will make possible the development of the attack towards the opponent's goal.

A goalkeeper may be called upon to take about twenty goal-kicks during a game. How the kick is taken should therefore merit careful consideration by the whole team.

ORGANISATION FOR PRACTICE

The practice must take place in an eleven-a-side game. At the outset, it may be necessary to take several goal-kicks in order to establish positions, give the goalkeeper practice in selecting the pass, and establish team confidence in the method. Play, therefore, can be restricted to one half of the field and stopped when an attacking player achieves a position on the half-way line in full control of the ball. The ball is then returned to the goalkeeper who should alternate the kick between the left and the right flanks.

Play should then be developed into a normal eleven-a-side game, sure in the knowledge that there will always be a sufficient number of goal-kicks to provide adequate practice.

POINTS FOR THE COACH TO OBSERVE

1. Observe that the attacking players spread out end-to-end and side-to-side.
2. Observe the options available to the goalkeeper.
3. Observe the quality of the pass in relation to:
    (i) Pace of the pass.
    (ii) Accuracy and angle – making receiving easy and challenging difficult.
4. Observe that the goalkeeper supports the pass if he plays the ball short.
5. Observe the movement of the attacking players:
    (i) To support the player receiving the pass.
    (ii) To create more space.

GLOSSARY

Angle, altering the A and passing in one movement: applied to a player controlling the ball and moving it two or three yards to the side and then passing on the second touch.

Angle, narrowing the: applied to defenders, especially the goalkeeper, moving nearer to the ball in order to reduce passing or shooting angles.

Angle of run: the angle at which a player runs, sometimes applied in relation to the ball and sometimes in relation to the goal.

Angle, passing: applied to the line of the pass, i.e. angling the ball to the right or left of a player.

Angle, widening the: usually applied to supporting players moving into a position where the point of attack can be changed, thereby creating a better angle for a forward pass.

Ball watching: watching the ball to the exclusion of one's opponent.

Blind side: the opposite side of a defender to the ball.

Checking: making a movement in one direction, stopping, and then moving off in the opposite direction.

Control, cushion: control of the ball by withdrawing the surface in contact with the ball on impact, e.g. the thigh.

Control, wedge: control of the ball with the use of a rigid surface, e.g. the sole of the boot.

Controlling surface: the surface of the body in contact with the ball to bring the ball under control.

Cross, diagonal: usually applied in the attacking third of the field to a pass played well infield from the touch-line and diagonally forward from right to left or left to right.

Cross, far-post: a pass made to the area, usually beyond the post, farthest from the point from which the ball was kicked.

Cross, flank: a pass made from near to a touch-line, in the attacking third of the field, to an area near to the goal.

Cross, mid-goal: a pass made to the area directly in front of the goal and some six to twelve yards from the goal-line.

Cross, near-post: a pass made to the area four to six yards infield from the post nearest to the point from which the ball was kicked.

Defence, back of the: the space between the goalkeeper and the defender nearest to him.

Defender, committing the: attracting the exclusive attention of a defender by moving towards him with or without the ball.

Disguise: concealing one's intentions by pretending to do one thing and then doing something else.

Dribble: applied to an attacker taking the ball past an opponent.

Dummy: applied in dribbling to feinting to move in one direction, to unbalance an opponent, before moving away in a different direction.

Feint: a deceptive movement which can be applied with or without the ball, e.g. feinting to kick the ball, or feinting to move in one direction.

Flank: the area of the field within fifteen yards or so of the touch-lines.

Flight, line of: applied to the trajectory of the ball.

Goal, mid-G area: an area in front of the goal and six to twelve yards out from the goal-line.

Goal side of the ball: a position between the ball and the goal one is defending.

Instep: the upper surface of the foot or boot, e.g. the laces.

Line of recovery: the path a defender takes when running back towards his goal to get on the goal side of the ball.

Line of retreat: the path a defender takes when moving back towards his goal from a position on the goal side of the ball.

Lofted drive: a powerful kick with the instep through the bottom half of the ball.

Mark: adopt a position, in relation to an opponent, which enables a player either to prevent the opponent from receiving the ball or, at least, to challenge for the ball.

Marking, man-to-man: marking a particular opponent in all the important defensive areas of the field.

Pass, chip: a pass made by a stabbing action of the kicking foot to the bottom part of the ball to achieve a steep trajectory and vicious back spin on the ball.

Pass, flick: a pass made by an outward rotation of the kicking foot, contact on the ball being made with the outside of the foot.

Pass, half-volley: a pass made by the kicking foot making contact with the ball at the moment the ball touches the ground.

Pass, push: a pass made with the inside of the kicking foot.

Pass, swerve: a pass made by imparting spin to the ball, thereby causing it to swerve from either right to left or left to right. Which way the ball swerves depends on whether contact with the ball is made with the outside or the inside of the kicking foot.

Pass, volley: a pass made before the ball touches the ground.

Play, conditioned: applying an artificial restriction, e.g. all players must pass the ball on the first touch.

Play, cross-over: applied to the movements of two attacking players moving in opposite directions past each other. These movements are usually made with the ball but can also be made without it.

Play, one-touch: passing the ball first time, i.e. without controlling the ball.

Play, shadow: a method of coaching which allows players to create movements without opposition.

Player, challenging: applied to a defending player attempting to dispossess an attacking player with the ball.

Player, covering: applied to a defending player who is assisting the challenging player by adopting a position which will enable him to challenge if the challenger is beaten.

Player, supporting: applied to an attacking player who has positioned to receive a pass from the player in possession of the ball. Usually, but not always, the supporting player is behind the ball.

Pressure training: a method of training players to perform a technique many times in rapid succession for a limited period of time.

Run, blind-side: a run by an attacker on the opposite side of a defender from the ball.

Run, cross-field: a run made side-to-side as opposed to end-to-end or diagonally.

Run, diagonal, inside-to-outside: a run made by an attacker, diagonally, from a central position towards a touch-line.

Run, diagonal, outside-to-inside: a run made by an attacker, diagonally, from a flank position towards a central position.

Run, overlap: the movement of an attacking player from a position behind the ball, outside the player with the ball and into a position ahead of the ball.

Runs, split: runs made usually by central forward players in opposite directions in order to create space in central attacking positions.

Run with the ball: movement, with the ball, without dribbling past an opponent.

Space, creating: increasing the distance between, to the side, in front of, or behind opponents.

Space, exploiting: utilising effectively in attack the space already created.

Skill: the application of the correct technique on demand.

Support, wide-angled: support at a sufficiently wide angle to give the greatest possibility for passing the ball forward.

Swerve – inswerve: a ball curling in towards the target, e.g. an inswerve corner swerving towards the goal.

Swerve – outswerve: a ball curling away from the target, e.g. an outswerve corner swerving away from the goal.

Tackle: a challenge, using the feet, to win the ball from an opponent.

Take-over: a term sometimes used to describe a cross-over movement where the player without the ball takes the ball from the dribbling player.

Taking players on: applied to dribbling past opponents.

Technique: a single performance, e.g. a push pass, a chest trap, a turn, a jump.

Thirds of the field: areas roughly 35 yards in length signifying the defending, the middle, and the attacking thirds of the field.

Turning one's opponent: causing an opponent to turn, usually by playing the ball past him, or by moving past him, or by both.

Turning with the ball: the act of receiving the ball when facing one's goal and turning, with the ball under control, to face the opponent's goal.

Volley, hook: a hooking or circular movement by the kicking leg where the leg is parallel with the ground when contact is made on the ball.

Wall pass: interpassing between two attacking players, where the player acting as the wall plays the ball first time and off at a similar angle at which the ball was received. The pass is usually made behind an opponent.

Wall player: the player acting as the wall in a wall pass.

Weight of the pass: a term quite frequently used to describe the pace of a pass.